Contemporary Theories of Learning

WITHDRAWN

In this definitive collection of today's most influential learning theorists, sixteen world-renowned experts present their understanding of what learning is and how human learning takes place.

Professor Knud Illeris has collected chapters that explain both the complex frameworks in which learning takes place and the specific facets of learning, such as the acquisition of learning content, personal development, and the cultural and social nature of learning processes. Each international expert provides either a seminal text or an entirely new précis of the conceptual framework they have developed over a lifetime of study.

Elucidating the key concepts of learning, *Contemporary Theories of Learning* provides both the perfect desk reference and an ideal introduction for students. It will prove an authoritative guide for researchers and academics involved in the study of learning and an invaluable resource for all those dealing with learning in daily life and work. It provides a detailed synthesis of current learning theories ... all in the words of the theorists themselves.

The theories of

KNUD ILLERIS • PETER JARVIS • ROBERT KEGAN • YRJÖ ENGESTRÖM •
BENTE ELKJAER • JACK MEZIROW • HOWARD GARDNER • PETER ALHEIT
• JOHN HERON • MARK TENNANT • JEROME BRUNER • ROBIN USHER •
THOMAS ZIEHE • JEAN LAVE • ETIENNE WENGER • DANNY WILDEMEERSCH
& VEERLE STROOBANTS

in their own words

Knud Illeris is Professor of Lifelong Learning at the Danish University of Education. He is internationally acknowledged as an innovative contributor to learning theory and adult education. In 2005 he became an Honorary Adjunct Professor of Teachers College, Columbia University, New York, and in 2006 he was inducted to The International Hall of Fame of Adult and Continuing Education. He is the author of numerous books, including *How We Learn*, which provides a comprehensive understanding of human learning and non-learning.

Contemporary Theories of Learning

Learning theorists ... in their own words

Edited by Knud Illeris

Routledge
Taylor & Francis Group

LONDON AND NEW YORK

First published 2009
by Routledge
2 Park Square, Milton Park, Abingdon, Oxon OX14 4RN

Simultaneously published in the USA and Canada
by Routledge
711 Third Ave, New York, NY 10017

Routledge is an imprint of the Taylor & Francis Group, an informa business

© 2009 Knud Illeris

Typeset in Garamond by Pindar NZ, Auckland, New Zealand
Printed and bound in Great Britain by CPI Antony Rowe,
Chippenham, Wiltshire

British Library Cataloguing in Publication Data
A catalogue record for this book is available from the British Library

Library of Congress Cataloging in Publication Data
Contemporary theories of learning: learning theorists—in their own
words / edited by Knud Illeris.—1st.
     p. cm.
  1. Learning—Philosophy. 2. Adult learning. I. Illeris, Knud.
  LB1060.C6558 2009
  370.15'23—dc22
  2008027878

ISBN10: 0-415-47343-8 (hbk)
ISBN10: 0-415-47344-6 (pbk)

ISBN13: 978-0-415-47343-9 (hbk)
ISBN13: 978-0-415-47344-6 (pbk)

Contents

Figures

Introduction

The idea of this book is to present an international selection of the most important contemporary learning theorists in one volume and in their own words in order to give an impression of the ongoing development and debate in this area.

During the last 10–15 years, learning has become a key topic, not only for professionals and students in the areas of psychology, pedagogy and education, but also in political and economic contexts. One reason for this is that the level of education and skills of nations, companies and individuals is considered a crucial parameter of competition in the present globalised market and knowledge society. It is, however, important to emphasise that the competitive functions of learning are merely a secondary, late-modern addition to the much more fundamental primary function of learning as one of the most basic abilities and manifestations of human life.

Learning is also a very complex matter, and there is no generally accepted definition of the concept. On the contrary, a great number of more-or-less special or overlapping theories of learning are constantly being developed, some of them referring back to more traditional understandings, others trying to explore new possibilities and ways of thinking. It is also worth noting that whereas learning traditionally has been understood mainly as the acquisition of knowledge and skills, today the concept covers a much larger field that includes emotional, social and societal dimensions. For example, learning sometimes takes on the nature of competence development, which has to do with the ability to manage different existing and future challenges in working life and many other fields of practice.

It is thus quite difficult to obtain an overview of the present situation of the understanding of the topic of learning. It is, first of all, characterised by complexity, which is also mirrored in the long story that lies behind the genesis of this book.

This story begins right back in 1998 when I was writing a book that was published in Danish in 1999 and in English in 2002 entitled *The Three Dimensions of Learning*. As I later stated, a little sentimentally perhaps, I experienced this work as 'a kind of voyage of discovery', and when I started on my journey, I had no idea of what I would find (Illeris 2007, p. xi).

A part of this journey led through the reading of a lot of writings by earlier and contemporary learning theorists as I tried to develop a framework that could cover the whole field of learning in a structured way. Later, when the book had been published, I came to think that it might be a good idea to pick out what I now could see were key articles or chapters by the various theorists and present them in a way that could form an overview for interested students and others. This was a much bigger task than I had expected. However, a year later the book called *Texts on Learning* appeared in Danish, with 31 chapters by old and new authors from 11 countries. This book has never been published in English; on the contrary, most of the chapters were translated into Danish from English and other languages. However, up to now almost 10,000 copies of it have been sold, which is quite a lot in a small country like Denmark.

Some years later I wrote another book called *Adult Education and Adult Learning*, which appeared in Danish in 2003 and in English in 2004, and the story was repeated. So in 2005, an edited book appeared in Danish called *Texts on Adult Learning* and containing 27 chapters by authors from 11 countries and three international bodies (UNESCO, OECD and the EU).

Finally, in 2006, I published a book in Danish that came out in English in 2007 with the title *How We Learn*. When this book was launched in Denmark, the Danish University of Education arranged a one-day conference with Peter Jarvis, Etienne Wenger and myself as keynote speakers. The conference was a great success. The assembly hall was packed with 420 participants, and during the closing discussion we were urged to make a publication out of the three keynotes. However, three chapters are not enough for a book, so I included another three relevant chapters (by Jack Mezirow, Yrjö Engeström and Thomas Ziehe), and this book was published in Danish in 2007 under the title *Learning Theories: Six Contemporary Approaches*. This volume also quickly became very popular in Denmark, selling more than 2,000 copies during its first year.

Thus, altogether in the three books, I had an international collection of 64 selected chapters presenting different understandings of learning by authors ranging from Grundtvig in 1838 to brand-new contributors in 2007. On this basis I proposed to Routledge that I should pick out some 14 to 16 of the most remarkable chapters of current interest and add a few new ones. This proposal was reviewed and accepted, and the editing process and enquiries about obtaining the necessary permissions commenced early in 2008.

The most fundamental question, of course, has been which authors and texts to select. In this context, first of all a practical interpretation of what is meant by 'contemporary' was needed. An examination of the material led me to choose to make 1990 the start date – i.e. that only contributions which appeared for the first time after 1990 could be accepted. Of course, a boundary of this kind is arbitrary and will always exclude some contributions that could be considered both 'contemporary' and important.

For example, in 1984, David Kolb published his book *Experiential Learning* (following a preliminary publication by Kolb and Fry in 1975), which has certainly made an important contribution to the understanding of learning but which, in my opinion, can hardly be regarded as contemporary and up to date. The concept of 'experiential learning' has been elaborated further by many other authors (cf. e.g. Weil and McGill 1989), and Peter Jarvis, in this book and many other writings, actually starts his deliberations by stating that he finds Kolb's theory much too simple to capture the complexity of learning. Other authors who made important contributions in the 1970s and 80s were Chris Argyris and Donald Schön with their concepts of 'single loop' and 'double loop' learning (Argyris and Schön 1978) and 'the reflective practitioner' (Schön 1983), and Hans Furth in his book *Knowledge As Desire* (1987).

On the other hand, some of the selected authors made their first contributions long before 1990. Thus, Jerome Bruner's first well-known publication in this connection dates right back to 1956 (Bruner *et al.* 1956), Thomas Ziehe's first work on learning in youth stems from 1975, Jack Mezirow launched his theory of 'transformative learning' for the first time in 1978, Robert Kegan's *The Evolving Self* appeared in 1982, Howard Gardner advanced his idea of 'multiple intelligences' in 1983, Peter Jarvis started publishing on learning in 1987 and Yrjö Engeström's dissertation *Learning by Expanding* is also from 1987. In general, most of the authors in this book published before 1990. However, the crucial point is that either their main theoretical contributions have been made, or they have renewed or expanded their understandings in decisive ways, after this date.

The other basic criterion of selection concerns what can be regarded as 'learning' and 'learning theory'. My decisions in this field are based on the definition of the concept of learning as 'any process that in living organisms leads to permanent capacity change and which is not solely due to biological maturation or ageing' (Illeris 2007, p. 3, repeated in my chapter later in this book). This very open definition is, as I see it, in line with important modern understandings of learning as something much broader and more complicated than the traditional conception of learning as 'the acquisition of knowledge and skills', and it has allowed me to select contributions ranging as widely as from Howard Gardner's 'Multiple Approaches to Understanding' to Thomas Ziehe's ideas of 'normal learning problems' and 'underlying cultural convictions'.

However, there are some types of possible contributions that have been avoided. First, readers will look in vain for chapters referring mainly to the classic behaviourist conception of learning – partly because not many new contributions by this school appear, and partly because, in my understanding, this school deals with such a small corner of the vast field of learning that, in relation to human learning, it is only of interest concerning some very special fields of early learning, re-training and certain groups of mentally handicapped learners. Similarly, there are also other areas of learning that once were important conquests but now have been overtaken by more inclusive and complicated approaches as, for example, the gestalt psychological interest in learning by problem solving, which today is integrated in such approaches as experiential learning and practice learning.

Second, I have avoided approaches in which the interest in learning is limited to some special sectors of life or society, such as school learning and especially organisational learning (not to speak of 'the learning organisation'). However, this does not mean that approaches taking their point of departure in, for example, adult education or workplace learning have been excluded if their understanding of learning is of general interest.

Third, I have not taken in contributions of a specific system theoretical approach such as the works of the German sociologist Niklas Luhmann (e.g. Luhmann 1995) and his many followers in particular, because I find this type of approach too dissociated and distant from the concrete learning of everyday life in modern society. There is in this case, as I see it, a tendency for the systematic features to become more important than the human learners and their complex life situations.

Fourth, I have not included any contributions from modern brain research. This is not because I do not find such contributions interesting or important – I actually use them quite a lot in my own work – but because I think that they are still too specialised to have the status of general understandings of learning.

All this has left me with the 16 chapters that make up the rest of this book. There are, of course, many others that I have had to omit in order not to make the volume too extensive or with too many overlaps and repetitions.

The next problem I have had to face in the editing process is how to arrange these 16 chapters. In this respect I have taken my point of departure in the learning dimensions that I have presented and explained in my own contribution. I have therefore placed this chapter first so that the reader can start by getting acquainted with the line of thinking lying behind the structure of the book.

Next, I have placed four other chapters that in very different ways also try to deal with and explain learning as a whole. These are first the chapters by Peter Jarvis and Robert Kegan, who from an existential and a psychological perspective, respectively, outline a general understanding of what learning is and involves. These are followed by the chapters by Yrjö Engeström and Bente Elkjaer, who are a bit more specific in their approaches as they represent the 'schools' of activity theory and pragmatism, respectively.

Then come two contributions which, while they certainly also are of a holistic nature, are to some extent more oriented towards the classic topic of the learning content, i.e. what is actually learned. These are the chapters by two of the most influential figures in the contemporary field of learning in America: Jack Mezirow, as the creator of the theory of transformative learning, and Howard Gardner, as the creator of the theory of multiple intelligences.

From there I turn to the incentive dimension of learning, i.e. theoretical approaches which have special focus on the interests, motivations and emotions that drive learning and the personal development that learning creates. I see the chapter by Peter Alheit, which describes the biographical approach to learning, as the most general contribution in this area. This is followed by the chapter by John Heron, who uses the example of learning to illustrate his general theory of 'feeling and personhood'. And, finally, there is the chapter by Mark Tennant, who discusses the development of the self in relation to the mainly French understandings of postmodernity.

The last six chapters all focus on the interaction dimension of learning. Three of them do this in a mainly cultural context. These are, first, the chapter by Jerome Bruner, who for more than 50 years has played a key role in the American learning landscape and gradually has moved from a behaviourist via a so-called 'science-centred' to a cultural psychological position. Second comes the chapter by Robin Usher, who describes four postmodern positions in relation to learning. And third follows the chapter by Thomas Ziehe, who digs deeply into the cultural conditions that set the scene for young people's learning today.

Finally, the last three chapters of the book deal with learning in a social context. Jean Lave takes up the approach of practice learning; Etienne Wenger, who has worked closely together with Lave, presents 'a social theory of learning'; and in the last chapter of the book, Danny Wildemeersch and Veerle Stroobants develop a model that illustrates how many different social influences are involved in modern learning processes.

In this way the book will take the reader through a broad variety of perspectives on learning. I have chosen not to divide the book into sections as each of the 16 contributions in a way forms its own section.

Some readers may disagree with the selections and dispositions I have made, and some may be disappointed, but all I can say is that in my editing I have tried to be stringent and to achieve a broad and adequate representation of contemporary approaches to the topic of learning. It is my hope that in this way I have succeeded in producing a volume that can provide an overview of the current situation and the multitude of learning theoretical understandings, thereby inspiring the readers to deal with this topic in qualified and differentiated ways.

Knud Illeris

References

Argyris, Chris and Schön, Donald A. (1978): *Organizational Learning: A Theory of Action and Perspective*. Reading, MA: Addison-Wesley.

Bruner, Jerome S., Goodnow, Jacqueline J., and Austin, George A. (1956): *A Study of Thinking*. New York: Wiley.

Engeström, Yrjö (1987): *Learning by Expanding: An Activity-Theoretical Approach to Developmental Research*. Helsinki: Orienta-Kunsultit.

Furth, Hans G. (1987): *Knowledge As Desire: An Essay on Freud and Piaget*. New York: Columbia University Press.

Gardner, Howard (1983): *Frames of Mind: The Theory of Multiple Intelligences*. New York: Basic Books.

Illeris, Knud (2002): *The Three Dimensions of Learning: Contemporary Learning Theory in the Tension Field between the Cognitive, the Emotional and the Social*. Copenhagen: Roskilde University Press, and Leicester: NIACE (American edition: Krieger Publishing, Malabar, FL, 2004).

Illeris, Knud (2004): *Adult Education and Adult Learning*. Copenhagen: Roskilde University Press, and Malabar, FL: Krieger Publishing.

Illeris, Knud (2007): *How We Learn: Learning and Non-learning in Schools and Beyond*. London/ New York: Routledge.

Jarvis, Peter (1987): *Adult Learning in the Social Context*. New York: Croom Helm.

Kegan, Robert (1982): *The Evolving Self: Problem and Process in Human Development*. Cambridge, MA: Harvard University Press.

Kolb, David A. (1984): *Experiential Learning: Experience as the Source of Learning and Development*. Englewood Cliffs, NJ: Prentice-Hall.

Kolb, David and Fry, Roger (1975): Toward an Applied Theory of Experiential Learning. In Cary L. Cooper (ed.): *Theories of Group Processes*. London: Wiley.

Luhmann, Niklas (1995 [1984]): *Social Systems*. Stanford, CA: Stanford University Press.

Mezirow, Jack (1978): *Education for Perspective Transformation: Women's Re-entry Programs in Community Colleges*. New York: Teachers College, Columbia University.

Schön, Donald A. (1983): *The Reflective Practitioner: How Professionals Think in Action*. San Francisco: Jossey-Bass.

Weil, Susan Warner and McGill, Ian (eds.) (1989): *Making Sense of Experiential Learning: Diversity in Theory and Practice*. Buckingham: Open University Press.

Ziehe, Thomas (1975): *Pubertät und Narzissmus* [Puberty and Narcissism]. Frankfurt a.M.: Europäische Verlagsanstalt.

Chapter I

A comprehensive understanding of human learning

Knud Illeris

Already in the 1970s Knud Illeris was well known in Scandinavia for his developing work on project studies in theory and practice. In this work, learning theory was applied, mainly by a combination of Jean Piaget's approach to learning and the so-called 'critical theory' of the German–American Frankfurt School that basically connected Freudian psychology with Marxist sociology. In the 1990s, Illeris returned to his learning theoretical roots, now involving many other theoretical approaches in the general understanding of learning, which was first presented in The Three Dimensions of Learning *and later fully worked out in* How We Learn: Learning and Non-learning in School and Beyond. *The following chapter presents the main ideas of this understanding and is an elaborated version of the presentation Illeris made at a conference in Copenhagen in 2006 when the Danish version of* How We Learn *was launched. The article has never before been published in English.*

Background and basic assumptions

Since the last decades of the nineteenth century, many theories and under-standings of learning have been launched. They have had different angles, different epistemological platforms and a very different content. Some of them have been overtaken by new knowledge and new standards, but in general we have today a picture of a great variety of learning theoretical approaches and constructions, which are more-or-less compatible and more-or-less competitive on the global academic market. The basic idea of the approach to learning presented in this chapter is to build on a wide selection of the best of these constructions, add new insights and perspectives and in this way develop an overall understanding or framework, which can offer a general and up-to-date overview of the field.

Learning can broadly be defined as *any process that in living organisms leads to permanent capacity change and which is not solely due to biological maturation or ageing* (Illeris 2007, p. 3). I have deliberately chosen this very open formulation because the concept of learning includes a very extensive and complicated set of processes, and a comprehensive understanding is not only a matter of the nature of the learning process itself. It must also include all the conditions that

STRUCTURE OF THE THEORY

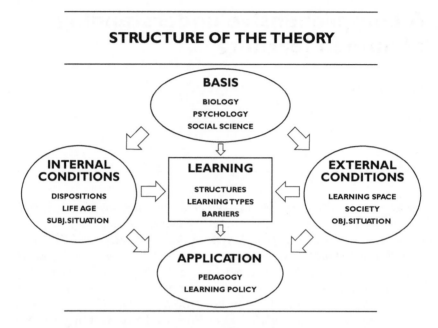

Figure 1.1 The main areas of the understanding of learning.

influence and are influenced by this process. Figure 1.1 shows the main areas which are involved and the structure of their mutual connections.

On the top I have placed the basis of the learning theory, i.e. the areas of knowledge and understanding which, in my opinion, must underlie the development of a comprehensive and coherent theory construction. These include all the psychological, biological and social conditions which are involved in any learning. Under this is the central box depicting learning itself, including its processes and dimensions, different learning types and learning barriers, which to me are the central elements of the understanding of learning. Further there are the specific internal and external conditions which are not only influencing but also directly involved in learning. And finally, the possible applications of learning are also involved. I shall now go through these five areas and emphasise some of the most important features of each of them.

The two basic processes and the three dimensions of learning

The first important condition to realise is that all learning implies the integration of two very different processes, namely an external interaction process between the learner and his or her social, cultural or material environment, and an internal psychological process of elaboration and acquisition.

Many learning theories deal only with one of these processes, which of course does not mean that they are wrong or worthless, as both processes can be studied separately. However, it does mean that they do not cover the whole field of learning. This may, for instance, be said of traditional behaviourist and cognitive learning theories focusing only on the internal psychological process. It can equally be said of certain modern social learning theories which – sometimes in explicit opposition to this – draw attention to the external interaction process alone. However, it seems evident that both processes must be actively involved if any learning is to take place.

When constructing my model of the field of learning (Figure 1.2), I started by depicting the external interaction process as a vertical double arrow between the environment, which is the general basis and therefore placed at the bottom, and the individual, who is the specific learner and therefore placed at the top.

Next I added the psychological acquisition process as another double arrow. It is an internal process of the learner and must therefore be placed at the top pole of the interaction process. Further, it is a process of integrated interplay between two equal psychological functions involved in any learning, namely the function of managing the learning content and the incentive function of providing and directing the necessary mental energy that runs the process. Thus the double arrow of the acquisition process is placed horizontally at the top of the interaction process and between the poles of content and incentive – and it should be emphasised that the double arrow means that these two functions are always involved and usually in an integrated way.

As can be seen, the two double arrows can now span out a triangular field between three angles. These three angles depict three spheres or dimensions of learning, and it is the core claim of the understanding that all learning will always involve these three dimensions.

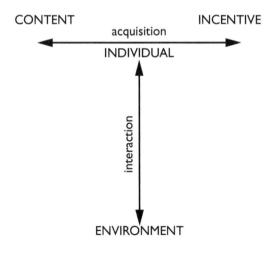

Figure 1.2 The fundamental processes of learning.

The content dimension concerns what is learned. This is usually described as knowledge and skills, but also many other things such as opinions, insight, meaning, attitudes, values, ways of behaviour, methods, strategies, etc. may be involved as learning content and contribute to building up the understanding and the capacity of the learner. The endeavour of the learner is to construct *meaning* and *ability* to deal with the challenges of practical life and thereby an overall personal *functionality* is developed.

The incentive dimension provides and directs the mental energy that is necessary for the learning process to take place. It comprises such elements as feelings, emotions, motivation and volition. Its ultimate function is to secure the continuous *mental balance* of the learner and thereby it simultaneously develops a personal *sensitivity*.

These two dimensions are always initiated by impulses from the interaction processes and integrated in the internal process of elaboration and acquisition. Therefore, the learning content is, so to speak, always 'obsessed' with the incentives at stake – e.g. whether the learning is driven by desire, interest, necessity or compulsion. Correspondingly, the incentives are always influenced by the content, e.g. new information can change the incentive condition. Many psychologists have been aware of this close connection between what

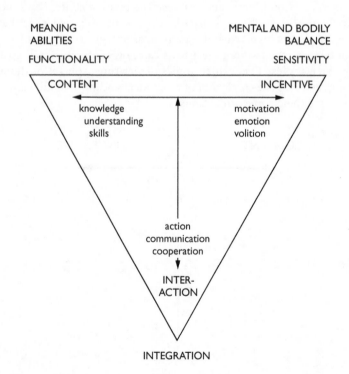

Figure 1.3 The three dimensions of learning and competence development.

has usually been termed the cognitive and the emotional (e.g. Vygotsky 1978; Furth 1987), and recently advanced neurology has proven that both areas are always involved in the learning process, unless in cases of very severe brain damage (Damasio 1994).

The interaction dimension provides the impulses that initiate the learning process. This may take place as perception, transmission, experience, imitation, activity, participation, etc. (Illeris 2007, pp. 100ff.). It serves the personal *integration* in communities and society and thereby also builds up the *sociality* of the learner. However, this building up necessarily takes place through the two other dimensions.

Thus the triangle depicts what may be described as the tension field of learning in general and of any specific learning event or learning process as stretched out between the development of functionality, sensibility and sociality – which are also the general components of what we term as competencies.

It is also important to mention that each dimension includes a mental as well as a bodily side. Actually, learning begins with the body and takes place through the brain, which is also part of the body, and only gradually is the mental side separated out as a specific but never independent area or function (Piaget 1952).

An example from everyday school life

In order to illustrate how the model may be understood and used, I shall take an everyday example from ordinary school life (which does not mean that the model only deals with school learning).

During a chemistry lesson in the classroom, a teacher is explaining a chemical process. The students are supposed to be listening and perhaps asking questions to be sure that they have understood the explanation correctly. The students are thus involved in an interaction process. But at the same time, they are supposed to take in or to learn what the teacher is teaching, i.e. psychologically to relate what is taught to what they should already have learned. The result should be that they are able to remember what they have been taught and, under certain conditions, to reproduce it, apply it and involve it in further learning.

But sometimes, or for some students, the learning process does not take place as intended, and mistakes or derailing may occur in many different ways. Perhaps the interaction does not function because the teacher's explanation is not good enough or is even incoherent, or there may be disturbances in the situation. If so, the explanation will only be picked up partially or incorrectly, and the learning result will be insufficient. But the students' acquisition process may also be inadequate, for instance because of a lack of concentration, and this will also lead to deterioration in the learning result. Or there may be errors or insufficiencies in the prior learning of some students, making them unable to understand the teacher's explanation and thereby also to learn what is being taught. Much of this indicates that acquisition is not only a cognitive matter. There is also another area or function involved concerning the students' attitudes to the intended learning: their interests and mobilisation of mental energy, i.e. the incentive dimension.

In a school situation, focus is usually on the learning content; in the case described it is on the students' understanding of the nature of the chemical process concerned. However, the incentive function is also still crucial, i.e. how the situation is experienced, what sort of feelings and motivations are involved, and thus the nature and the strength of the mental energy that is mobilised. The value and durability of the learning result is closely related to the incentive dimension of the learning process.

Further, both the content and the incentive are crucially dependent on the interaction process between the learner and the social, societal, cultural and material environment. If the interaction in the chemistry lesson is not adequate and acceptable to the students, the learning will suffer, or something quite different may be learned, for instance a negative impression of the teacher, of some other students, of the subject or of the school situation in general.

The four types of learning

What has been outlined in the triangle model and the example above is a concept of learning which is basically constructivist in nature, i.e. it is assumed that the learner him- or herself actively builds up or construes his/her learning as mental structures. These structures exist in the brain as dispositions that are usually described by a psychological metaphor as *mental schemes*. This means that there must in the brain be some organisation of the learning outcomes since we, when becoming aware of something – a person, a problem, a topic, etc. – in fractions of a second are able to recall what we subjectively and usually unconsciously define as relevant knowledge, understanding, attitudes, reactions and the like. But this organisation is in no way a kind of archive, and it is not possible to find the different elements at specific positions in the brain. It has the nature of what brain researchers call 'engrams', which are traces of circuits between some of the billions of neurons that have been active at earlier occasions and therefore are likely to be revived, perhaps with slightly different courses because of the impact of new experiences or understandings.

However, in order to deal systematically with this, the concept of schemes is used for what we subjectively tend to classify as belonging to a specific topic or theme and therefore mentally connect and are inclined to recall in relation to situations that we relate to that topic or theme. This especially applies to the content dimension, whereas in the incentive and interaction dimensions we would rather speak of *mental patterns*. But the background is similar in that motivations, emotions or ways of communication tend to be organised so that they can be revived when we are oriented towards situations that 'remind' us of earlier situations when they have been active.

In relation to learning, the crucial thing is that new impulses can be included in the mental organisation in various ways, and on this basis it is possible to distinguish between four different types of learning which are activated in different contexts, imply different kinds of learning results and require more or less energy. (This is an elaboration of the concept of learning originally developed by Jean Piaget (e.g. Piaget 1952; Flavell 1963).)

When a scheme or pattern is established, it is a case of *cumulative* or mechanical learning. This type of learning is characterised by being an isolated formation, something new that is not a part of anything else. Therefore, cumulative learning is most frequent during the first years of life, but later occurs only in special situations where one must learn something with no context of meaning or personal significance, for example a PIN code. The learning result is characterised by a type of automation that means that it can only be recalled and applied in situations mentally similar to the learning context. It is mainly this type of learning which is involved in the training of animals and which is therefore also referred to as conditioning in behaviourist psychology.

By far the most common type of learning is termed *assimilative* or learning by addition, meaning that the new element is linked as an addition to a scheme or pattern that is already established. One typical example could be learning in school subjects that are usually built up by means of constant additions to what has already been learned, but assimilative learning also takes place in all contexts where one gradually develops one's capacities. The results of learning are characterised by being linked to the scheme or pattern in question in such a manner that it is relatively easy to recall and apply them when one is mentally oriented towards the field in question, for example a school subject, while they may be hard to access in other contexts. This is why problems are frequently experienced in applying knowledge from a school subject to other subjects or in contexts outside of school (Illeris 2008).

However, in some cases, situations occur where something takes place that is difficult to immediately relate to any existing scheme or pattern. This is experienced as something one cannot really understand or relate to. But if it seems important or interesting, if it is something one is determined to acquire, this can take place by means of *accommodative* or transcendent learning. This type of learning implies that one breaks down (parts of) an existing scheme and transforms it so that the new situation can be linked in. Thus one both relinquishes and reconstructs something, and this can be experienced as demanding or even painful, because it is something that requires a strong supply of mental energy. One must cross existing limitations and understand or accept something that is significantly new or different, and this is much more demanding than just adding a new element to an already existing scheme or pattern. In return, the results of such learning are characterised by the fact that they can be recalled and applied in many different, relevant contexts. It is typically experienced as having understood or got hold of something which one really has internalised.

Finally, over the last few decades it has been pointed out that in special situations there is also a far-reaching type of learning that has been variously described as significant (Rogers 1951, 1969), expansive (Engeström 1987), transitional (Alheit 1994) or transformative learning (Mezirow 1991). This learning implies what could be termed personality changes, or changes in the organisation of the self, and is characterised by simultaneous restructuring of a whole cluster of schemes and patterns in all of the three learning dimensions – a break of orientation that typically occurs as the result of a crisis-like situation caused by challenges experienced as urgent and unavoidable, making it necessary to change oneself in order to get any further. Transformative learning is thus both profound and extensive, it demands a lot of mental energy and when accomplished it can often be experienced physically, typically as a feeling of relief or relaxation.

As has been demonstrated, the four types of learning are widely different in scope and nature, and they also occur – or are activated by learners – in very different situations and connections. Whereas cumulative learning is most important in early childhood, and transformative learning is a very demanding process that changes the very personality or identity and occurs only in very special situations of profound significance for the learner, assimilation and accommodation are, as described by Piaget, the two types of learning that characterise general, sound and normal everyday learning. Many other learning theorists also point to two such types of learning; for example, Chris Argyris and Donald Schön have coined the well-known concepts of single and double loop learning (Argyris 1992; Argyris and Schön 1996), Per-Erik Ellström (2001) speaks about adaptation-oriented and development-oriented learning, and also Lev Vygotsky's idea (1978) of transition into the 'zone of proximal development' may be seen as a parallel to accommodative learning.

However, ordinary discussions of learning and the design of many educational and school activities are concentrated on and often only aimed at assimilative learning, as this is the sort of learning that the usual understanding of the concept of learning is about. But today this understanding is obviously insufficient, and the much-demanded generic competencies can only be built up by a combination of assimilative, accommodative and, eventually, transformative learning processes.

Barriers to learning

Another problem is that much intended learning does not take place or is incomplete or distorted. In schools, in education, at workplaces and in many other situations, very often people do not learn what they could learn or what they are supposed to learn. Therefore I find it important also to discuss briefly what happens in such cases.

Of course, it cannot be avoided that we all sometimes learn something that is wrong (cf. Mager 1961) or something that is inadequate for us in some way or another. In the first instance, this concerns matters such as mislearning, which can be due to misunderstandings, lack of concentration, insufficient prior learning and the like. This may be annoying and in some cases unlucky, but simple mislearning due to 'practical' reasons is not a matter of great interest to learning theory as such mislearning can usually be corrected rather easily, if necessary.

However, today much non-learning and mislearning are not so simple, but have a background in some general conditions that modern society creates, and in some respects the investigation and understanding of such processes are definitely as important as more traditional learning theory to understand what is happening and to cope with it in practice.

The central point is that in our complex late-modern society, what Freud called *defence mechanisms* – which are active in specific personal connections (cf. Anna Freud 1942) – must necessarily be generalised and take more systematised forms because nobody can manage to remain open to the gigantic volumes and impact of influences we are all constantly faced with.

This is why today people develop a kind of semi-automatic sorting mechanism vis-à-vis the many influences, or what the German social psychologist Thomas Leithäuser (1976) has analysed and described as an *everyday consciousness*. This functions in the way that one develops some general pre-understandings within certain thematic areas, and when one meets with influences within such an area, these pre-understandings are activated so that if elements in the influences do not correspond to the pre-understandings, they are either rejected or distorted to make them agree. In both cases, this results in no new learning but, on the contrary, often the cementing of the already-existing understanding.

Thus, through everyday consciousness we control our own learning and non-learning in a manner that seldom involves any direct positioning while simultaneously involving a massive defence of the already-acquired understandings and, in the final analysis, our very identity. (There are, of course, also areas and situations where our positioning takes place in a more target-oriented manner, consciously and flexibly.)

However, not only the volume but also the kind of influence can be overwhelming. Not least, on television we are faced every day with so much cruelty, wickedness and similar negative impact that it is absolutely impossible to really take it in – and people who cannot protect themselves from this are doomed to end up in some kind of psychological breakdown. Other new forms of similar overloading are caused by the endless changes and reorganisations many people experience at their workplaces, social institutions, etc. or by the helplessness that can be felt when consequences of the decisions of those in power encroach on one's life situation and possibilities.

In the most important cases, for instance when a change to a basically new situation in a certain life area must be overcome, most people react by mobilising a genuine *identity defence* which demands very hard work of a more-or-less therapeutic character to break through, usually by a transformative learning process. This happens typically in relation to a sudden situation of unemployment or other fundamental changes in the work situation, divorce, death of closely related persons or the like, and it is worth realising that such situations happen much more frequently in the modern globalised market society of today than just a generation ago.

Another very common form of defence is *ambivalence*, meaning that in a certain situation or connection one is both wanting and not wanting to learn or do something. A typical example is that people who unwillingly and without any personal fault have become unemployed on the one hand know very well that they must engage themselves in some retraining or re-education, and on the other hand strongly wish that this was not the case. So they go or are sent to some courses but it is difficult for them to concentrate on the learning and they use any possible excuse to escape, mentally or physically.

In all such defence situations, learning is obstructed, hindered, derailed or distorted if it is not possible for the learner to break through the defence, and the task of a teacher or instructor will often be to support and encourage such a breakthrough before more goal-directed and constructive training or education can take place. But teachers are usually not trained for such functions, although they quite frequently are necessary if the intended learning shall be promoted.

Another psychological mechanism which may block or distort relevant learning is *mental resistance*. This is not, in itself, so very time-specific, as all human beings in any society will experience situations where what they try to accomplish cannot be carried through, and if they cannot understand or accept the barriers they will naturally react with some sort of resistance.

In practice it is sometimes quite difficult to distinguish between non-learning caused by defence and non-learning caused by resistance. However, psychologically there is a great and important difference. Whereas the defence mechanisms exist prior to the learning situation and function reactively, resistance is caused by the learning situation itself as an active response. Thus resistance contains a strong mental mobilisation and therefore also a strong learning potential, especially for accommodative and even transformative learning. Often when one does not just accept something, the possibility of learning something significantly new emerges. And most great steps forward in the development of mankind and society have taken place when someone did not accept a given truth or way of doing or understanding things.

In everyday life, resistance is also a most important source of transcendent learning, although it may be both inconvenient and annoying, not least for teachers. In any event, today it should be a central qualification of teachers to be able to cope with and even inspire mental resistance, as precisely such personal competencies which are so much in demand – for example, independence, responsibility, flexibility and creativity – are likely to be developed in this way. This is why conflict or dilemma raising may be taken in as effective but demanding techniques in some particularly challenging educational situations.

Internal and external learning conditions

What has been discussed in the above – the processes, dimensions, types and barriers of learning – I regard as features which should be included in any learning theory that aims at covering the whole field of the concept. However, there are also other issues that influence learning without being directly involved in learning as such and thus can be termed the conditions of learning. These issues are also taken up in my book *How We Learn* (Illeris 2007), but in this article I shall only shortly indicate what they are about.

The internal conditions of learning are features of or in the learner that influence learning possibilities and are involved in the learning processes. *Intelligence* is supposed to be a measure of the general ability to learn, but it has always been disputed whether or not a general and measurable instance of this kind exists, and there is certainly not a general agreement about its definition. Since 1983, American psychologist Howard Gardner (1983, 1993, 1999) has claimed that there are several independent intelligences – a view which to some extent corresponds to the understanding of learning presented here because it includes not only cognitive but also emotional and social abilities. A somewhat similar concept is about individual *learning styles*, but the nature and existence of these still seem to be more an open question. In contrast to these general measures, it is obvious that the more specific individual features of gender and life age to some degree influence the learning possibilities.

The external conditions of learning are features outside the learner that influence learning possibilities and are involved in the learning processes. These can roughly be divided into features of the immediate learning situation and learning space and more general cultural and societal conditions. The kind of learning space makes up for differences between everyday learning, school learning, workplace learning, net-based learning, interest-based learning, etc. and for difficulties in applying learning outcomes across the borders of these spaces – the so-called 'transfer problem' of learning (Eraut 1994; Illeris *et al.* 2004; Illeris 2008). General societal conditions are dependent on time and place: obviously the learning possibilities are much more wide-ranging today than a century ago and they also differ between the countries and cultures of today.

Finally, some important questions about the use and applicability of learning theory, especially in the areas of educational practice and policy, are also briefly discussed in the book. Some very common misunderstandings in these areas are pointed out, as well as some typical connections between different understandings of learning, different schools of pedagogy and different fundamental assumptions of learning policy. In the last chapter, the book concludes by mapping the most important understandings and theorists of learning in relation to the learning triangle shown in Figure 1.3.

Conclusion

The general conclusion is that learning is a very complicated matter, and analyses, programmes and discussions of learning must consider the whole field if they are to be adequate and reliable. This implies, for instance, that all three learning dimensions must be taken into account, that the question of relevant learning types must be included, that possible defence or resistance must be considered and that internal as well as external learning conditions must also be dealt with. This is, of course, a very wide-ranging demand. To word it differently, it could be said that if for some reason it is not possible or appropriate to include all these areas, it must be clear that the situation or process has not been fully covered, and an open question will remain as to what happens in the areas that are not discussed.

I shall round off by illustrating this more concretely through two examples from my own research and practice.

The first example has to do with youth education. Many Western countries have a high ambition to the effect that all or the great majority of young people should complete some academically or practically qualifying post-16 education programme. The goal of the Danish government is for 95 per cent to receive such qualifications, but although 95 per cent commence a programme, less than 80 per cent complete it.

This, of course, has been the subject of a great deal of research, debate, reforms, etc. but with almost no or even negative effect. From a learning point of view, it would seem not to have been fully realised that today young people of this age are highly engaged in a process of personal identity development, which is an absolute necessity to be able to navigate in the late-modern, globalised market society. Therefore, young people fundamentally meet all learning initiatives – consciously or unconsciously – with such questions as: What does this mean *to me?* or What can *I* use this for? – implying that it is only worth paying attention to if it is subjectively accepted as a usable contribution to the present demands of the identity process. And the premises of this judgement lie equally in all three learning dimensions, i.e. the programme offered must not only have an acceptable, interesting and challenging content, it must also contribute to an acceptable positioning in relation to contemporary trends on the youth lifestyle market, and it must be organised in ways and by teachers or other persons who are in harmony with the personal needs of the young learners. One may think that such demands are not relevant or acceptable, and many people in the educational field are of this opinion, but the inevitable consequence will then be a continued high drop-out rate (see e.g. Illeris 2003, 2007).

The second example is about retraining of low-skilled workers who against their will have become unemployed – which is a very frequent state of affairs in today's society. These adults are very often referred to various practical courses to acquire a basis for employment in a new trade where it is possible to get a job. But the process leading to this has been experienced not as guidance (as it is officially called) but as placement. Furthermore, even when the person in question realises that the training may lead to a return to the labour market, which is usually a very strong wish, their identity is tied to their former trade and a strong defence blocks the engagement in new learning. If the guidance received had made time for personal reflection and participation in the decision, this defence could have been overcome. When asked, the great majority of people in this situation answer that they would probably have chosen the same course, but they had not been given the opportunity to make the mental switch before the course. Now they are forced to undergo a demanding transformative learning process at the same time as they are expected to acquire a great many new practical qualifications (see e.g. Illeris 2006).

In learning terms, in both of these examples a lot of resources are invested in endeavours that have little or no chance of success because the considerations of the 'system' or the authorities have not included an adequate and realistic analysis of the learning situation.

References

Alheit, Peter (1994): The 'Biographical Question' as a Challenge to Adult Education. *International Review of Education*, 40(3/5), pp. 283–98.

Argyris, Chris (1992): *On Organizational Learning*. Cambridge, MA: Blackwell.

Argyris, Chris and Schön, Donald A. (1996): *Organizational Learning II – Theory, Method, and Practice*. Reading, MA: Addison-Wesley.

Damasio, Antonio R. (1994): *Descartes' Error: Emotion, Reason and the Human Brain*. New York: Grosset/Putnam.

Ellström, Per-Erik (2001): Integrating Learning and Work: Conceptual Issues and Critical Conditions. *Human Resource Development Quarterly*, 12(4), pp. 421–35.

Engeström, Yrjö (1987): *Learning by Expanding: An Activity-Theoretical Approach to Developmental Research*. Helsinki: Orienta-Kunsultit.

Eraut, Michael (1994): *Developing Professional Knowledge and Competence*. London: Falmer.

Flavell, John H. (1963): *The Developmental Psychology of Jean Piaget*. New York: Van Nostrand.

Freud, Anna (1942): *The Ego and the Mechanisms of Defence*. London: Hogarth Press.

Furth, Hans G. (1987): *Knowledge As Desire: An Essay on Freud and Piaget*. New York: Columbia University Press.

Gardner, Howard (1983): *Frames of Mind: The Theory of Multiple Intelligences*. New York: Basic Books.

Gardner, Howard (1993): *Multiple Intelligences: The Theory in Practice*. New York: Basic Books.

Gardner, Howard (1999): *Intelligence Reframed: Multiple Intelligences for the 21st Century*. New York: Basic Books.

Illeris, Knud (2003): Learning, Identity and Self-Orientation in Youth. *Young – Nordic Journal of Youth Research*, 11(4), pp. 357–76.

Illeris, Knud (2006): Lifelong Learning and the Low-Skilled. *International Journal of Lifelong Education*, 25(1), pp. 15–28.

Illeris, Knud (2007): *How We Learn: Learning and Non-learning in School and Beyond*. London/New York: Routledge.

Illeris, Knud (2008): Transfer of Learning in the Learning Society. *International Journal of Lifelong Education* (in press).

Illeris, Knud *et al.* (2004): *Learning in Working Life*. Copenhagen: Roskilde University Press.

Leithäuser, Thomas (1976): *Formen des Alltagsbewusstseins* [The Forms of Everyday Consciousness]. Frankfurt a.M.: Campus.

Mager, Robert F. (1961): On the Sequencing of Instructional Content. *Psychological Reports*, 9, pp. 405–13.

Mezirow, Jack (1991): *Transformative Dimensions of Adult Learning*. San Francisco: Jossey-Bass.

Piaget, Jean (1952 [1936]): *The Origins of Intelligence in Children*. New York: International Universities Press.

Rogers, Carl R. (1951): *Client-Centered Therapy*. Boston: Houghton Mifflin.

Rogers, Carl R. (1969): *Freedom to Learn: A View of What Education Might Become*. Columbus, OH: Charles E. Merrill.

Vygotsky, Lev S. (1978): *Mind in Society: The Development of Higher Psychological Processes*. Cambridge, MA: Harvard University Press.

Chapter 2

Learning to be a person in society
Learning to be me

Peter Jarvis

Briton Peter Jarvis is today one of the best-known figures of international learning research. He was trained as both a theologian and a sociologist, but only later did he take up the topic of learning theory, primarily in relation to adult education. However, since the late 1980s Jarvis has been extremely productive in these areas, and since 2006 he has worked out a trilogy, Lifelong Learning and the Learning Society, *summing up his extensive understandings of learning. He has also for many years been the chief editor of the well-reputed* International Journal of Lifelong Education. *The following chapter stems, like the previous one, from the one-day conference on learning theory in Copenhagen in 2006. At the same time it presents the main ideas of the first volume of the mentioned trilogy:* Towards a Comprehensive Theory of Human Learning. *His presentation is here published internationally for the first time.*

Introduction

Many years ago I used to be invited to speak at pre-retirement courses, and one of the exercises that I asked the participants to undertake was that well-known psychological one on identity. I would put on the flip chart the question, 'Who am I?' and the response which began 'I am (a) ...'. Then I asked the participants to complete the answer ten times. We took feedback, and on many occasions the respondents placed their occupation high on the list – usually in the top three. I would then ask them a simple question: 'Who will you be when you retire?'

If I were now to be asked to answer that question, I would respond that 'I am learning to be me'. But, as we all know, 'me' exists in society and so I am forced to ask four further questions:

- What or who is me?
- What is society?
- How does the one interact with the other?
- What do I mean by 'learning'?

This apparently simple answer to the question actually raises more profound questions than it answers, but these are four of the questions that, if we could answer them, would help us to understand the person. I want to focus on the 'learning' for the major part of this chapter, but in the final analysis it is the 'me' that becomes just as important. This is also a chapter that raises questions about both 'being' and 'becoming' and this takes us beyond psychology, sociology and social psychology to philosophy and philosophical anthropology and even to metaphysics.

My interest in learning began in the early 1980s, but my concern with the idea of *disjuncture* between me and my world goes back a further decade to the time when I began to focus upon those unanswerable questions about human existence that underlie all religions and theologies of the world. It is, therefore, the process of me interacting with my life-world that forms the basis of my current thinking about human learning, but the quest that I began then is one that remains incomplete and will always be so. I do not want to pursue the religious/theological response to disjuncture (the gap between biography and my current experience) here but I do want to claim that all human learning begins with disjuncture – with either an overt question or with a sense of un-knowing. I hope that you will forgive me for making this presentation a little personal – but it will also demonstrate how my work began and where I think it is going, and in this way it reflects the opening chapter of my recent book on learning (Jarvis, 2006). In the process of the chapter, I will outline my developing theory and relate it to other theories of learning. The chapter falls into three parts: developing the theory, my present understanding of learning and learning throughout the lifetime.

Developing my understanding of human learning

As an adult educator I had a number of experiences in the early 1980s that sparked off my interest in learning, but the one which actually began my research was unintentional. I was invited to speak at an adult education workshop about the relationship between teaching and learning. In those days, that was a most insightful topic to choose since most of the books about teaching rarely mentioned learning and most of the texts about learning rarely mentioned teaching. I decided that the best way for me to tackle the topic was to get the participants to generate their own data, and so at the start of the workshop each participant was asked to write down a learning experience. It was a difficult thing to do – but after 20 or 30 minutes, everybody had a story, and I then asked them to pair up and discuss their learning experiences. We took some feedback at this stage, and I then put the pairs into fours and they continued to discuss, but by this time some of their discussion was not so much about their stories as about learning in general. At this point I introduced them to Kolb's learning cycle (1984).

I told the groups that the cycle was not necessarily correct – indeed, I have always maintained that it is too simple to reflect the reality of the complex

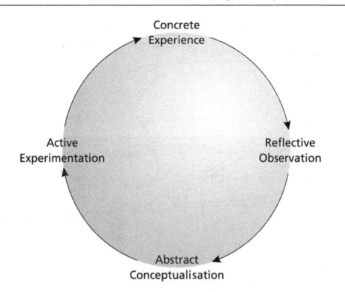

Figure 2.1 Kolb's learning cycle.

social process of human learning – and so I asked them to re-draw it to fit their four experiences. We took feedback and produced four totally different diagrams. By good fortune, I had the opportunity over the next year to conduct this workshop in the UK and USA on eight more occasions and, by the third, I realised that I had a research project on adult learning. During all the workshops, I collected all the feedback and, after the second one, I told the participants that I was also using the outcome of their discussions for research. Nobody objected, but rather they started making even more suggestions about my work. By 1986, I had completed the research and wrote it up, and it contained my own model of learning based upon over 200 participants in nine workshops all undertaking this exercise. In 1987, the book *Adult Learning in the Social Context* (Jarvis, 1987) appeared, in which I offered my own learning cycle.

As a sociologist, I recognised that all the psychological models of learning were flawed, including Kolb's well-known learning cycle, in as much as they omitted the social and the interaction. Hence my model included these, and the book discussed the social functions of learning itself, as well as many different types of learning. However, it is possible to see the many routes that we can take through the learning process if we look at the following diagram – I actually mentioned 12 in the book. I tried this model out in many different workshops, including two very early on in Denmark, and over the following 15 years I conducted the workshop many times, and in different books variations on this theme occurred.

However, I was always a little concerned about this model, which I regarded as a little over-simple, but far more sophisticated than anything that had

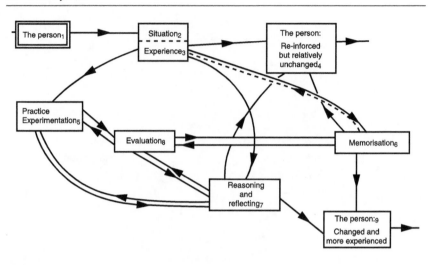

Figure 2.2 Jarvis' 1987 model of learning.

gone before. While I was clear in my own mind that learning always started with experience and that experience is always social, I was moving towards a philosophical perspective on human learning, and so an existentialist study was then undertaken – *Paradoxes of Learning* (Jarvis, 1992). In this, I recognised that, although I had recognised it in the 1987 model, the crucial philosophical issue about learning is that it is the person who learns, although it took me a long time to develop this. What I also recognised was that such concepts as truth and meaning also needed more discussion within learning theory since they are ambiguous and problematic.

To my mind, the move from experientialism to existentialism has been the most significant in my own thinking about human learning and it occupies a central theme of my current understanding (Jarvis, 2006). It was this recognition that led to another recent book in which Stella Parker and I (Jarvis and Parker, 2005) argued that since learning is human, then every academic discipline that focuses upon the human being has an implicit theory of learning, or at least a contribution to make to our understanding of learning. Fundamentally, it is the person who learns and it is the changed person who is the outcome of the learning, although that changed person may cause several different social outcomes. Consequently, we had chapters from the pure sciences, such as biology and neuroscience, and from the social sciences and from metaphysics and ethics. At the same time, I was involved in writing another book on learning with two other colleagues (Jarvis, Holford and Griffin, 2003) in which we wrote chapters about all the different theories of learning, most of which are still psychological or experiential. What was becoming apparent to me was that we needed a single theory that embraced all the other theories, one that was multi-disciplinary.

Over the years my understanding of learning developed and was changed, but in order to produce such a theory it was necessary to have an operational definition of human learning that reflected that complexity – a point also made by Illeris (2002). Initially, I had defined learning as 'the transformation of experience into knowledge, skills and attitudes' (Jarvis, 1987, p. 32) but after a number of metamorphoses I now define it in the following manner:

> Human learning is the combination of processes throughout a lifetime whereby the whole person – body (genetic, physical and biological) and mind (knowledge, skills, attitudes, values, emotions, beliefs and senses) – experiences social situations, the perceived content of which is then transformed cognitively, emotively or practically (or through any combination) and integrated into the individual person's biography resulting in a continually changing (or more experienced) person.

What I have recounted here has been a gradual development of my understanding of learning as a result of a number of years of research and the realisation that it is the whole person who learns and that the person learns in a social situation. It must, therefore, involve a number of academic disciplines including sociology, psychology and philosophy. These have all come together recently in my current study of learning (Jarvis, 2006, 2007).

Towards a comprehensive theory of human learning

As I have thus far argued, learning is both existential and experiential. In a sense, I would want to argue that learning occurs from before birth – for we do learn pre-consciously from experiences that we have in the womb, as a number of different disciplines indicate – and continues to the point when we lose consciousness before death. However, the fact that the individual is social is crucial to our understanding of learning, but so is the fact that the person is both mind and body. All of our experiences of our life-world begin with bodily sensations which occur at the intersection of the person and the life-world. These sensations initially have no meaning for us as this is the beginning of the learning process. Experience begins with disjuncture (the gap between our biography and our perception of our experience) or a sense of not-knowing, but in the first instance experience is a matter of the body receiving sensations, e.g. sound, sight, smell and so on, which appear to have no meaning. Thereafter, we transform these sensations into the language of our brains and minds and learn to make them meaningful to ourselves – this is the first stage in human learning. However, we cannot make this meaning alone; we are social human beings, always in relationship with us, and as we grow, we acquire a social language, so that nearly all the meanings will reflect the society into which we are born. I depict this first process in Figure 2.3.

Significantly, as adults we live a great deal of our lives in situations which we

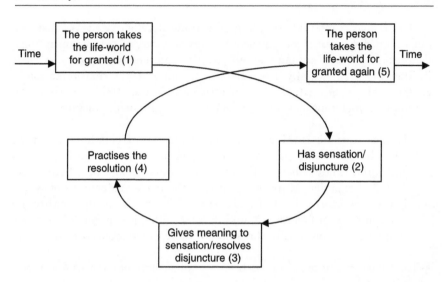

Figure 2.3 The transformation of sensations: learning from primary experience.

have learned to take for granted (Box 1), that is, we assume that the world as we know it does not change a great deal from one experience to another similar one (Schutz and Luckmann, 1974), although as Bauman (2000) reminds us, our world is changing so rapidly that he can refer to it as 'liquid'. Over a period of time, however, we actually develop categories and classifications that allow this taken-for-grantedness to occur. Falzon (1998, p. 38) puts this neatly:

> Encountering the world ... necessarily involves a process of ordering the world in terms of our categories, organising it and classifying it, actively bringing it under control in some way. We always bring some framework to bear on the world in our dealings with it. Without this organisational activity, we would be unable to make any sense of the world at all.

However, the same claim cannot be made for young children – they frequently experience sensations about which they have no meaning or explanation and they have to seek meanings and ask the question that every parent is fearful of: Why? They are in constant disjuncture or, in other words, they start much of their living reflecting Box 2, but as they develop, they gain a perception of the life-world and of the meanings that society gives to their experiences, and so Box 1 becomes more of an everyday occurrence. However, throughout our lives, however old and experienced we are, we still enter novel situations and have sensations that we do not recognise – what is that sound, smell, taste and so on? Both adult and child have to transform the sensation to brain language and eventually to give it meaning. It is in learning the meaning, etc. of the sensation that we incorporate the culture of our life-world into ourselves; this we do in most, if not all, of our learning experiences.

Traditionally, however, adult educators have claimed that children learn differently from adults, but the processes of learning from novel situations is the same throughout the whole of life, although children have more new experiences than adults do and this is why there appears to be some difference in the learning processes of children and adults. These are primary experiences and we all have them throughout our lives; we all have new sensations in which we cannot take the world for granted – when we enter a state of disjuncture and immediately we raise questions: What do I do now? What does that mean? What is that smell? What is that sound? and so on. Many of these queries may not be articulated in the form of a question, but there is a sense of unknowing (Box 2). It is this disjuncture that is at the heart of conscious experience – because conscious experience arises when we do not know and when we cannot take our world for granted. Through a variety of ways we give meaning to the sensation and our disjuncture is resolved. An answer (not necessarily a correct one, even if there is one that is correct) to our questions may be given by a significant other in childhood, by a teacher, incidentally in the course of everyday living, through discovery learning or through self-directed learning and so on (Box 3). However, there are times when we just cannot give meaning to primary experiences like this – when we experience beauty, wonder and so on – and it is here that we may begin to locate religious experiences – but time and space forbid us to continue this exploration today (see Jarvis and Hirji, 2006).

When we do get our disjunctures resolved, the answers are social constructs, and so immediately our learning is influenced by the social context within which it occurs. We are encapsulated by our culture. Once we have acquired an answer to our implied question, however, we have to practise or repeat it in order to commit it to memory (Box 4). The more opportunities we have to practise the answer to our initial question, the better we will commit it to memory. Since we do this in our social world, we get feedback, which confirms that we have gotten a socially acceptable resolution or else we have to start the process again, or be different from those people around us. A socially acceptable answer may be called correct, but here we have to be aware of the problem of language – conformity is not always 'correctness'. This process of learning to conform is 'trial and error' learning – but we can also learn to disagree, and it is in agreeing and disagreeing that aspects of our individuality emerge. However, once we have a socially acceptable resolution and have memorised it, we are also in a position to take our world for granted again (Box 5), provided that the social world has not changed in some other way. Most importantly, however, as we change and others change as they learn, the social world is always changing and so our taken-for-grantedness becomes more suspect (Box 5) since we always experience slightly different situations. The same water does not flow under the same bridge twice and so even our taken-for-grantedness is relative.

The significance of this process in contemporary society, however, is that once we have given meaning to the sensation and committed a meaning to our memories then the significance of the sensation itself recedes in future experiences as the socially acceptable answer (meaning) dominates the process, and when disjuncture then occurs it is more likely because we cannot understand the meaning, we do not know the meaning of the word and so on, than it is about the sensation itself. Naturally the sensation still occurs but we are less conscious of it. In this sense, we carry social meaning within ourselves – whatever social reality is, it is incorporated in us through our learning from the time of our birth onwards. Indeed, this also reflects the thinking of Bourdieu (1992, p. 127) when he describes habitus as a 'social made body' and he goes on in the same page to suggest that '[s]ocial reality exists, so to speak, twice, in things and in minds, in fields and in habitus, outside and inside of agents'. There is a sense then in which we might, unknowingly, be imprisoned behind the bars of our own minds – a phrase which I think was originally termed by Peter Berger. Significantly, this is the type of learning that adult educators have assumed that adults but not children have: these experiences are secondary ones which occur as a result of language or other forms of mediation – secondary experiences are mediated experiences of the world. These always occur in conjunction with primary ones, although we are not always conscious of the primary ones; for instance, when we are listening to someone speak we are not always conscious of how comfortable the chair is, and so on.

We have a continuing ambivalent relationship with our life-world – both in experiencing sensations and in experiencing meaning, both in knowing and not knowing. We have already described the primary experience since it is about experiencing with the senses, and we can continue to have primary experiences throughout our lives so that Figure 2.3 is as relevant for adults as it is for children when the senses are at the heart of the learning. But when the senses are relegated and we are more concerned with the cultural meanings, when we do not know the meanings or words rather than the sounds etc., then we have secondary experiences – these are mediated experiences which are often through speech and the written word, although we are becoming increasingly aware of visual mediation through television and the Web. These are becoming an everyday feature for many of us. Nevertheless, cognition becomes central to learning and while we still have the primary experience, it is relegated to a subsidiary position in the hierarchy of human learning, and in the following diagram I have depicted this secondary process in which we have certain forms of cognitive disjuncture. In Box 1, the whole person is in the life-world and at the point of disjuncture has an experience (Box 2).

Having had an experience (Box 2), which might occur as a result of disjuncture, we can reject it, think about it, respond to it emotionally or do something about it – or any combination of these (Boxes 3–5). But there is a double arrow here since there is always feedback at every point in learning as well as a progressive act. What is important about this observation is that we

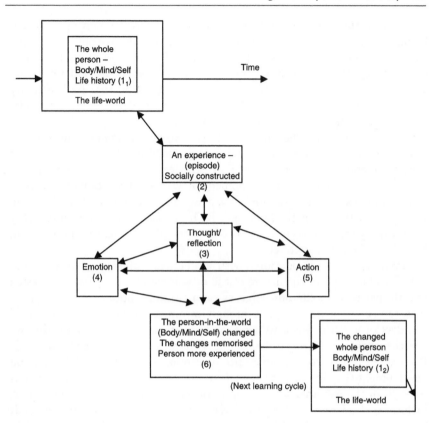

Figure 2.4 The transformation of the person through learning.

actually learn from the experience and not from the social situation in which the experience occurs, nor from the sensation once meaning has been attributed to it. As a result of the learning we become changed persons (Box 6) but, as we see, learning is itself a complex process. Once the person is changed, it is self-evident that the next social situation into which the individual enters is changed. And so, we can return to my experiences – I do not need to have a meaning to learn from the experience, although I might want to give meaning to my experiences as I reflect upon them (Box 3). However, my emotions are transformed (Box 4), my beliefs are affected and so are many attitudes and values (Box 3) and so on. I might even want to do something about them (Box 5). Finally, we see that as a result of learning (Box 6), we become changed persons and so only in being can we become and in learning we experience the process of becoming. Indeed, I am changed and so, therefore, is the situation in which I interact. Consequently, we can conclude that learning involves three transformations: the sensation, the person and then the social situation.

In Figure 2.4, I have tried to capture the continuous nature of learning by pointing to the second cycle (Box 1_2). However, this diagram must always be understood in relation to Figure 2.3, since it is only by combining them that we can begin to understand the process of human learning. These two diagrams together depict the complex process of experiencing both sensations and meanings simultaneously; it is also a recognition that both primary and secondary experiences occur simultaneously. However, there is a fundamental issue here about the person becoming more experienced which tells us something more about the nature of the person. For as long as I can continue to learn, I remain an unfinished person – the possibility of more growth, more experience and so on remains – or I am still learning to be me! Philosophically speaking, I only am at the moment 'now' and since I cannot stop time I am always becoming; paradoxically, however, through all that becoming I always feel that I am the same self. Being and becoming are inextricably intertwined, and human learning is one of the phenomena that unite them, for it is fundamental to life itself.

I am now, therefore, confronted with another issue in learning to be me and that is to be found in the nature of the person who learns: I have suggested that the person is about knowledge, skills, attitudes, emotions, beliefs, values, senses and even identity and that through learning each of these can be changed and develop further. But if we look carefully at the literature on learning we find that there is work on personal and cognitive development (Erikson, 1963; Piaget, 1929), work on religious faith development (Fowler, 1981), on moral development (Kohlberg, 1981) and so on. In precisely the same way, there is research in the way that we develop both our personal and social identities, including Mead (Strauss, 1964) and Wenger (1998) in their different ways. If we are to understand how the person learns to become a whole person, then we need to combine all of these theories, and that is where the book that I am just beginning will take us.

A person's lifetime learning

Since learning is an existential phenomenon, my starting point is the whole person – that is, body and mind. We can describe this process as that of the human essence emerging from the human existent, a process that continues throughout the whole of life, and that essence is moulded through interaction with the world. But that essence does not just emerge unaided, as it were – like the physical body needs food in order to mature, so that human existent needs to have experiences and learn if the human essence is to emerge and develop. The stimulus for this learning is our experience of the world – the point at which we intersect with the world (both physical and social). The only way that we can experience these moments of intersection is through our senses – we see, hear, feel, smell and taste. These then are the beginning of every learning experience, so that the bodily sensations are fundamental to the whole of the learning process. Fundamental to our understanding of learning, therefore, is our understanding of the whole person in the social situation – it is a philosophical anthropology but also a sociology and psychology. Once we recognise that learning is not just psychological and that the exclusive claims of psychology detract from the fullness of our understanding of learning, we can look afresh at human learning.

But before we do, we need to note that the person is both body and mind and that these are not separate entities – they are interrelated. Therefore, once we have recognised the significance of the senses in our learning theory, we need to examine the relationship between body and mind. There have been many volumes written on this topic and so there is no place to review the relationship in depth here. Suffice to note that there are five major sets of theory about the body–mind relationship. Maslin (2001), for instance, suggests five main theories:

- Dualism: the human person is a composite of two completely separate entities: body and mind. However, contemporary brain scanning techniques have demonstrated that brain activity can be seen as a result of the body receiving sensations, which suggests that there is a close interconnection between them;
- Mind/brain identity: a monist theory that claims that only physical substances exist and that human beings are just part of the material world; therefore, mental states are identical with physical ones, which raises fundamental problems about the nature of culture and meaning;
- Logical or analytical behaviourism: 'statements about the mind and mental states turn out, after analysis, to be statements that describe a person's actual and potential public behaviour' (Maslin 2001, p. 106). The objections include rejecting the idea that behaviour is the driving force of human being, and other forces, such as meaning or even thought itself, are significant;
- Functionalism: the mind is a function of the brain. Such a theory rules out meaning, intentionality, irrationality and emotion;
- Non-reductive monism: Maslin (2001, p. 163) describes it thus:

It is non-reductive because it does not insist that mental properties are nothing over and above physical properties. On the contrary, it is willing to allow that mental properties are different in kind from physical properties, and not ontologically reducible to them. It is clusters and series of these mental properties which constitute our psychological lives ... property dualism dispenses with the dualism of substances and physical events, hence it is a form of monism. But these physical substances and events possess two very different kinds of property, namely physical properties and, in addition, non-physical, mental properties.

Having examined five different ways of looking at the body–mind relationship we can find no simple theory that allows us to explain it. Exclusive claims should not logically be made for any single theory, although they are made quite widely in contemporary society. Some of the theories, however, appear to be much weaker than others, such as mind/brain identity, behaviourism and functionalism. This is unfortunate since these are the ones most widely cited and used in contemporary society. We have accepted a form of dualism that may best be explained as a form of non-reductive monism, although we are less happy with dualism *per se.* Yet we have to acknowledge that none of the theories can claim universal allegiance and in each there are problems that appear insurmountable.

From the above brief philosophical discussion we can see immediately that profound doubt is cast on many contemporary theories of learning as providing logical understanding of human learning, including behaviourism, information processing and all forms of cognitive theory. This is not to say that they are not valid in as far as they go, simply that they do not go far enough: they all have an incomplete theory of the person. Clearly experientialism comes much closer because it situates the learning in the social context, but even experiential learning theories do not go sufficiently far since they also build on an incomplete theory of the person and few of them actually examine the social context within which the experience occurs. Two theories which offer a great deal of insight into human learning – in fact to my mind the most comprehensive – are those of Illeris (2002) and Wenger (1998).

Conclusion

As with many other learning theories, the two last mentioned start from the psychological and the sociological angle, respectively. Each of them provides tremendous insights into human learning and points us beyond its own boundaries. Both raise profound questions and both include the idea of the human being in relation to the social world which I try to depict in Figure 2.5.

The psychologist traces the arrows out from the person to the external, objectified culture, while the sociologist starts with the objectified culture and points inwards to the individual person. A person's learning must be seen from both perspectives! This leaves us with major problems about how we study learning. I would argue that we need to start with an understanding of the person – the learner – which is a philosophical perspective that has been sadly lacking from studies of learning, and, thereafter, begin to explore the psychological and the sociological aspects of the leaning process in tandem. But standing in the middle is the person – and analysis of the person calls for a philosophical anthropology. This also leads us to recognising the inter-subjectivity of social living and human learning – well captured by Buber's (1994) *I and Thou* – and I believe that this broader perspective will help us understand learning better, although it is impossible to have a theory that explains the learning process in every detail. Paradoxically, despite all that we

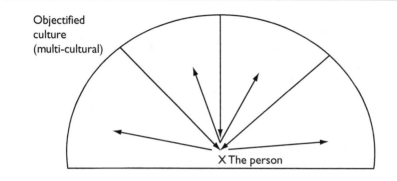

Figure 2.5 The internalisation and externalisation of culture.

know and all that we have learned, we will spend the reminder of our lives
learning to be ourselves – people in society.

References

Arendt, H. (1978) *The Life of the Mind.* San Diego: Harvest Book, Harcourt.

Bauman, Z. (2000) *Liquid Modernity.* Cambridge, UK: Polity.

Bourdieu, P. (1992) The Purpose of Reflexive Sociology. In Bourdieu, P. and Wacquant, L (eds).
An Invitation to Reflexive Sociology. Cambridge, UK: Polity.

Buber, M. (1994 [1923]) *I and Thou.* Edinburgh: T&T Clark.

Erikson, E. (1963) *Childhood and Society.* New York: Norton.

Falzon, C. (1998) *Foucault and Social Dialogue: Beyond Fragmentation.* London: Routledge.

Fowler, J. (1981) *Stages of Faith: The Psychology of Human Development and the Quest for Meaning.*
New York: Harper and Row.

Illeris. K (2002) *The Three Dimensions of Learning: Contemporary Learning Theory in the Tension Field
Between the Cognitive, the Emotional and the Social.* Leicester: NIACE.

Jarvis, P. (1987) *Adult Learning in the Social Context.* London: Croom Helm.

Jarvis, P. (1992) *Paradoxes of Learning: On Becoming an Individual in Society.* San Francisco: Jossey-
Bass.

Jarvis, P. (2001) *Learning in Later Life: An Introduction for Educators & Carers.* London: Kogan Page.

Jarvis, P. (2006) *Towards a Comprehensive Theory of Human Learning.* London: Routledge.
(Vol 1 of *Lifelong Learning and the Learning Society*).

Jarvis, P. (2007) *Globalisation, Lifelong Learning and the Learning Society: Sociological Perspectives.*
London: Routledge. (Vol 2 of *Lifelong Learning and the Learning Society*).

Jarvis, P., Holford, J. and Griffin, C. (2003) *Theory and Practice of Learning (2nd edition).* London:
Routledge.

Jarvis, P. and Hirji, N. (2006) Learning the Unlearnable – Experiencing the Unknowable. *Journal
for Adult Theological Education*, 1, pp. 88–94.

Jarvis, P. and Parker, S. (eds) (2005) *Human Learning: An Holistic Approach.* London:
Routledge.

Kohlberg, L. (1981) *The Philosophy of Moral Development: Moral Stages and the Idea of Justice.*
San Francisco: Harper & Row.

Kolb, D. (1984) *Experiential Learning: Experience as the Source of Learning and Development.* Englewood Cliffs, NJ: Prentice-Hall.

Loder, J. (1998) *The Logic of the Spirit: Human Development in Theological Perspective.* San Francisco: Jossey-Bass.

Maslin, K. T. (2001) *An Introduction to the Philosophy of Mind.* Cambridge, UK: Polity.

Piaget, J. (1929) *The Child's Conception of the World.* London: Routledge and Kegan Paul.

Schutz, A. and Luckmann, T. (1974) *The Structures of the Life-world.* London: Heinemann.

Strauss, A. (ed) (1964) *George Herbert Mead on Social Psychology.* Chicago: University of Chicago Press.

Wenger, E (1998) *Communities of Practice: Learning, Meaning, and Identity.* Cambridge, UK: Cambridge University Press.

Chapter 3

What "form" transforms?

A constructive-developmental approach to transformative learning

Robert Kegan

Robert Kegan is a trained psychologist and Professor of Adult Learning and Professional Development at Harvard University. In 1982 he presented his advanced stage model of human development in his book The Evolving Self, *and in 1994 he elaborated the model further in another important book,* In Over Our Heads: The Mental Demands of Modern Life. *Later, leadership, change, and professional learning and training have become the focus of his work. His interest in the transformations that lead from one developmental stage to the next has led him to take up Jack Mezirow's concept of "transformative learning" (see Mezirow's chapter later in this book), as can be seen in the following chapter, which is a slightly abridged version of Kegan's chapter in Jack Mezirow* et al. *(2000),* Learning as Transformation: Critical Perspectives on a Theory in Progress.

Introduction

Consider the case of Peter and Lynn as they tumble out of bed. "These days," each could say, "my work is too much with me." Different as their work is, they have noticed that in each of their jobs a similar circumstance has stirred them up.

Lynn has been at Highland Junior High School for twelve years, originally as an English teacher. Three years ago she became chair of the English department, and last year it was decided that chairpersons would become part of the principal's newly formed Leadership Council. The school had decided to adopt a site-based management (SBM) philosophy in which the responsibility and authority for running the school would no longer be vested only in the principal, Carolyn Evans, but shared mainly among the principal and the faculty or its representatives.

Peter has worked at BestRest Incorporated for nineteen years. A bedding manufacturer with twelve regional factories, BestRest hired Peter during the summers while he was still in college. He caught the eye of Anderson Wright, then a plant manager, who became his mentor. As Anderson rose through the ranks he brought Peter along. Eventually, when he became a corporate vice president, he put Peter in charge of an independent product line. Peter enjoyed the continuing close association with Anderson, whom he consulted frequently and easily.

But life became more complicated for Peter when Anderson decided to make the independent product line a separate company division and Peter its new head. "If you're game, Peter," said Anderson, "and I think you're ready, I want you to think of the new line as a company on its own – SafeSleep Products – and I want you to run it." Peter could hear the excitement in Anderson's voice, his pleasure in offering Peter what Anderson clearly regarded as a wonderful present. So Peter, without hesitation or conscious deliberation, moved himself to rejoin Anderson in this new place.

Thus Lynn and Peter, the teacher and the business executive who seldom feel their work has anything in common, find themselves contending with a similar circumstance: worker-participation initiatives have recast the issues of responsibility, ownership, and authority at work. Both are miserable and de- moralized about the changes at work. Let's take a closer look to find out why.

"I can give you an example of why this thing is not working at Highland," Lynn says. "Probably every department chair and most of the faculty would agree that there are big flaws in the way we do faculty evaluations. First of all, faculty evaluations are based on two class visits by the principal. They are announced visits, so teachers end up preparing for a performance and they don't feel that the principal gets a fair sample of their work. The kids know what's going on and act weird – they're on 'good behavior' too, and completely un- spontaneous. The principal writes up a generally innocuous report. Nobody is learning a thing, but at least the principal can tell the central office that 'everyone's been evaluated' and she has the paperwork to prove it.

"I went along with this, but by the time I'd become the English department chair I got the idea that the school should be a learning place for everyone. I decided that if we want kids to be learning in school it would help them if we modeled learning ourselves. It was actually some version of this that got me excited about being on the Leadership Council in the first place. I had some different ideas about faculty evaluation. I wanted to return the emphasis to learning, not file-filling.

"So when Carolyn proposed site-based management to our faculty, I admired her for being willing to let some other voices come into the leadership of the school, but I wasn't thinking, 'Good, now we're going to take over.' I don't want to take over. I don't want to be the principal. But I don't want Carolyn being the department chair either, and I felt that we had a better chance of clearing these things up in group discussions, like we'd have on the council, than in one-on-one meetings in Carolyn's office.

"The whole thing started to fall apart for me this semester around just this issue of faculty evaluation, and it wasn't even my initiative. When Alan – he's the history chair – brought in his proposal, it was a complete surprise to me. Basically, his proposal was that the history department be allowed to run a one-year experiment on evaluation. He wanted to get the performance-anxiety, test-taking dimension out of it. He wanted people to have the option of entering supervisory relationships with him or a few other senior members of the department that would really be more consultative than supervisory. The supervisor/consultant would, in effect, be 'hired' by the faculty member to advance the faculty member's learning goals. The teacher could 'fire' the consultant without consequences. No file entries for one year. Try to get a sense of how the faculty used it and how much and what kind of learning was going on, but all anonymously, evaluating the experiment, not the teachers.

"I loved the idea, of course. I was envious that I hadn't thought of it myself. It seemed like a good way of putting into operation my idea that the faculty member should run his evaluation, that the evaluation should be aimed at learning, not putting on a show, that the chair could serve as a consultant and a resource to self-directed learning.

"We've now had three long discussions about this on the council, and we still haven't had the first word about the real merits of Alan's proposal. As I now realize, the issue for Carolyn had less to do with promoting faculty learning than with the precedent it sets about accountability in general and accountability to her specifically. Stop visits by the principal? Let the faculty decide what they need to learn? No evaluations for the files by anybody! These didn't go down easily with Carolyn. Rather than take her usual stance of speaking last in a conversation, she was the first to speak after Alan made his proposal, and what she had to say pretty much silenced the rest of us. She didn't identify any merits in the proposal. She didn't even acknowledge the implicit problems the proposal was at least trying to address. She just said basically, 'This is something we can't do.'

"I'm not proud of the way I responded, but it was just such a unilateral and imperial stance for her to take, and I guess I got mad. What I said was, 'Why, Carolyn? Is it illegal what Alan is proposing?' and everyone else laughed and I could see that Carolyn was very angry. I hadn't meant it exactly the way it came out. I didn't mean she was out of line to object to the proposal. I was reacting to the way she framed it. I didn't feel she had the right to just shut down the conversation. At the time I attributed my overreaction and sarcasm to the fact this was an especially important issue to me personally, and I resented how it was being dismissed. That didn't justify my sarcasm, but it did dignify it somehow.

"Anyhow, after that council session Carolyn asked to meet with me in her office, and she read me the riot act: How could I do that to her? Didn't I know how much she counted on my loyalty? Didn't I realize how powerful I was as a department chair, and that to take such a doubting view when she had clearly committed herself was terribly undermining? That she thought of us as partners, that we had worked so well together all these years, and how it was even more important with SBM that we read each other's signals well and be a good team. I had to say, 'Whoa, Carolyn, time out, I'm having too many reactions to all this.'

"We ended up having a good conversation, actually, one of our best in years, but it was really difficult. I had to tell her I thought it was unfair of her to trade on my loyalty to her, that I *did* respect her and I was grateful to her for her support to me professionally over the years, but that I was sure she was not interested in a friend who was a clone. This got us into the whole SBM, Leadership Council thing, and whether that was itself a team, and what were the expectations about how we functioned as members of that council. Carolyn broke down and cried and said she was finding SBM terribly hard, that she had had no idea what she was getting into, that half the time she had nightmares that the school was going to fall apart because there was more chaos than leadership, and the other half of the time she had nightmares that the school was getting along too well without her running things, that SBM was about gradually making the principal irrelevant."

Were Peter to tell us what his new role as head of a division really felt like, he might say something like this: "Honestly? It's definitely a different ball game! What game is it? Well, let's see. I guess you could say before I was president, I was playing a game of catch. Anderson would throw things at me and I'd catch them, I'd throw things back at him and he'd catch them. And now? Now I'd say I'm a juggler. There's not one ball, there are five, and then there are ten, and then there are fifteen! People keep tossing more in to me to add to those I'm juggling. But I'm not throwing to anyone. I'm just throwing them into the air. And my job as the juggler is to keep them all going up there, to not let any of them drop to the ground.

"You couldn't believe the number of things that come across my desk. 'Anderson says to take this to you now.' 'Anderson says he's not the guy on this anymore; you are.' If it isn't one thing, it's another. You have to deal with a lot of people's feelings about this change. Everybody thought the company concept for SafeSleep was a hot idea when Anderson proposed it, but now that we're actually doing it, a lot of people aren't so sure. I'm not even sure Anderson's so sure at this point. People keep asking me how I feel about the change, but I don't have time to think about how I feel about it because I spend half my day dealing with how everybody else feels about it.

"Take Ted, for example. He's one of our salespeople. I've known Ted ten years in this business. Ted's putting a lot of pressure on me not to separate him from the SafeSleep line. Ted's a mattress salesman and a damn good one. He does excellent work for his customers. They love him and he loves them. The SafeSleep line got its start by accident, or what Anderson called 'entrepreneurial jujitsu,' turning a weakness into a strength. New government codes mandated that we manufacture flame-retardant mattresses, and it cost millions of dollars to set up the capacity. Since we had the capacity, Anderson reasoned, why not use it for other things, too? Presto! The SafeSleep line. But originally these products were just an extra that the mattress salespeople offered their furniture stores. The store used them as 'sweeteners' to sell their customers our top-of-the-line mattresses. Everybody was happy. The furniture store's customer liked the freebie; the store liked the mattress sale; our salespeople liked the increased mattress orders they got from the stores. 'So why are you ruining a nice thing?' Ted wants to know. 'Peter, I'm family,' he says to me. 'And Harold is not,' which is true. 'So why are you letting this guy take the bread off my table?' he says.

"I hired Harold soon after I became president of SafeSleep because Harold had sales experience in bedclothes. He was the first nonmattress salesperson in the place, and I thought we needed that for the new company. He's turned out to be a dynamo. The guy's got more ideas per square inch than I've ever seen, and most of them make sense. But they're also making some people, like Ted, mad. And I'm not so sure Anderson's very keen about him either.

"Harold's take was that BestRest was choking SafeSleep, that the best reason for setting up SafeSleep as a separate company was that its growth was stunted in the shadow of the mattress company. Furniture stores, he said, were not the place to be selling pajamas and not even the best place to sell quilts. And on and on. It all made sense to me, but whenever you start talking about doing things differently people get worried about what it means for them. His view is that if SafeSleep is really going to be its own company, it needs its own *identity*, its own *purpose*. It has to get out of the hip pocket of BestRest.

"The problem with this is that as soon as you pull the SafeSleep line away from the mattress sales force, a guy like Ted, who has gotten a lot of mileage out of it, yells 'Ouch.' I think Harold's basically right, but Ted's probably right, too, that his mattress orders will go down, at least for a while, if we pull the SafeSleep line from him. Ted's not just worried about his volume, he's worried about his bonus benefits. Why doesn't he go make his stores feel guilty? It's their fault if they short-order him, not mine. Give me a break!

"I consider Ted and Anderson two of my best friends, and if this new job ruins both of these friendships I won't be surprised. When Anderson offered me the presidency he said it was a way to move our relationship to a whole new level, that we were becoming true colleagues. It's a whole new level all right! I guess if you never want to see a guy again you should become true colleagues with him! But I know if you ask Anderson he'll say he's just as available, that it's *me*, that I don't call. And that's true. I just stay away from him these days and figure that when he needs to tell me something he will. I'd leave our meetings feeling as if we'd talked a lot but I had no clearer idea where I was when I left.

"It was very clear that he didn't want to be asked straight out what he thought we should do. It was very clear that he wanted me to have a plan. But it was also clear that he liked some plans better than others. He'd dump all over a lot of Harold's ideas. I'd leave his office and find myself down on Harold for the next three days. I'd feel that he was trying to warn me away from Harold but wouldn't come right out and say so. What I'd always liked about Anderson was that he was a straight shooter. He'd always tell you exactly what he wanted. I want Anderson to sign on to my plans, and he keeps saying, 'If this is where you want to put your chips.' A fat lot of help that is! When I tell him it must be nice for him to be out of it, he gets annoyed and says, 'Don't think for a minute I'm out of it! You're turning SafeSleep from a cute afterthought into a corporate factor, and if it goes down the tubes they'll be asking me what happened.' And then I feel even less reassured because now I'm responsible for Anderson's not getting hurt. That's a lot of what's different about being the president. I've got to worry about Ted. I've got to worry about Anderson. And I'm not exactly sure what I did to deserve this wonderful job."

Peter and Lynn are dealing with what we might call the hidden curriculum of adult life as it expresses itself here in the world of work. If we were to look at the whole of contemporary culture in the West as a kind of school, and consider adult roles as the courses in which we are *enrolled*, most adults have a full and demanding schedule. The "courses" of parenting, partnering, working, and living in an increasingly diverse society are demanding ones, yet most adults are enrolled in all of them. What does it take to succeed in these courses? What is the nature of the change struggling students would have to undergo to become successful students?

These are the kinds of questions I posed in my book *In Over Our Heads* (1994), of which Peter and Lynn are the heroes. In the last several years since the book has been published, I have heard the thinking of a few thousand adult educators about Peter and Lynn in various workshops, institutes, and summer conferences. Most people see Lynn as more capable and handling better the new demands at work. Although people often want to claim that Peter has a number of external problems that Lynn does not – he has more at stake, they say; his organizational culture is less supportive, they say; he has a male boss, they say, who isn't as open to conversation as Lynn's boss – most people do not attribute Lynn's greater success to these external advantages alone.

Without using the terms, people find Lynn more capable in each of four familiar quadrants of the psychological self: *cognitive* ("Lynn seems to have more of a mind of her own"; "She has a Big Picture and an overall 'take' on things, but Peter seems lost and overwhelmed"), *affective* ("Lynn takes responsibility for how she feels, understands why she feels that way, and can even step out of being controlled by her feelings"; "Peter seems swamped and overrun by his feelings"; "He blames other people for how he feels"), *interpersonal* ("Peter is like a victim"; "He's too dependent"; "Lynn is able to set clear boundaries in a complicated multidimensional relationship, but Peter is not, and seems run by his relationships to people at work who are his friends"), and *intrapersonal* ("Peter doesn't seem very self-reflective"; "He's thinking about what other people are thinking, and she's thinking about her own thinking").

What sort of transformation would it take for Peter to exercise the capabilities people see in Lynn? What capabilities does Peter already possess and what prior transformations in his learning might their presence imply? Why don't his present capabilities serve him in his new circumstances?

Transformational learning and the problem of its success

Some academic writing – that which is most frequently parodied and ridiculed – uses obscure language to hide the fact that nothing terribly original is being expressed. Some unappealingly obscure academic language is in the service of genuinely new ideas; the thinkers are just better at creating new thinking than at devising the language required to express it. And on occasion a richly heuristic set of novel ideas finds an appealing language for its expression and the field takes off. In psychology, Erikson's concepts of identity and identity crisis are examples. Gardner's multiple intelligences is a more recent one. And surely transformational learning is another. Jack Mezirow's genius and our good fortune derive from this double-header ability to provide accessible new language in service of valuable new ideas. But as Mezirow well knows, this kind of success spawns its own problems. The language can become so appealing it begins to be used for myriad purposes; its meaning can be distorted, its distinct ideas lost. It can take on quasi-religious qualities, in this case of dramatic "conversion." Transformation begins to refer to any kind of change or process at all. Piaget (1954) distinguished between assimilative processes, in which new experience is shaped to conform to existing knowledge structures, and accommodative processes, in which the structures themselves change in response to new experience. Ironically, as the language of transformation is more widely assimilated, it risks losing its genuinely transformative potential!

In this chapter I try to protect the genuinely landscape-altering potential in the concept of transformational learning by suggesting several of its distinct features that I believe need to be more explicit:

- Transformational kinds of learning need to be more clearly distinguished from informational kinds of learning, and each needs to be recognized as valuable in any learning activity, discipline, or field.
- The *form* that is undergoing trans*form*ation needs to be better understood; if there is no form, there is no transformation.
- At the heart of a form is a way of knowing (what Mezirow calls a "frame of reference"); thus genuinely transformational learning is always to some extent an epistemological change rather than merely a change in behavioral repertoire or an increase in the quantity or fund of knowledge.
- Even as the concept of transformational learning needs to be *narrowed* by focusing more explicitly on the epistemological, it needs to be *broadened* to include the whole lifespan; transformational learning is not the province of adulthood or adult education alone.
- Adult educators with an interest in transformational learning may need a better understanding of their students' current epistemologies so as not to create learning designs that unwittingly presuppose the very capacities in the students their designs might seek to promote.

- Adult educators may better discern the nature of learners' particular needs for transformational learning by better understanding not only their students' present epistemologies but also the epistemological complexity of the present learning challenges they face in their lives.

The remainder of this chapter addresses each of these points in the context of the predicaments of Peter and Lynn.

Informational learning and transformational learning

Learning aimed at increasing our fund of knowledge, at increasing our repertoire of skills, at extending already established cognitive structures all deepen the resources available to an existing frame of reference. Such learning is literally in-*form*-ative because it seeks to bring valuable new contents into the existing form of our way of knowing.

No learning activity, discipline, or field is well nourished without continuous opportunities to engage in this kind of learning. Certainly no passenger wants an airline pilot whose professional training was long on collaborative reflective dialogue leading to ever more complex apprehensions of the phenomena of flight but short on the technique of landing a plane in a crosswind; no patient wants a doctor well trained in such dialogue but unable to tell a benign lump from a cancerous tumor.

However, learning aimed at changes not only in *what* we know but changes in *how* we know has an almost opposite rhythm about it and comes closer to the etymological meaning of *education* ("leading out"). "Informative" learning involves a kind of leading in, or filling of the form (see Figure 3.1). Trans-*form*-ative learning puts the form itself at risk of change (and not just change but increased capacity). If one is bound by concrete thinking in the study of, say, history, then yes, further learning of the informative sort might involve the mastery of more historical facts, events, characters, and outcomes. But further learning of a transformative sort might also involve the development of a capacity for abstract thinking so that one can ask more general, thematic questions *about* the facts, or consider the perspectives and biases of those who wrote the historical account *creating* the facts. Both kinds of learning are expansive and valuable, one within a preexisting frame of mind and the other reconstructing the very frame.

But only the latter would I call transformative or transformational. Trans-formation should not refer to just any kind of change, even to any kind of dramatic, consequential change. I know a 10-year-old who decided to read the entire encyclopedia, A through Z, for a summer project. His appetite and his recall were certainly impressive. His ability even to sustain his interest in a series of very short-term exposures was commendable. But I see nothing transformational about his learning.

Changes in one's fund of knowledge, one's confidence as a learner, one's self-

Informative: Changes in *what* we know

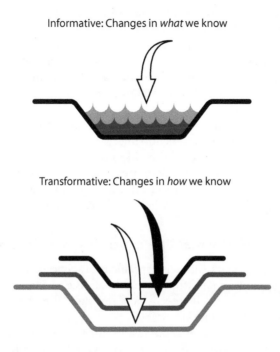

Transformative: Changes in *how* we know

Figure 3.1 Two kinds of learning: informative and transformative.

perception as a learner, one's motives in learning, one's self-esteem – these are all potentially important kinds of changes, all desirable, all worthy of teachers thinking about how to facilitate them. But it is possible for any or all of these changes to take place without any transformation because they could all occur within the existing form or frame of reference.

And much of the time there would be no problem whatever in this being exactly what occurs. Lynn, for example, already demonstrates the complex capacity to set boundaries, to keep separate her simultaneous relationship to Carolyn as friend and as colleague so that the claims from one sphere are not inappropriately honored in another. She demonstrates the capacity to generate an internal vision that guides her purposes and allows her to sort through and make judgments about the choices, expectations, and proposals of others. Although it would certainly be possible for the underlying form of her way of knowing to undergo further transformation, it may not be necessary at the moment. She may be in greater need of learning additional skills at detecting more readily circumstances that are likely to risk such boundary violations, or how one more effectively gathers a consensus to bring to life the vision she is able intellectually to create. Such learnings could be extremely valuable, make her even more effective, and increase her enjoyment of work and her circumstances – and none of that learning need be transformational.

Peter, on the other hand, would be ill-served by a kind of learning that was only informative. He is overreliant on the opinion of others, too dependent on signals from others to direct his own choices and behaviors. He could experience a kind of learning that might dramatically enhance his signal-detecting capabilities in twelve different ways. But dramatic as such changes might be, I would not call them transformational because they do not give Peter the opportunity to reconstruct the very role of such signals in his life. Given his current work circumstances, if he cannot effect this change he is going to continue to have a difficult time.

Informational and transformational kinds of learning are each honorable, valuable, meritable, dignifiable activities. Each can be enhancing, necessary, and challenging for the teacher to facilitate. In given moments or contexts, a heavier weighting of one or the other may be called for.

What form transforms? The centrality of epistemology

As the foregoing suggests, the saving specificity of a concept like transformational learning may lie in a more explicit understanding of the form we believe is undergoing some change. If there is no form, there is no transformation. But what really constitutes a form?

Mezirow's term *frame of reference* is a useful way to engage this question. Its province is necessarily epistemological. Our frame of reference may be passionately clung to or casually held, so it clearly has an emotional or affective coloring. Our frame of reference may be an expression of our familial loyalties or tribal identifications, so it clearly has a social or interpersonal coloring. Our frame of reference may have an implicit or explicit ethical dimension, so it clearly has a moral coloring. But what is the phenomenon itself that takes on all these colorings? Mezirow says a frame of reference involves both a habit of mind and a point of view. Both of these suggest that, at its root, a frame of reference is a way of knowing.

"Epistemology" refers to precisely this: not *what* we know but our way of knowing. Attending to the epistemological inevitably involves attending to two kinds of processes, both at the heart of a concept like transformational learning. The first is what we might call *meaning-forming*, the activity by which we shape a coherent meaning out of the raw material of our outer and inner experiencing. Constructivism recognizes that reality does not happen preformed and waiting for us merely to copy a picture of it. Our perceiving is simultaneously an act of conceiving, of interpreting. "Percept without concept is blind," Kant said. "Our experience," Huxley said, "is less what happens to us, and more what we make of what happens to us."

The second process inherent in the epistemological is what we might call *reforming our meaning-forming*. This is a metaprocess that affects the very terms of our meaning-constructing. We do not only form meaning, and we do not only change our meanings; we change the very form by which we are making our meanings. We change our epistemologies.

These two processes inherent in epistemology are actually at the heart of two lines of social-scientific thought that should be in much closer conversations with each other: the educational line of thought is transformational learning, and the psychological line of thought is constructive developmentalism. Constructive developmental psychology (Kegan, 1982, 1994; Piaget, 1954; Kohlberg, 1984; Belenky *et al.*, 1986) attends to the natural evolution of the forms of our meaning-constructing (hence "constructive-developmental"). A more explicit rendering of transformational learning, I suggest, attends to the deliberate efforts and designs that support changes in the learner's form of knowing. Adult educators with an interest in supporting transformational learning can look to constructive-developmental theory as a source of ideas about (1) the dynamic architecture of "that form which transforms," that is, a form of knowing; and (2) the dynamic architecture of "reforming our forms of knowing," that is, the psychological process of transformations in our knowing.

Constructive-developmental theory invites those with an interest in transformational learning to consider that a form of knowing always consists of a relationship or temporary equilibrium between the subject and the object in one's knowing. The subject–object relationship forms the cognate or core of an epistemology. That which is "object" we can look at, take responsibility for, reflect upon, exercise control over, integrate with some other way of knowing. That which is "subject" we are run by, identified with, fused with, at the effect of. We cannot be responsible for that to which we are subject. What is "object" in our knowing describes the thoughts and feelings we say we have; what is "subject" describes the thinking and feeling that has us. We "have" object; we "are" subject.

Constructive-developmental theory looks at the process it calls development as the gradual process by which what was "subject" in our knowing becomes "object." When a way of knowing moves from a place where we are "had by it" (captive of it) to a place where we "have it," and can be in relationship to it, the form of our knowing has become more complex, more expansive. This somewhat formal, explicitly epistemological rendering of development comes closest, in my view, to the real meaning of transformation in transformational learning theory.

Transformational learning as a lifelong phenomenon

As all good teachers know, every student comes with a "learning past" that is an important part of his or her present and future learning. Important features of this past – for adult learners especially, and their teachers – include the history of their relationship to the subject at hand and the history of their personal disposition toward the enterprise of learning itself. But for the adult educator with an interest in supporting transformative learning, an important and often overlooked feature of their students' learning pasts is their history of prior transformations.

Although the more explicitly epistemological definition of transformative learning this chapter advances is intended to limit our definition of transformation (so that not every kind of change, even important change, constitutes transformation), it also expands our exploration of the phenomenon to the entire lifespan. Much of the literature on transformational learning really constitutes an exploration of what constructive-developmental theory and research identifies as but one of several gradual, epochal transformations in knowing of which persons are shown to be capable throughout life. This particular transformation, reflected in the contrast between Peter's and Lynn's constructions of their similar predicaments at work, is empirically the most widespread gradual transformation we find in adulthood, so it is not surprising that adult educators have come to focus on it. But constructive-developmental theory suggests that (a) it is not the only transformation in the form of our knowing possible in adulthood; (b) even this transformation will be better understood and facilitated if its history is better honored and its future better appreciated; and (c) we will better discern the nature of learners' particular needs for transformational learning by better understanding not only their present epistemologies but the epistemological complexity of the present learning challenges they face in their lives.

The transformation that Peter would undergo were he to construct experience more like Lynn is a shift away from being "made up by" the values and expectations of one's "surround" (family, friends, community, culture) that get uncritically internalized and with which one becomes identified, toward developing an internal authority that makes choices about these external values and expectations according to one's own self-authored belief system. One goes from being psychologically "written by" the socializing press to "writing upon" it, a shift from a socialized to a self-authoring epistemology, in the lingo of constructive-developmental theory.

As pervasive and powerful as this gradual transformation may be, it is only one of several shifts in the deep underlying epistemology (the form that transforms) we use to organize meaning. Longitudinal and cross-sectorial research, using a reliable interview instrument to discern what epistemologies an individual has access to (Lahey and others, 1988), identifies five distinctly different epistemologies (Kegan, 1994). As Figure 3.2 suggests, each of these can be described with respect to what is subject and what is object, and each shift entails the movement of what had been subject in the old epistemology to what is object in the new epistemology. Thus the basic principle of complexification of mind here is not the mere addition of new capacities (an aggregation model), nor the substitution of a new capacity for an old one (a replacement model), but the subordination of once-ruling capacities to the dominion of more complex capacities, an evolutionary model that again distinguishes transformation from other kinds of change.

An array of increasingly complex epistemologies, such as those described in Figure 3.2, works against the unhelpful tendency to see a person like Peter, who

	SUBJECT	OBJECT	UNDERLYING STRUCTURE
	PERCEPTIONS Fantasy SOCIAL PERCEPTIONS/ IMPULSES	Movement Sensation	Single point/immediate/atomistic

	CONCRETE
	  Actuality
	  Data, cause-and-effect
	POINT OF VIEW
	  Role-concept
	  Simple reciprocity (tit-for-tat)
	ENDURING DISPOSITIONS
	  Needs, preferences
	  Self-concept
		Perceptions
		
		Social perception
		
		Impulses
			Durable category 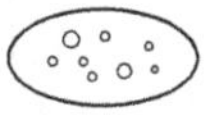

The socialized mind / TRADITIONALISM	ABSTRACTIONS
	  Ideality
	  Inference, generalization
	  Hypothesis, proposition
	  Ideals, values
	MUTUALITY/INTERPERSONALISM
	  Role consciousness
	  Mutual reciprocity
	INNER STATES
	  Subjectivity, self-consciousness
		Concrete
		
		Point of view
		
		Enduring dispositions
		Needs, preferences
			Cross-categorical
			Trans-categorical 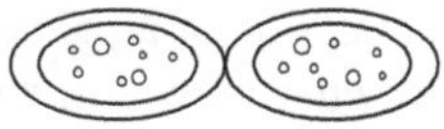

The self-authoring mind / MODERNISM	ABSTRACT SYSTEMS
	  Ideology
	  Formulation, authorization
	  Relations between abstractions
	INSTITUTION
	  Relationship-regulating forms
	  Multiple-role consciousness
	SELF-AUTHORSHIP
	  Self-regulation, self-formation
	  Identity, autonomy, individuation
		Abstractions
		
		Mutuality
		Interpersonalism
		
		Inner states
		Subjectivity
		Self-consciousness
			System/complex 

The self-transforming mind / POST-MODERNISM	DIALECTICAL
	  Trans-ideological/post-ideological
	  Testing formulation, paradox
	  Contradiction, oppositeness
	INTER-INSTITUTIONAL
	  Relationship between forms
	  Interpenetration of self and other
	SELF-TRANSFORMATION
	  Interpenetration of selves
	  Inter-individuation
		Abstract system
		ideology
		
		Institution
		relationship-
		regulating forms
		
		Self-authorship
		Self-regulation
		Self formation
			Trans-system
			Trans-complex 

LINES OF DEVELOPMENT	
K	COGNITIVE
E	**INTERPERSONAL**
Y	*INTRAPERSONAL*

Figure 3.2 Five increasingly complex epistemologies.

orders experience predominantly from the socialized epistemology, only in terms of what he cannot do, and to see a person like Lynn, who predominantly orders experience from the self-authoring epistemology, only in terms of what she can.

Surely any educator who wished to be helpful to Peter, especially one wishing to facilitate transformational learning, would do well to know and respect where Peter is coming from, not just where it may be valuable for him to go. A constructive-developmental perspective on transformational learning creates an image of this kind of learning over a lifetime as the gradual traversing of a succession of increasingly elaborate bridges. Three injunctions follow from this image. First, we need to know which bridge we are on. Second, we need to know how far along the learner is in traversing that particular bridge. Third, we need to know that, if it is to be a bridge that is safe to walk across, it must be well anchored on both sides, not just the culminating side. We cannot overattend to where we want the student to be – the far side of the bridge – and ignore where the student is. If Peter is at the very beginning – the near side – of the bridge that traverses the socialized and the self-authoring epistemologies, it may be important to consider that this also means he is at the far side of a prior bridge. Only by respecting what he has already gained and what he would have to lose were he to venture forth is it likely we could help him continue his journey.

Although it is easy and tempting to define Peter by what he does not or cannot do (especially in comparison to Lynn), it is also true that his socialized epistemology permits him all the following capacities: he can think abstractly, construct values and ideals, introspect, subordinate his short-term interests to the welfare of a relationship, and orient to and identify with the expectations of those social groups and interpersonal relationships of which he wishes to feel himself a part.

From the vantage point of empirical research we know that it ordinarily takes the first two decades of living to develop these complex capacities, and some people have not developed them even by then (Kegan, 1982, 1994). Many parents, for example, would be overjoyed were their teenagers to have these capacities. Consider as an example parents' wish that their children be trustworthy and hold up their end of family agreements, such as abiding by a curfew on Saturday night. What appears to be a call for a specific behavior ("Be home by midnight or phone us") or the acquisition of a specific knowledge ("Know that it is important to us that you do what you say you will") actually turns out to be something more epistemological. Parents do not simply want their kids to get themselves home by midnight on Saturday night; they want them to do it for a specific reason. If their kids abide by a curfew only because the parents have an effective enough monitoring system to detect if they do not and a sufficiently noxious set of consequences to impose when they do not, the parents would ultimately be disappointed even though the kids are behaving correctly. Parents of teens want to resign from the role of "parent police." They want their kids to hold up their end of the agreement, not simply because they can frighten them into doing so but because the kids have begun to intrinsically prioritize the importance of being trustworthy. This is not first of all a claim on their kids' behavior; it is a claim on their minds. Nor will the mere acquisition of the knowledge content ("It is important to my parents that I do what I say I will") be sufficient to bring the child home by midnight. Many non-behaving teens know precisely what their parents value. They just do not themselves hold these values! They hold them extrinsically, as landmines they need to take account of, to maneuver around so they do not explode.

What the parents are really hoping for from their teens is a transformation, a shift away from an epistemology oriented to self-interest, the short term, and others-as-supplies-to-the-self. This epistemology they ordinarily develop in late childhood. Rather they need to relativize or subordinate their own immediate interests on behalf of the interests of a social relationship, the continued participation in which they value more highly than the gratification of an immediate need. When they make this epistemological shift, sustaining a mutual bond of trust with their parents becomes more important than partying till dawn.

And when adolescents do make this shift (to the socialized mind in Figure 3.2), interestingly, we consider them to be responsible. For a teen, the very capacity to be "written upon," to be "made up by," constitutes responsibility. It is Peter's misfortune that this perfectly dignifiable and complicated epistemology is a better match with the hidden curriculum of adolescence than that of modern adulthood, which makes demands on us to win some distance from the socializing press and actually regards people who uncritically internalize and identify with the values and expectations of others as insufficiently responsible! Parents who, for example, cannot set limits on their children, who cannot defy them, or who are susceptible to being "made up" by their wishes we regard as irresponsible. To master this new curriculum, Peter needs a new epistemology. But this does not mean that he did not earlier undergo an important transformation (to the socialized epistemology), and it does not mean he did not learn well or did not learn enough. In fact, by all accounts he was a very successful learner. His present difficulties arise because the complexity of the "life curriculum" he faces has gotten qualitatively more challenging. In the words of Ronald Heifetz (1995), what he faces are not technical challenges (the sort that can be addressed by what I call "informational learning"), but adaptive challenges, the kind that require not merely knowing more but knowing differently. For this reason he is in need of supports to transformational learning.

The particular epistemological transformation Peter needs help to begin – the transformation to a self-authoring frame of reference – is the particular transformation we often find unwittingly privileged in writings on adult learning. Mezirow (2000) talks about our need to pierce a taken-for-granted relationship to the assumptions that surround us. "We must become critically reflective of the assumptions of the person communicating" with us, he says.

"We need to know whether the person who gives us a diagnosis about our health is a trained medical worker, or that one who gives us direction at work is authorized to do so." In essence, Mezirow says, we need to "take as object ... what is taken for granted, like conventional wisdom; [or] a particular religious worldview," rather than being subject to it. This is not only a call for an epistemological shift; it is a call for a *particular* epistemological shift, the move from the socialized to the self-authoring mind. This is a call that makes nothing but good sense provided the adult learner is not too far from the entrance to this particular epistemological bridge (nor has already traversed it).

And even when it does make good curricular sense, we must be careful not to create learning designs that get out too far ahead of the learner. For example, when Mezirow says transformational educators want to support the learner's ability "to negotiate his or her own purposes, values, feelings, and meanings rather than simply to act on those of others," he again sounds the call for the move toward self-authoring, and he quite understandably invokes a model of education that will support this shift: "The generally accepted model of adult education involves a transfer of authority from the educator to the learners." But even when this particular shift is the appropriate transformational bridge for our student, all of us, as adult educators, need help in discerning how rapidly or gradually this shift in authority will optimally take place for that student, which is a function of how far he or she is along this particular bridge.

The shift in authority to which Mezirow refers reflects the familiar call in the adult education literature for us to regard and respect all our adult students as self-directed learners, almost by virtue of their adult status alone. Gerald Grow (1991) defines self-directed learners as those who are able to:

> examine themselves, their culture and their milieu in order to understand how to separate what they feel from what they should feel, what they value from what they should value, and what they want from what they should want. They develop critical thinking, individual initiative, and a sense of themselves as co-creators of the culture that shapes them.

But when the adult education experts tell us they want students to "understand how to separate what they feel from what they should feel, what they value from what they should value, and what they want from what they should want," do they take seriously enough the possibility that when the socialized mind dominates our meaning-making, what we should feel is what we do feel, what we should value is what we do value, and what we should want is what we do want? Their goal therefore may not be a matter of getting students merely to identify and value a distinction between two parts that already exist, but of fostering a qualitative evolution of mind that actually creates the distinction. Their goal may involve something more than the cognitive act of "distinction," a bloodless word that fails to capture the human wrenching of the self from its cultural surround. Although this goal is perfectly suited to assisting adults in meeting the bigger culture-wide "curriculum" of the modern world, educators may need a better understanding of how ambitious their aspiration is and how costly the project may seem to their students.

Adult students are not all automatically self-directing merely by virtue of being adults, or even easily trained to become so. Educators seeking self-direction from their adult students are not merely asking them to take on new skills, modify their learning style, or increase their self-confidence. They are asking many of them to change the whole way they understand themselves, their world, and the relationship between the two. They are asking many of them to put at risk the loyalties and devotions that have made up the very foundation of their lives. We acquire personal authority, after all, only by relativizing – that is, only by fundamentally altering – our relationship to public authority. This is a long, often painful voyage, and one that, much of the time, may feel more like mutiny than a merely exhilarating (and less self-conflicted) expedition to discover new lands.

Note how lost at sea Peter becomes when his long-time mentor unwittingly assumes his capacity for self-directed learning. Anderson no doubt sees himself as an emancipatory, empowering employer-as-adult-educator who scrupulously and consistently stands by his transfer of authority, taking care not to undermine Peter by taking on business that should properly be referred to him and refusing even Peter's veiled requests to step in and once again provide a map and a destination. What Anderson sees as his testimony to Peter's capacity for self-direction, Peter sees as a bewildering vacuum of externally supplied expectation and an indirect message from his boss that he no longer cares that much what happens to Peter. I have heard countless complaints about Anderson's ineffectiveness as a good leader, that he has asked too much of Peter all at once; and yet when we have the opportunity to examine our own leadership as adult educators, few of us can escape the conclusion that we have ourselves – on many occasions with the most emancipatory of intentions – been Andersons in our own classrooms.

Finally, an array of epistemologies such as that depicted in Figure 3.2 reminds us that even as our designs can get too far ahead of where some of our students are, so they can also fall too far behind; even as we can fail to do Peter justice by seeing him only in terms of what he cannot do, we can fail to do justice to Lynn's learning opportunities by seeing her only in terms of those capacities she has already developed. The move toward the self-authoring mind – valorized though it may unwittingly be in the subtexts of our aspirations for transformational learning – is not the only fundamental epistemological shift in adulthood. Nor are the learning challenges that call for the self-authoring mind the only challenges adults of this new century will face.

The self-authoring mind is equipped, essentially, to meet the challenges of modernism. Unlike traditionalism, in which a fairly homogeneous set of definitions of how one should live is consistently promulgated by the cohesive arrangements, models, and codes of the community or tribe, modernism is characterized by ever-proliferating pluralism, multiplicity, and competition for our loyalty to a given way of living. Modernism requires that we be more than well socialized; we must also develop the internal authority to look at and make judgments about the expectations and claims that bombard us from all directions. Yet adult learners today and tomorrow encounter not only the challenges of modernism but of postmodernism as well. Postmodernism calls on us to win some distance even from our own internal authorities so that we are not completely captive of our own theories, so that we can recognize their incompleteness, so that we can even embrace contradictory systems simultaneously. These challenges – a whole different "curriculum" – show up in as private a context as our conflicted relationships, where we may or may not be able to hold the embattled sides internally rather than projecting one side onto our adversary, and in as public a context as higher education itself, where we may or may not be able to see that our intellectual disciplines are inevitably, to some extent, ideological procedures for creating and validating what counts as real knowledge. Lynn too, it seems, has further bridges to cross. She has her own particular needs for transformational learning, however different from Peter's these may be. She challenges educators to create yet another set of learning designs should they seek to support her own bigger becoming.

"The spirit," Hegel wrote in *The Phenomenology of Mind*, "is never at rest but always engaged in ever progressive motion, in giving itself a new form." How might we understand transformational learning differently – and our opportunities as educators – were we better to understand the restless, creative processes of development itself, in which all our students partake before, during, and after their participation in our classrooms?

References

Belenky, M. F., Clinchy, B. McV., Goldberger, N. R., and Tarule, J. M. *Women's Ways of Knowing: The Development of Self, Voice, and Mind.* New York: Basic Books, 1986.

Grow, G. "Teaching Learners to Be Self-Directed." *Adult Education Quarterly*, 1991, 41(3), 125–49.

Heifetz, R. A. *Leadership Without Easy Answers.* Cambridge, MA: Harvard University Press, 1995.

Kegan, R. *The Evolving Self: Problem and Process in Human Development.* Cambridge, MA: Harvard University Press, 1982.

Kegan, R. *In Over Our Heads: The Mental Demands of Ordinary Life.* Cambridge, MA: Harvard University Press, 1994.

Kohlberg, L. *The Psychology of Moral Development: The Nature and Validity of Moral Stages.* New York: HarperCollins, 1984.

Lahey, L., and others. *A Guide to the Subject-Object Interview: Its Administration and Interpretation.* Cambridge, MA: Subject-Object Workshop, 1988.

Mezirow, J. "Learning to Think Like an Adult – Core Concepts of Transformation Theory." In J. Mezirow and Associates: *Learning as Transformation: Critical Perspectives on a Theory in Progress.* San Francisco: Jossey-Bass, 2000.

Piaget, J. *The Construction of Reality in the Child.* New York: Basic Books, 1954.

Chapter 4

Expansive learning

Toward an activity-theoretical reconceptualization

Yrjö Engeström

Yrjö Engeström is the founder and leader of the Center for Activity Theory and Developmental Work Research at the University of Helsinki in Finland and is at the same time Professor at the University of California, San Diego. He fundamentally builds his theoretical work on the so-called cultural-historical or activity-theoretical approach to learning and mental development, which was first launched in the Soviet Union in the 1920s and 30s by Lev Vygotsky. However, in his dissertation on "expansive learning" in 1987, he combined this approach with the system theoretical work of Briton Gregory Bateson on double-bind situations and learning levels and thereby introduced the notion of conflicts which were absent in Vygotsky's framework. In the following slightly abridged version of an article, Engeström sums up the historical development and current status of activity theory and illustrates its potential with a case story from the work at his Boundary Crossing Laboratory in Helsinki.

Introduction

Any theory of learning must answer at least four central questions: (1) Who are the subjects of learning – how are they defined and located? (2) Why do they learn – what makes them make the effort? (3) What do they learn – what are the contents and outcomes of learning? (4) How do they learn – what are the key actions of processes of learning? In this chapter, I will use these four questions to examine the theory of expansive learning (Engeström, 1987) developed within the framework of cultural-historical activity theory.

Before going into expansive learning, I will briefly introduce the evolution and five central ideas of activity theory. The four questions and the five principles form a matrix which I will use to systematize my discussion of expansive learning.

I will concretize the theoretical ideas of this chapter with the help of examples and findings from an ongoing intervention study we are conducting in the multi-organizational field of medical care for children in the Helsinki area in Finland. After presenting the setting and the learning challenge it was facing, I will discuss each of the four questions in turn, using selected materials from the project to highlight the answers offered by the theory of expansive learning.

I will conclude by discussing the implications of the theory of expansive learning for our understanding of directionality in learning and development.

Generations and principles of activity theory

Cultural-historical activity theory was initiated by Lev Vygotsky (1978) in the 1920s and early 1930s. It was further developed by Vygotsky's colleague and disciple Alexei Leont'ev (1978, 1981). In my reading, activity theory has evolved through three generations of research (Engeström, 1996). The first generation, centered around Vygotsky, created the idea of *mediation*. This idea was crystallized in Vygotsky's (1978, p. 40) famous triangular model in which the conditioned direct connection between stimulus (S) and response (R) was transcended by "a complex, mediated act" (Figure 4.1A). Vygotsky's idea of cultural mediation of actions is commonly expressed as the triad of subject, object, and mediating artifact (Figure 4.1B).

The insertion of cultural artifacts into human actions was revolutionary in that the basic unit of analysis now overcame the split between the Cartesian individual and the untouchable societal structure. The individual could no longer be understood without his or her cultural means; and the society could no longer be understood without the agency of individuals who use and produce artifacts. This meant that objects ceased to be just raw material for the formation of logical operations in the subject as they were for Piaget. Objects became cultural entities and the object-orientedness of action became the key to understanding human psyche.

The limitation of the first generation was that the unit of analysis remained individually focused. This was overcome by the second generation, centered around Leont'ev. In his famous example of "primeval collective hunt" (Leont'ev, 1981, pp. 210–213), Leont'ev explicated the crucial difference between an individual action and a collective activity. However, Leont'ev never graphically expanded Vygotsky's original model into a model of a collective activity system. Such a modeling is depicted in Figure 4.2.

The uppermost sub-triangle of Figure 4.2 may be seen as the "tip of the iceberg" representing individual and group actions embedded in a collective

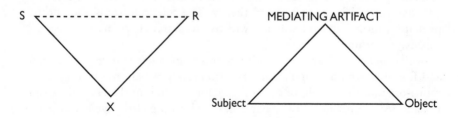

Figure 4.1 (A) Vygotsky's model of mediated act and (B) its common reformulation.

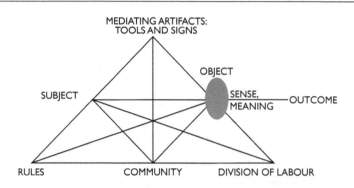

Figure 4.2 The structure of a human activity system (Engeström, 1987, p. 78).

activity system. The object is depicted with the help of an oval indicating that object-oriented actions are always, explicitly or implicitly, characterized by ambiguity, surprise, interpretation, sense-making, and potential for change.

The concept of activity took the paradigm a huge step forward in that it turned the focus on complex interrelations between the individual subject and his or her community. In the Soviet Union, the societal activity systems studied concretely by activity theorists were largely limited to play and learning among children, and contradictions of activity remained an extremely touchy issue. Since the 1970s, the tradition was taken up and recontextualized by radical researchers in the West. New domains of activity, including work, were opened up for concrete research. A tremendous diversity of applications of activity theory began to emerge, as manifested in recent collections (e.g. Chaiklin *et al.*, 1999; Engelsted *et al.*, 1993; Engeström *et al.*, 1999). The idea of internal contradictions as the driving force of change and development in activity systems, so powerfully conceptualized by Il'enkov (1977), began to gain its due status as a guiding principle of empirical research.

Ever since Vygotsky's foundational work, the cultural-historical approach was very much a discourse of vertical development toward "higher psychological functions." Luria's (1976) cross-cultural research remained an isolated attempt. Michael Cole (1988) was one of the first to clearly point out the deep-seated insensitivity of the second-generation activity theory toward cultural diversity. When activity theory went international, questions of diversity and dialogue between different traditions or perspectives became increasingly serious challenges. It is these challenges that the third generation of activity theory must deal with.

The third generation of activity theory needs to develop conceptual tools to understand dialogue, multiple perspectives, and networks of interacting activity systems. Wertsch (1991) introduced Bakhtin's (1981) ideas on dialogicality as a way to expand the Vygotskian framework. Ritva Engeström (1995) went a step further by pulling together Bakhtin's ideas and Leont'ev's concept of activity, and others have developed notions of activity networks, discussed Latour's actor-network theory, and elaborated the concept of boundary crossing within activity theory.

These developments indicate that the door is open for the formation of the third generation of activity theory. In this mode of research, the basic model is expanded to include minimally two interacting activity systems (Figure 4.3).

In Figure 4.3, the object moves from an initial state of unreflected, situationally given "raw material" (object 1; e.g. a specific patient entering a physician's office) to a collectively meaningful object constructed by the activity system (object 2; e.g. the patient constructed as a specimen of a biomedical disease category and thus as an instantiation of the general object of illness/health), and to a potentially shared or jointly constructed object (object 3; e.g. a collaboratively constructed understanding of the patient's life situation and care plan). The object of activity is a moving target, not reducible to conscious short-term goals.

In its current shape, activity theory may be summarized with the help of five principles (for earlier summaries, see Engeström, 1993, 1995, 1999a).

The first principle is that a collective, artifact-mediated and object-oriented activity system, seen in its network relations to other activity systems, is taken as the prime unit of analysis. Goal-directed individual and group actions, as well as automatic operations, are relatively independent but subordinate units of analysis, eventually understandable only when interpreted against the background of entire activity systems. Activity systems realize and reproduce themselves by generating actions and operations.

The second principle is the multi-voicedness of activity systems. An activity system is always a community of multiple points of view, traditions, and interests. The division of labor in an activity creates different positions for

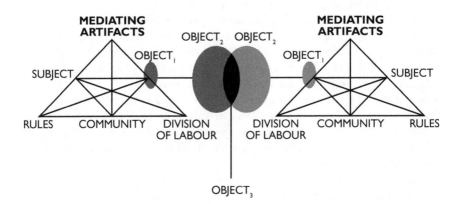

Figure 4.3 Two interacting activity systems as minimal model for the third generation of activity theory.

the participants, the participants carry their own diverse histories, and the activity system itself carries multiple layers and strands of history engraved in its artifacts, rules, and conventions. The multi-voicedness is multiplied in networks of interacting activity systems. It is a source of trouble and a source of innovation, demanding actions of translation and negotiation.

The third principle is historicity. Activity systems take shape and get transformed over lengthy periods of time. Their problems and potentials can only be understood against their own history. History itself needs to be studied as local history of the activity and its objects, and as history of the theoretical ideas and tools that have shaped the activity. Thus, medical work needs to be analyzed against the history of its local organization and against the more global history of the medical concepts, procedures, and tools employed and accumulated in the local activity.

The fourth principle is the central role of contradictions as sources of change and development. Contradictions are not the same as problems or conflicts. Contradictions are historically accumulating structural tensions within and between activity systems. The primary contradiction of activities in capitalism is between the use value and exchange value of commodities. This primary contradiction pervades all elements of our activity systems. Activities are open systems. When an activity system adopts a new element from the outside (for example, a new technology or a new object), it often leads to an aggravated secondary contradiction where some old element (for example, the rules or the division of labor) collides with the new one. Such contradictions generate disturbances and conflicts, but also innovative attempts to change the activity.

The fifth principle proclaims the possibility of expansive transformations in activity systems. Activity systems move through relatively long cycles of qualitative transformations. As the contradictions of an activity system are aggravated, some individual participants begin to question and deviate from its established norms. In some cases, this escalates into collaborative envisioning and a deliberate collective change effort. An expansive transformation is accomplished when the object and motive of the activity are reconceptualized to embrace a radically wider horizon of possibilities than in the previous mode of the activity. A full cycle of expansive transformation may be understood as a collective journey through the *zone of proximal development* of the activity:

> It is the distance between the present everyday actions of the individuals and the historically new form of the societal activity that can be collectively generated as a solution to the double bind potentially embedded in the everyday actions.

> (Engeström, 1987, p. 174)

Expansive learning – a new approach

Standard theories of learning are focused on processes where a subject (traditionally an individual, more recently possibly also an organization) acquires some identifiable knowledge or skills in such a way that a corresponding, relatively lasting change in the behavior of the subject may be observed. It is a self-evident presupposition that the knowledge or skill to be acquired is itself stable and reasonably well defined. There is a competent "teacher" who knows what is to be learned.

The problem is that much of the most intriguing kinds of learning in work organizations violates this presupposition. People and organizations are all the time learning something that is not stable, not even defined or understood ahead of time. In important transformations of our personal lives and organizational practices, we must learn new forms of activity which are not yet there. They are literally learned as they are being created. There is no competent teacher. Standard learning theories have little to offer if one wants to understand these processes.

Gregory Bateson's (1972) theory of learning is one of the few approaches helpful for tackling this challenge. Bateson distinguished between three levels of learning. Learning I refers to conditioning, acquisition of the responses deemed correct in the given context – for instance, the learning of correct answers in a classroom. Bateson points out that wherever we observe Learning I, Learning II is also going on: people acquire the deep-seated rules and patterns of behavior characteristic to the context itself. Thus, in classrooms, students learn the "hidden curriculum" of what it means to be a student: how to please the teachers, how to pass exams, how to belong to groups, etc. Sometimes the context bombards participants with contradictory demands: Learning II creates a double bind. Such pressures can lead to Learning III, where a person or a group begins to radically question the sense and meaning of the context and to construct a wider alternative context. Learning III is essentially a collective endeavor. As Bateson points out, processes of Learning III are rare and dangerous:

> Even the attempt at Level III can be dangerous, and some fall by the wayside. These are often labeled by psychiatry as psychotic, and many of them find themselves inhibited from using the first person pronoun.
>
> (Bateson, 1972, pp. 305–306)

Bateson's conceptualization of Learning III was a provocative proposal, not an elaborated theory. The theory of expansive learning develops Bateson's idea into a systematic framework. Learning III is seen as learning activity which has its own typical actions and tools (these will be discussed later in this chapter). The object of expansive learning activity is the entire activity system in which the learners are engaged. Expansive learning activity produces culturally new patterns of activity.

The learning challenge in children's health care in Helsinki

In Finland, public health care services are principally funded by taxation, and the patient typically pays a nominal fee for a visit. A critical structural issue in the Helsinki area is the excessive use of high-end hospital services, historically caused by a concentration of hospitals in this area. In children's medical care, the high-end of medicine is represented by the Children's Hospital, which has a reputation of monopolizing its patients and not actively encouraging them to use primary care health center services. Due to rising costs, there is now much political pressure to change this division of labor in favor of increased use of primary care services.

The problem is most acute among children with long-term illnesses, especially those with multiple or unclear diagnoses. Children with asthma and severe allergies are a typical and rapidly growing group. Such children often drift between caregiver organizations without anyone having overview and overall responsibility of the child's care trajectory. This puts a heavy burden on the families and on the society.

The Children's Hospital decided to respond to the pressures by initiating and hosting a collaborative redesign effort, facilitated by our research group using a method called *Boundary Crossing Laboratory*. Approximately 60 invited representatives of physicians, nurses, other staff, and management from primary care health centers and hospitals responsible for children's health care in the Helsinki area met in ten three-hour sessions, the last one of which was held in mid-February 1998. The participants viewed and discussed a series of patient cases videotaped by the researchers. The cases demonstrated in various ways troubles caused by lack of coordination and communication between the different care providers in the area. The troubles took the form of excessive numbers of visits, unclear *loci* of responsibility, and failure to inform other involved care providers (including the patient's family) of the practitioner's diagnoses, actions, and plans.

The *learning challenge* in this setting was to acquire a new way of working in which parents and practitioners from different caregiver organizations will collaboratively plan and monitor the child's trajectory of care, taking joint responsibility for its overall progress. There was no readily available model that would fix the problems; no wise teacher had the correct answer.

Who and where are the subjects of learning?

This learning challenge could not be met by training individual practitioners and parents to adopt some new skills and knowledge. The issue at stake was organizational, not resolvable by a sum total of separate individuals.

On the other hand, there was no mythical collective subject that we could approach and push to take charge of the transformation. Top-down commands and guidelines are of little value when the management does not know what the content of such directives should be. The management of the Children's Hospital – as competent and experienced as it was – was conscious of its own limitations in the situation and asked us to help.

Recent theories of situated learning (Lave and Wenger, 1991; Wenger, 1998) and distributed cognition (Hutchins, 1995) tell us to look for well-bounded *communities of practice* or *functional systems*, such as task-oriented teams or work units, to become collaborative subjects of learning. But in the multi-organizational field of children's medical care in Helsinki, there is no well-bounded work unit that could conceivably be the center of coordination. In each individual patient case, the combination of institutions, specialties, and practitioners involved in the delivery of care is different, and it is seldom possible to name a stable *locus* of control.

Latour's (1987) *actor-network theory* recommends that we locate learning in a heterogeneous network of human and non-human actors. This is fine, but Latour's principle of generalized symmetry turns all the actors (or actants, as he prefers to call them) into black boxes without identifiable internal systemic properties and contradictions. If we want to successfully confront the various actors involved in the care, we must be able to touch and trigger some internal tensions and dynamics in their respective institutional contexts, dynamics that can energize a serious learning effort on their part.

In our case, learning needs to occur in a changing mosaic of *interconnected activity systems* which are energized by their own inner contradictions. A minimal constellation of activity systems includes the activity system of the Children's Hospital, the activity system of the primary care health center, and the activity system of the child's family. In each particular patient case, the specific instantiation of the three activity systems is different. Yet, the general structural characteristics and network positions of each one of them remain sufficiently stable to allow analysis and redesign.

In the Boundary Crossing Laboratory, the basic constellation of the three activity systems was implemented so that hospital practitioners sat on one side of the room and primary care health center practitioners sat on another side of the room. The voices of patients' families came from the front of the room, from videotapes made by following patients through their hospital and health center visits and also from actual parents we invited to join in the sessions.

In the first session of the Boundary Crossing Laboratory, we presented the case of a prematurely born boy who was suffering from asthma symptoms and repeated respiratory infections. His care had been initiated at the Children's Hospital in August. By mid-November, his personal physician at the health center had not received any information on the initiation of hospital care or on plans for continued care. As the health center personal physician was unable to attend the Laboratory session in person, we showed her videotaped interview to the participants. The personal physician's use of reported speech – borrowing the voice of an imagined hospital physician – made her statement particularly poignant:

Excerpt 1 (Boundary Crossing Laboratory, session 1)

INTERVIEWER I'm thinking to myself, would there be any room for negotiation, I mean, is it always so that one-sidedly one party, the hospital, decides that OK, now this is at such a stage that we can send him to primary care ... Is there any discussion on this?

PERSONAL PHYSICIAN Nobody has ever asked me, "Would you take this patient for follow-up?" But then again, I am not specialized in pediatrics.

In the Laboratory session, practitioners from the Children's Hospital by and large denied that patient information is not sent to the health centers and maintained that the papers must have gotten lost at the health center. Health center practitioners on the other hand claimed that it was in fact common that the Children's Hospital would not send patient papers to the health center. In other words, at this point the multi-voicedness of the interaction took the shape of interlocking defensive positions. Toward the end of the first session, the head physician of the Children's Hospital opened a first crack in the defensive deadlock:

Excerpt 2 (Boundary Crossing Laboratory, session 1)

HEAD PHYSICIAN OF THE CHILDREN'S HOSPITAL And here I think we now have a pretty obvious issue, we just have to ask whether the patient record is actually sent to the primary care.

While expansive learning was firmly distributed within and between the three key activity systems, actions like the one taken by the head physician demonstrate that individual agency is also involved. However, different individuals speaking in different voices take the leading subject position in the activity at different moments. The leading subject role and agency is not fixed, it keeps shifting.

Why do they learn – what makes them make the effort?

For situated learning theory (Lave and Wenger, 1991), motivation to learn stems from participation in culturally valued collaborative practices in which something useful is produced. This seems a satisfactory starting point when we look at novices gradually gaining competence in relatively stable practices. However, motivation for risky expansive learning processes associated with major transformations in activity systems are not well explained by mere participation and gradual acquisition of mastery.

As I pointed out earlier, Bateson (1972) suggested that expansive Learning III is triggered by double binds generated by contradictory demands imposed on the participants by the context. In the Boundary Crossing Laboratory, we made the participants face and articulate the contradictory demands inherent in their work activity by presenting a series of troublesome patient cases captured on videotape. In several of these cases, the patient's mother was also present. This made it virtually impossible for the participants to blame the clients for the problems and added greatly to the urgency of the double bind.

Despite overwhelming evidence, the acknowledgment and articulation of the contradictions was very difficult for the practitioners. The first statements to that effect began to emerge in the third session of the Boundary Crossing Laboratory:

Excerpt 3 (Boundary Crossing Laboratory, session 3)

HOSPITAL NURSE A chronically ill child who has several illnesses does not necessarily have a clearly defined physician in charge. The care is fragmented. The information is terribly fragmented in the patient's medical record. It is not necessarily easy to draw conclusions as to what has happened to this child in the previous visit, not to speak of finding information about visits to another hospital, for example what shared guidance and counseling practices the family would need. And one doesn't necessarily even find information on the current medications. They are merely in the parents' memory or written on some piece of paper. So the information on the care of the illness compared to the clinical situation and urgent care situation can be detective work ...

To make analytical sense of the situation, we need to look at the recent *history* of the activity systems involved. Since the late 1980s, in municipal primary care health centers, the personal doctor principle and multi-professional teams have effectively increased the continuity of care, replacing the isolated *visit* with the long-term *care relationship* as the object of the practitioners' work activity. The notion of care relationship has gradually become the key conceptual tool for planning and recording work in health centers.

A parallel development has taken place in Finnish hospitals. Hospitals grew bigger and more complicated in the postwar decades. Fragmentation by specialties led to complaints and was seen to be partially responsible for the rapidly rising costs of hospital care. In the late 1980s, hospitals began to design and implement *critical paths* or *pathways* for designated diseases or diagnostic groups. At the beginning of the Boundary Crossing Laboratory work, the head physician of the Children's Hospital made it clear to the participants that he saw critical pathways as the solution to the problems:

Excerpt 4 (Boundary Crossing Laboratory, session 1)

HEAD PHYSICIAN OF THE CHILDREN'S HOSPITAL Why critical pathways, that has surely been explained sufficiently, and now I'll only tell you that in the spring we started this activity. That is, the planning of critical pathways for children and adolescents in Uusimaa county. And we have a basic working group which has representatives from both the health center level and the central hospital level and from here and from all parties, that is, representatives of both nursing and physicians.

With these reforms spreading and taking root, shouldn't the problems with coordination and collaboration be under control? Evidence presented and discussed in Boundary Crossing Laboratory sessions led to the conclusion that this is not the case. Care relationships and critical paths were solutions created in response to particular historical sets of contradictions. These contradictions are rapidly being superseded by a new, more encompassing configuration of contradictions.

Care relationships and critical paths respond to contradictions *internal* to the respective institutions. Care relationships are seen as a way to conceptualize, document, and plan long-term interactions with a patient inside primary health care. Their virtue is that the patient can be seen as having multiple interacting problems and diagnoses that evolve over time; their limitation is that responsibility for the patient is practically suspended when the patient enters a hospital. Correspondingly, critical paths are constructed to give a normative sequence of procedures for dealing with a given disease or diagnosis. They do not help in dealing with patients with unclear and multiple diagnoses, and they tend to impose their disease-centered worldview even on primary care practitioners. Fundamentally, both care relationships and critical paths are *linear* and *temporal* constructions of the object. They have great difficulties in representing and guiding *horizontal* and *socio-spatial* relations and interactions between care providers located in different institutions, including the patient and his/her family as the most important actors in care.

Asthmatic and allergic children with repeated respiratory problems are a clear case in point. Such a child may have more than a dozen hospital visits, including some stays of a few days in a ward, and even more numerous visits to a primary care health center in one year. Some of these visits are serious emergencies, some of them are milder but urgent infections, some are for tests, control and follow-ups.

One of the cases we presented in the Boundary Crossing Laboratory was Simon, age 3. In 1997, he had three visits to the district hospital of his municipality, 11 visits to the Helsinki University Central Hospital (HUCH) ear clinic, 14 visits to his personal physician at the local health center, and one visit to the outpatient clinic of the HUCH Children's Hospital. Another case we presented, Andrew, age 4, had in 1997 four visits to the HUCH hospital for skin and allergic diseases, nine visits to his local district hospital, and 14 visits to his primary care health center.

After we presented yet another such case in the Boundary Crossing Laboratory, the head physician of the Children's Hospital turned to the hospital physician who was in charge of designing the critical pathway for allergic children and asked her to explain how the implementation of the critical pathway will solve this child's problem. The response was something of a turning point for the head physician:

Excerpt 5 (Boundary Crossing Laboratory, session 7)

HOSPITAL PHYSICIAN 1 Here is first of all ... the care for asthma and then there is the care for food allergy. So in the case of one child, this cannot really be presented on one overhead, how this goes ...

HEAD PHYSICIAN (IN AGGRAVATED TONE) But isn't it quite common that children with allergies have these other problems? So surely they, surely you will plan some sort of a process which guarantees that these children do not belong to many critical pathways but ...?

HOSPITAL PHYSICIAN 2 Well, unfortunately these children will indeed belong to multiple critical pathways ...

The constellation of contradictions in this field of activity systems is schematically depicted in Figure 4.4. In both the hospital and the health center, a contradiction emerges between the increasingly important *object* of patients moving between primary care and hospital care and the *rule* of cost-efficiency implemented in both activity systems. In Helsinki, the per capita expenditure on health care is clearly above national averages, largely due to the excessive use

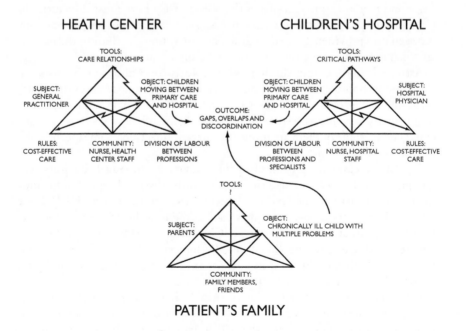

Figure 4.4 Contradictions in children's health care in the Helsinki area.

and high cost of services provided by the central university hospital of which the Children's Hospital is a part. Thus, there is an aggravated tension between the primary care health center and the university hospital. Health centers in the Helsinki area are blaming the university hospital for high costs, while the university hospital criticizes health centers for excessive referrals and for not being able to take care of patients who do not necessarily need hospital care.

A contradiction also emerges between the new *object* (patients moving between primary care and hospital care) and the recently established *tools*, namely care relationships in primary care and critical paths in hospital work. Being linear–temporal and mainly focused on care inside the institution, these tools are inadequate for dealing with patients who have multiple simultaneous problems and parallel contacts to different institutions of care. In the activity system of the patient's family, the contradiction is also between the complex object of multiple illnesses and the largely unavailable or unknown tools for mastering the object.

As different aspects of these contradictions were articulated in the Boundary Crossing Laboratory, we observed a shift among the participants from initial defensive postures toward a growing determination to do something about the situation. The determination was initially fuzzy, as if a need state looking for an identifiable object and corresponding concept at which the energy could be directed:

Excerpt 6 (Boundary Crossing Laboratory, session 5)

HOSPITAL PHYSICIAN I kind of woke up when I was writing the minutes [of the preceding session]. ... What dawned on me concerning B [name of the patient in the case discussed] is, I mean, a central thing ... for the mastery of the entire care. How will it be realized and what systems does it require? I think it was pretty good, when I went back through our discussion, I think one finds clear attempts at solving this. It is sort of a foundation, which we must erect for every patient.

RESEARCHER That seems to be a proposal for formulating the problem. What is ... or how do we want to solve it in B's case? I mean, is it your idea that what we want to solve is the mastery of the entire care?

HOSPITAL PHYSICIAN I think it's just that. I mean that we should have ... or specifically concerning these responsibilities and sharing of responsibility and of practical plans, and tying knots, well, we should have some kind of arrangement in place. Something that makes everyone aware of his or her place around this sick child and the family.

What are they learning?

Above in excerpt 6, a physician from the Children's Hospital used the expression "tying of knots." He referred to a preceding discussion in the same

Boundary Crossing Laboratory session in which the researcher suggested the term "knotworking" to capture the idea of the new pattern of activity needed to achieve collaborative care of children with multiple illnesses across institutional boundaries. The practitioners should be able to connect and coordinate with one another and with the parents quickly "on the spot" when needed, but also on the basis of a shared and mutually monitored long-term plan. The notion of knotworking served as one link in an emerging configuration of concepts that was to define the expanded pattern of activity.

Later in session 4, a task force of four practitioners, led by a hospital head nurse, presented their proposal for the improvement of feedback between the Children's Hospital and the health centers:

Excerpt 7 (Boundary Crossing Laboratory, session 4)

HOSPITAL HEAD NURSE Well, this is the title— Proposal for a trial period for the month of January, and a trial must always be evaluated, whether it succeeds or not, and what needs to be improved. And I say already at this point that this trial requires additional work, it brings more work. For the outpatient clinic, we propose a procedure in which the outpatient clinic during the entire month sends written feedback on every patient visit regardless of the continuation. To whom, to the home, to the personal primary care physician, to the physician who wrote the referral ...

The proposal met with a range of objections, largely centering on the excessive amount of work the feedback system was expected to cause. The head physician of the Children's Hospital joined in the chorus of objections, employing the available concept of critical pathways as a warrant in his argument:

Excerpt 8 (Boundary Crossing Laboratory, session 4)

HOSPITAL HEAD PHYSICIAN We have these task force groups for the critical pathways in place, and they have also discussed this matter, and without exception they have the opinion that definitely not for every visit – I, too, would be afraid that if there is feedback for every visit, there will be so many pieces of paper that the essential information gets easily lost, so surely it would be better that the sender, that is those who are in charge of the care of the patient, should themselves assess when feedback needs to be sent.

The proposal was rejected. In the fifth session of the Boundary Crossing Laboratory, the task force came back with a new proposal. In the discussion, the new proposal was mainly referred to as "care responsibility negotiation." The term "care agreement" was also mentioned. The proposal emphasized communication and negotiation between the parents and the different practitioners involved in a child's care.

This proposal had a favorable response. It was elaborated further in the sixth session. In this session, the "care agreement" emerged as the central new concept. The older concept of critical pathways was still used side by side with the new idea of the care agreement:

Excerpt 9 (Boundary Crossing Laboratory, session 6)

HOSPITAL HEAD NURSE Then an important thing in this is the division of care responsibility which we have discussed, which is difficult to chew on. Now this also takes a stand with regard to the division of care responsibility, and at the end there is the important point that parents have accepted the plan, and the concept of feedback refers simply to a copy of the medical record text which contains necessary contact information. And in our opinion this would mean additional work but this would be simple enough, flexible and possible to realize if we embark on this, and the goal is to develop dialogue ...

DATA SECURITY SPECIALIST Well, if I may comment on this. This would in my opinion be exactly building the critical pathway model, finding ways to improve the critical pathway and the work within it.

HOSPITAL PHYSICIAN 1 An agreement is made only if the hospital care exceeds two visits or goes beyond a standard protocol, so in fact we imagine that the majority of visits will fall into those not exceeding two visits or the protocol.

HOSPITAL PHYSICIAN 2 What may be new in this is that in the second visit, or the visit when the outpatient clinic physician makes the care agreement proposal, which is a kind of a vision for continuation of care, so he or she kind of presents this vision also to the parents sitting there, who become committed this way to this continuation of care and to the distribution of care responsibility, however the distribution is defined, something that probably has not been talked about so clearly to the parents. That's what makes this excellent.

INFORMATION SYSTEMS SPECIALIST In my opinion, this is a great system, and as an outsider, I say, implement this as soon as possible so that after a sufficient trial period we can duplicate this system elsewhere. This is a great system.

Under the umbrella of care agreement, four interconnected solutions were created. First, the patient's personal physician – a general practitioner in the local health center – is designated as the *coordinator* in charge of the patient's network and trajectory of care across institutional boundaries. Secondly, whenever a child becomes a patient of the Children's Hospital for more than a single visit, the hospital physician and nurse in charge of the child draft a *care agreement* which includes a plan for the patient's care and the division of labor between the different care providers contributing to the care of the child. The draft agreement is given to the child's family and sent to the child's personal health center physician (and when appropriate, to the physicians in charge of the child in other hospitals) for their scrutiny. Thirdly, if one or more of the parties find it necessary, they will have a *care negotiation* (by e-mail, by telephone, or face to face) to formulate a mutually acceptable care agreement. Fourthly, *care feedback,* in the form of a copy of the patient's medical record, is automatically and without delay given or sent to the other parties of the care agreement after the patient's unplanned visit or changes in diagnoses or care plans. Figure 4.5 depicts a simplified model of the care agreement, produced and used by the practitioners in the Boundary Crossing Laboratory.

The care agreement practice aims at resolving the contradictions depicted in Figure 4.4 by creating a new instrumentality. This instrumentality, when shared by parents and practitioners across institutional boundaries, is supposed to expand the object of their work by opening up the dimension of horizontal, socio-spatial interactions in the patient's evolving network of care, making the parties conceptually aware of and practically responsible for the coordination of multiple parallel medical needs and services in the patient's life. This does not replace but complements and extends the linear and temporal dimension of care. The solution also aims at relieving the pressure coming from the rule of cost-efficiency and the tension between the Children's Hospital and health centers by eliminating uncoordinated excessive visits and tests and by getting the health center general practitioners involved in making joint care decisions that are acceptable to all parties.

The new instrumentality is supposed to become a germ cell for a new kind of collaborative care, "knotworking," in which no single party has a permanent dominating position and in which no party can evade taking responsibility over the entire care trajectory. The model implies a radical expansion of the object of activity for all parties: from singular illness episodes or care visits to a long-term trajectory (temporal expansion), and from relationships between the patient and a singular practitioner to the joint monitoring of the entire network of care involved with the patient (socio-spatial expansion).

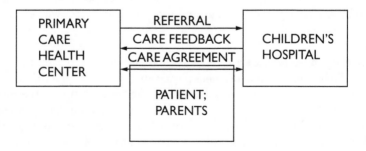

Figure 4.5 Conceptual model of the care agreement practice.

How do they learn – what are the key actions?

Theories of organizational learning are typically weak in spelling out the specific processes or actions that make the learning process. One of the more interesting attempts to open up this issue is Nonaka and Takeuchi's (1995) framework of cyclic knowledge creation, based on conversions between tacit and explicit knowledge. Their model posits four basic moves in knowledge creation: socialization, externalization, combination, and internalization.

A central problem with Nonaka and Takeuchi's model, and with many other models of organizational learning, is the assumption that the assignment for knowledge creation is unproblematically given from above. In other words, what is to be created and learned is depicted as a management decision that is outside the bounds of the local process (see Engeström, 1999b). This assumption leads to a model in which the first step consists of smooth, conflict-free socializing, the creation of "sympathized knowledge" as Nonaka and Takeuchi call it.

In contrast, a crucial triggering action in the expansive learning process discussed in this chapter, as in other analogous processes we have analyzed, is the conflictual *questioning* of the existing standard practice. In the Boundary Crossing Laboratory, this questioning was invoked by the troublesome patient cases, to be defensively rejected time and again. The practitioners did also begin to produce questioning actions in their own voices; a small example of this was shown in excerpt 2. The analysis of contradictions culminated much later as the conflict between critical pathways (available tool) and patients with multiple illnesses (new object) was articulated in excerpt 5. Actions of questioning and analysis are aimed at finding and defining problems and contradictions behind them. If the management tries to give a fixed learning assignment from above in this type of process, it is typically rejected (Engeström, 1999b). Out of these debates, a new direction begins to emerge, as seen in excerpt 6.

The third strategic action in expansive learning is *modeling*. Modeling is already involved in the formulation of the framework and the results of the analysis of contradictions, and it reaches its fruition in the modeling of the new solution, the new instrumentality, the new pattern of activity. In the Boundary Crossing Laboratory, the first proposal of the project group in session 4 was the first attempt at such modeling (see excerpt 7). The critical discussion and rejection of this proposal (excerpt 8) is an example of the action of *examining the new model*. The second, successful proposal, presented in session 5, is again an example of modeling, and the ensuing elaboration in session 6 (excerpt 9) again represents examining the new model.

The care agreement model has been implemented in practice since May 1998. The manifold *implementation* opens up a whole different story of tensions and disturbances between the old and the new practice, a story too large and complex to be entered in this paper. The cycle of expansion (Figure 4.6) is not completed yet. Our research group continues to follow and document the implementation and to feed back intermediate findings to the practitioners.

Conclusion: directionality in learning development

We habitually tend to depict learning and development as vertical processes, aimed at elevating humans upward, to higher levels of competence. Rather than simply denounce this view as an outdated relic of enlightenment, I suggest that we construct a complementary perspective, namely that of horizontal or sideways learning and development. The case discussed in this paper provides rich indications of such a complementary dimension.

In particular, the construction of the concept of care agreement (with the related concepts of care responsibility negotiation and knotworking) by the participants of the Boundary Crossing Laboratory is a useful example of developmentally significant sideways learning. In his classic work on concept formation, Vygotsky (1987) basically presented the process as a creative meeting between everyday concepts growing upward and scientific concepts growing downward. While this view opened up a tremendously fertile field of inquiry into the interplay between different types of concepts in learning, it did retain and reproduce the basic singular directionality of vertical movement. Later works by such Western scholars as Nelson (1985,

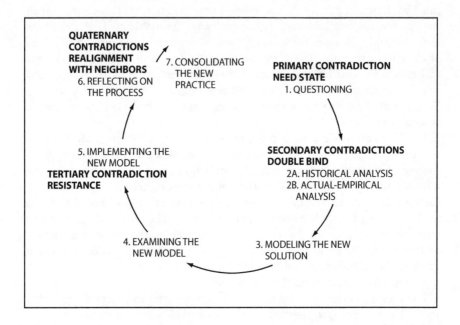

Figure 4.6 Strategic learning actions and corresponding contradictions in the cycle of expansive learning.

1995) and also by the greatest Russian analyst of learning, V. V. Davydov (1990), enriched and expanded Vygotsky's ideas, but the issue of directionality remained intact.

How does this image correspond to the data on expansive learning in the Boundary Crossing Laboratory? Concept formation in the laboratory sessions started out with the "scientific concept" proposed by the management: *critical pathways*. Instead of identifiable everyday concepts, it was met and confronted by our videotaped cases and live parents, telling about children with *multiple illnesses* and *fragmented care*. The meeting was uneasy, if not outright conflictual.

What followed was a sideways move. Instead of trying to merge the possibly incompatible worlds of the "scientific concept" of critical pathways and the everyday experience of the patients, a group of practitioners presented a series of alternative conceptualizations. This sideways move started with the poorly articulated idea of *automatic feedback* on every patient visit from the hospital to the primary care health center. This attempt at formulating a new deliberate concept was rejected "from below," using the experiential threat of *excessive paperwork* as the main conceptual argument.

The proponents of the new idea did not give up. They initiated another sideways move and proposed a new concept: *care responsibility negotiation*. This was met more favorably. The practitioners used their experiences of the need for *parent involvement* (see excerpt 9) to elaborate, refine, and concretize the concept. This led to yet another sideways move: the formulation of the concept of care agreement. Since the spring of 1998, through their actions of implementing this concept in practice, practitioners and parents have accumulated experiences to challenge and transform this concept again in new sideways moves.

This account leads us to a new, two-dimensional view of concept formation (Figure 4.7).

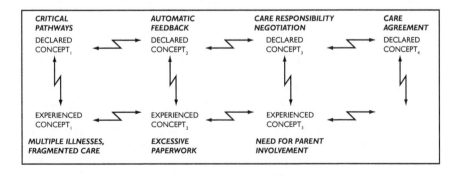

Figure 4.7 Expanded view of directionalities in concept formation.

References

Bakhtin, M. M. (1981). *The dialogic imagination: Four essays*. M. Holquist (Ed.). Austin: University of Texas Press.

Bateson, G. (1972). *Steps to an ecology of mind: Collected essays in anthropology, psychiatry, evolution, and epistemology*. New York: Ballantine Books.

Chaiklin, S., Hedegaard, M. and Jensen, U. J. (Eds.) (1999). *Activity theory and social practice: Cultural-historical approaches*. Aarhus, Denmark: Aarhus University Press.

Cole, M. (1988). Cross-cultural research in the sociohistorical tradition. *Human Development*, 31, 137–51.

Davydov, V. V. (1990). *Types of generalization in instruction: Logical and psychological problems in the structuring of school curricula*. Reston, VA: National Council of Teachers of Mathematics.

Engelsted, N., Hedegaard, M., Karpatschof, B. and Mortensen, A. (Eds.) (1993). *The societal subject*. Aarhus, Denmark: Aarhus University Press.

Engeström, R. (1995). Voice as communicative action. *Mind, Culture, and Activity*, 2, 192–214.

Engeström, Y. (1987). *Learning by expanding: An activity-theoretical approach to developmental research*. Helsinki: Orienta-Konsultit.

Engeström, Y. (1993). Developmental studies on work as a testbench of activity theory. In S. Chaiklin and J. Lave (Eds.), *Understanding practice: Perspectives on activity and context*. Cambridge, UK: Cambridge University Press.

Engeström, Y. (1995). Objects, contradictions and collaboration in medical cognition: An activity-theoretical perspective. *Artificial Intelligence in Medicine*, 7, 395–412.

Engeström, Y. (1996). Developmental work research as educational research. *Nordisk Pedagogik: Journal of Nordic Educational Research*, 16, 131–143.

Engeström, Y. (1999a). Activity theory and individual and social transformation. In Y. Engeström, R. Miettinen and R.-L. Punamäki (Eds.), *Perspectives on activity theory*. Cambridge, UK: Cambridge University Press.

Engeström, Y. (1999b). Innovative learning in work teams: Analyzing cycles of knowledge creation in practice. In Y. Engeström, R. Miettinen and R.-L. Punamäki (Eds.), *Perspectives on activity theory*. Cambridge, UK: Cambridge University Press.

Engeström, Y., Miettinen, R. and Punamäki, R.-L. (Eds.) (1999). *Perspectives on activity theory*. Cambridge, UK: Cambridge University Press.

Hutchins, E. (1995). *Cognition in the wild*. Cambridge, MA: MIT Press.

Il'enkov, E. V. (1977). *Dialectical logic: Essays in its history and theory*. Moscow: Progress.

Latour, B. (1987). *Science in action: How to follow scientists and engineers through society*. Cambridge, MA: Harvard University Press.

Lave, J. and Wenger, E. (1991). *Situated learning: Legitimate peripheral participation*. Cambridge, UK: Cambridge University Press.

Leont'ev, A. N. (1978). *Activity, consciousness, and personality*. Englewood Cliffs, NJ: Prentice-Hall.

Leont'ev, A. N. (1981). *Problems of the development of the mind*. Moscow: Progress.

Luria, A. R. (1976). *Cognitive development: Its cultural and social foundations*. Cambridge, MA: Harvard University Press.

Nelson, K. (1985). *Making sense: The acquisition of shared meanings*. New York: Academic Press.

Nelson, K. (1995). From spontaneous to scientific concepts: continuities and discontinuities from childhood to adulthood. In L. M. W. Martin, K. Nealson and E. Tobach (Eds.), *Sociocultural psychology: Theory and practice of knowing and doing*. Cambridge, UK: Cambridge University Press.

Nonaka, I. and Takeuchi, H. (1995). *The knowledge-creating company: How Japanese companies create the dynamics of innovation.* New York: Oxford University Press.

Vygotsky, L. S. (1978). *Mind in society: The development of higher psychological processes.* Cambridge, MA: Harvard University Press.

Vygotsky, L. S. (1987). *Thinking and speech.* New York: Plenum.

Wenger, E. (1998). *Communities of practice: Learning, meaning, and identity.* Cambridge, UK: Cambridge University Press.

Wertsch, J. V. (1991). *Voices of the mind: A sociocultural approach to mediated action.* Cambridge, MA: Harvard University Press.

Chapter 5

Pragmatism
A learning theory for the future

Bente Elkjaer

Dane Bente Elkjaer holds a chair in learning theory at the University of Aarhus. She is also Editor-in-Chief of the journal Management Learning. *Her main focus is working life learning, and her theoretical approach is inspired by the works of the American pragmatist philosopher and educator John Dewey. In 2005 she published a book,* When Learning Goes to Work: A Pragmatist Gaze at Working Life Learning *(in Danish). In the following chapter, which is published for the first time here, Elkjaer gives an interpretation of Dewey's understanding of learning grounded in his particular notion of the concept of experience. She discusses how a pragmatist perspective on learning can elaborate contemporary learning theory by being linked to the notion of practice-based learning as introduced by the works of Jean Lave and Etienne Wenger.*

Introduction

A theory of learning for the future advocates the teaching of a preparedness to respond in a creative way to difference and otherness. This includes an ability to act imaginatively in situations of uncertainties. John Dewey's pragmatism holds the key to such a learning theory and reflects his view of the continuous meetings of individuals and environments as experimental and playful.

That pragmatism has not yet been acknowledged as a relevant learning theory for the future may be due to the immediate connotation and the many interpretations associated with the term 'experience', which is at the heart of Dewey's educational thinking. Dewey defined experience in a way that is not well understood within educational research, and in a way that is easily confused with the term 'experiential learning'. The latter refers to the importance of participants' 'experiences' derived from bodily actions and stored in memory as more or less tacit knowledge.

Experience is, according to Dewey, not primarily associated with knowledge but with human beings' lives and living. In Dewey's terms, living is the continuous interaction (later: 'transaction') between individuals and their environments. Transaction holds the same meaning as experience, but also includes emotion, aesthetics and ethics as well as knowledge. To become knowledgeable is only a part of experience. Cognition and communication are still important parts of transaction, and as such are part of experiencing and not merely an outcome of experience.

Experience is the relation between individual and environments, 'subject' and 'worlds', which are the terms I use to connote the socialised individual and the interpreted world. The subject-worlds relation makes experience possible. Experience is both the process of experiencing and the result of the process. It is in experience, in transaction, that difficulties arise, and it is with experience that problems are resolved by inquiry. Inquiry (or critical and reflective thinking) is an experimental method by which new experience may be had not only through action but also by using ideas and concepts, hypotheses and theories as 'tools to think with' in an instrumental way. Inquiry concerns consequences, and pragmatism views subjects as future-oriented rather than oriented towards the past. This is evident from subjects exercising playful anticipatory imagination ('what-if') rather than causal thinking based upon a priori propositions ('if-then'). The consequence of the orientation towards the future is that knowledge (in Dewey's terms: 'warranted assertibilities') is provisional, transient and subject to change ('fallible') because future experience may act as a corrective to existing knowledge.

The view of experience as encompassing the relation between subject and worlds, inquiry as experimental and instrumental and knowledge as fallible means that pragmatism can be called a learning theory for the future. This means a learning theory that helps educators and learners develop a responsiveness towards challenges through the method of inquiry and an open-ended understanding of knowledge. I believe, in other words, that taking a closer look at the Deweyan notion of experience may be helpful for the creation of a learning theory that answers the cry for creativity and innovation that, at least rhetorically, is in demand in contemporary knowledge societies.

This chapter contains a brief background on how pragmatism should be understood in its everyday and philosophical meaning. Then I introduce Dewey's notion of experience as based on transaction between subject and worlds as well as in the relation between action and thinking. Third is a section on the differences between a Deweyan and a traditional understanding of experience. This is to create some background for understanding what happens when a non-Deweyan definition of 'experience' is used. Dewey was (late in life) well aware that the use of experience as a theoretical term created a lot of confusion and he would have used the term 'culture' had he known. This would not have been of any help today, as culture is also a term with many definitions. The term 'practice' may be a candidate for a contemporary theoretical term for what Dewey wanted to say with his 'experience'. I return to this issue in my conclusion and discussion.

In a fourth section, I return to the relation between action and thinking, but as the relation between transaction (i.e. experience) and thinking. I show that inquiry into a difficult situation in experience can result both in resolution of the situation and in new possible avenues for solving future problems by way of conceptual development. Fifth, I include a brief section on David Kolb's notion of experiential learning, because his use of experience is very different from Dewey's, although he is inspired by Dewey and often read like that.

In the final section, I discuss whether Dewey missed something when he talked about experience, inquiry, learning and becoming knowledgeable. I think that Deweyan philosophy is insufficient to describe how power is a key to understanding how learning is also a matter of access to participation in educational activities and to being able to respond to challenges (Biesta, 2006). I claim that a practice-based view of learning may help to incorporate the importance of power in theories of learning. Thus, a practice-based view of learning includes awareness of the need to include a conceptual understanding of the institutional order as transcending subjects' power to think and to act.

A pragmatist and pragmatism

In everyday language, a 'pragmatist' is a person who is focused on results, someone who gets things done and finds solutions to problems despite ideological and political differences. The pragmatist is often criticised for her or his apparent willingness to abandon ideals and moral standards in exchange for results. This commonly accepted meaning of the pragmatism of a pragmatist is, of course, not completely wrong, but it is not entirely in accordance with the philosophical interpretation of pragmatism. In this latter domain, and despite inevitable debates, there is widespread agreement that pragmatism concerns the understanding of the meanings of phenomena in terms of their consequences. That is, meaning is not ascribed in a priori terms ('if-then'); rather, it is identified by anticipating 'what-if' consequences to potential actions and conduct. Thus, the everyday results-oriented pragmatist echoes scholarly definitions of pragmatism to the extent that both are concerned with the consequences of actions and the attributions of meanings to phenomena.

American pragmatism emerged as a philosophical trend near the end of the nineteenth century, at a time when the US was still a 'new world' filled with adventure and the promise of new ways of life. The immigrants were looking to the future and its possibilities, and not towards the past they had left behind. The class-divided society of Europe was based upon traditions and family relations, but in the New World, at least in a rhetorical sense, one had to prove one's worth through values and actions rather than any privileges bestowed by birth. The US was a country in which the boundaries towards the West were still open and fascinating, but also a country in which industrialisation and mass production were rapidly influencing the development of society. Philosophically, this period was characterised by a range of contradictions that set science versus religion, positivism versus romanticism, intuition versus empiricism and the democratic ideals of the Age of Enlightenment versus aristocracy. In this context, pragmatism served as a mediating or consensual method of philosophy that sought to unite these various contradictions (Scheffler, 1974 [1986]).

One important contributor to the development of pragmatism was John Dewey (1859–1952), whose philosophical interests spanned many areas, including psychology, education, ethics, logic and politics. He insisted that philosophy must be practically useful in people's lives rather than a purely intellectual endeavour. In his view, the promise of a better world rests upon people's ability to respond 'in an intelligent way' to difficult situations that need to be resolved. Dewey argued that inquiry is a method in which working hypotheses are generated through anticipatory imagination of consequences, which may be tested in action. This experimental way of dealing with change does not merely happen through trial and error, because anticipatory imagination guides the process (Dewey, 1933 [1986], 1938 [1986]). In Dewey's version, pragmatism is a method to think and act in a creative (imaginative) and future-oriented (i.e. consequential) manner.

Where as the pragmatist in the everyday meaning of the term cares little for the ideological foundations of the results, Dewey's pragmatism examines how the use of different ideas and hypotheses, concepts and theories affects the result of inquiry. Thinking is to use concepts and theories to define a problem and, as such, is part of the result of inquiry. Thinking, i.e. critical anticipation of and reflection on the relation between defining and solving a problem, is part of pragmatism in the philosophical definition of the term. The pragmatist philosophical view of thinking is to help define the uncertainties that occur in experience. A pragmatist researcher cannot resort to general theoretical rules and maxims from the Grand Theories (Marxism, psychoanalysis, etc.) when s/he wants to understand a phenomenon. The situation determines which concepts and theories are useful for an analysis of a given problem. One can often use various theories and concepts as tools ('instruments') in an experimental process, the aim of which is to transform a difficult situation to one that is manageable and comfortable for the subject.

I have stressed the differences between an everyday understanding of a pragmatist and philosophical pragmatism because, in educational thinking, the latter is often associated with insufficient (theoretical) background. One example of this is when educationalists associate pragmatism with 'learning by doing' or as mere 'trial and error'. This view separates action from thinking, which for Dewey prevents learning in an informed (or 'intelligent') way. In order for learning to be still more informed, the use of concepts and theories are needed because they allow us to think about, anticipate and reflect on action and upon ourselves as acting. In the philosophical interpretation of pragmatism, cognition is closely related to action and is not to be understood by means of abstract and general theories. The understanding of learning as innovative is grounded in this open-ended and creative relation between thinking and action as both anticipatory and reflective. This does not mean that learning cannot be habitual (or 'reproductive'). This will indeed often be the case as most actions are habitual and only involve incremental adjustments. The philosophical pragmatism, however, provides a way to understand learning as an experimental responsiveness to change and as such it facilitates creative action and thinking. The key to this understanding of learning is Dewey's notion of experience, which is closely connected to his notion of inquiry and knowledge.

Experience as transactions between subject and worlds

Dewey worked all his life on refining his notion of experience and defined it first as interactional (resting on a principle of causal relations between subject and worlds) and later as a transactional concept (resting on a principle of mutual relations between subject and worlds) (Dewey and Bentley, 1949 [1991]). Experience concerns living, the continuous response to and feedback between subject and worlds, as well as the result of this process. It is within experience that difficulties arise and are resolved by way of inquiry. Experience is the concept Dewey used to denote the relation between subject and worlds as well as between action and thinking, between human existence and becoming knowledgeable about selves and the worlds of which they are a part.

Dewey laid the foundation for his concept of experience in 1896 with a groundbreaking article, in which he criticised how the concept of the 'reflex arc' was used to interpret the relation between action and thinking, between being and knowing (Dewey, 1896 [1972]). In this article, Dewey argued against the notion that it is possible to analyse human action as a mechanical sequence, a 'reflex arc', consisting of three separate events in the following order: sensory stimulus, idea and action. Dewey called the reflex arc a patchwork of separate parts, a mechanical juxtaposition without connection, instead of seeing action and thinking as parts of an integrated organic whole (see also Elkjaer, 2000). The 'organic' refers to the fact that subjects are always part of social and natural worlds, and it is as participants of these worlds that acting and knowing takes place. Action and thinking are not separate and clearly defined processes, but are integrated and connected. This integration of knowing and acting is mirrored in concrete action, both bodily and verbal.

Dewey argues that stimulus, idea and action are functional elements in a division of labour, which together makes up a whole, a situation or an event. Action and thinking are, in other words, elements of an organic coordination rather than a reflex arc. One example of the situatedness of stimulus is hearing a sound:

> If one is reading a book, if one is hunting, if one is watching in a dark place on a lonely night, if one is performing a chemical experiment, in each case, the noise has a very different psychical value; it is a different experience. In any case, what precedes the 'stimulus' is a whole act, a sensori-motor co-ordination. What is more to the point, the 'stimulus' emerges out of this co-ordination; it is born from it as its matrix; it represents as it were an escape from it.

(Dewey, 1896 [1972]: 100)

A sound is not an independent stimulus, because the meaning of it depends upon the situation in which it is heard. Nor is the response an independent event that merely follows from a stimulus. The response is part of defining the stimulus, and a sound has to be classified as a specific kind of sound (from an animal or a violent assault) in order to be followed by a relevant response. This classification has to be sufficiently exact to hold throughout the response in order to maintain it. It is not possible to aim a shot, shoot and run away at the same time. The response is therefore a reaction within the sound and not to the sound. The solution is, in other words, embedded in the definition of the problem. This is why Dewey prefers the term 'organic circle' rather than 'reflex arc' as a metaphor for the relation between being and knowing.

Dewey's notion of the organic circle contains the outline of his work with defining his notion of experience. Thus, experience is a series of connected organic circles, it is transaction, and it is the continuous relation between subject and worlds. Experience is an understanding of the subject as being in the world, not outside and looking into the world, as a spectator theory of knowledge would imply. The subject-in-world is the foundation for becoming knowledgeable of the world and of selves, because is rests upon a bond between action and thinking, being and knowing.

The equivocality of experience

About 20 years after Dewey wrote his article on the reflex arc, he made a comparison between his conception of experience and the commonplace meaning of experience. This led him to the following five differences between a commonplace interpretation of experience and his concept of experience (Dewey, 1917 [1980]). First, experience is traditionally understood as an epistemological concept in which the purpose is production and acquisitions of knowledge for example, through reflection on action (cf. Kolb). In contrast to this, Dewey's concept of experience is ontological and based upon the transactional relation between subject and worlds. The epistemological orientation of experience means that it is possible to overlook situations in which knowledge is not the primary content or purpose, and not be able to see that experience is also emotional and aesthetic. There is a difference between enjoying a painting because of its aesthetic value and studying the painting as an art reviewer (see also Bernstein, 1966 [1967]). There are no experiences without some form of knowing, but the meaning of the concept of experience is distorted if the paradigm for all experience becomes an issue of conscious thinking. Most of human lives consist of non-cognitive experiences as subjects continuously act, enjoy and suffer, and this is experience.

It is not possible to understand the meaning of Dewey's concept of inquiry if the value of the aesthetic and emotional experiences in Dewey's concept of experience is not recognised, because inquiry is an answer to a felt ('emotional') encounter with a conflict. Inquiry begins with an emotionally felt difficulty, an uncertain situation, and inquiry is a method to resolve this conflict. When something is experienced with the 'stomach' or an emotional response is exhibited in a situation, then inquiry is a way to help define experience in a cognitive sense and create meaning. To do so, it may be necessary to activate former similar experiences by experimenting with different possible ways of attributing meaning to the situation at hand and, through that, transform the emotional experience into something that can be comprehended as a cognitive and communicative experience. This is how an emotional experience becomes a reflective one; it becomes a learning experience, and may become knowledge, which in turn can be part of informing experience in the next similar experience of an emotionally difficult situation.

Secondly, experience is traditionally understood as an inner mental and subjective relation rather than a part of the objective conditions for human action that undergoes changes through human response. When experience is interpreted as subjective, then experience is trapped in the privacy of subjects' action and thinking. There is no experience without a subject experiencing it but it does not mean that experiencing is solely subjective and private. Sharing experience is more than a metaphor, because the objective world is always woven into the subjective experience.

Third, experience is traditionally viewed in the past tense, the given rather than the experimental and future oriented. Dewey's concept of experience, on the contrary, is characterised by reaching forward towards the unknown. In Dewey's definition, experience is connected to the future because 'we live forward'. Anticipatory and forward thinking is more important for action and cognition than recollection. Subjects are not passive spectators who look into the world from the outside, but powerful and future-oriented participants in natural and social worlds.

Fourth, experience is traditionally viewed as isolated and specific rather than as continuous and connected. For Dewey, however, experience is a series of connected situations (organic circles) and even if all situations are connected to other situations, every situation has its own unique character. Experience, nevertheless, is so connected that it is possible to use experience as a foundation for knowledge and to guide future actions.

Finally, experience has traditionally been viewed as beyond logical reasoning. Dewey argued, however, that there is no conscious experience without this kind of reasoning. Anticipatory thinking and reflection is always present in conscious experience by way of theories and concepts, ideas and hypotheses. This latter is the most important contrast to the traditional interpretation of experience. By on the one hand stressing that experience is not primarily an epistemological matter, and on the other hand claiming that the systematic process of knowledge is one form of experience, Dewey wanted to show how inquiry is the only method for having an experience. Inquiry is triggered by difficult situations, and inquiry is the means through which it is possible to transform these situations through the mediation of thinking and action.

Further, experience and inquiry are not limited to what is mental and private. Situations always have both subjective and objective elements, and through inquiry it is possible to change the direction of experience. Subjects are living, acting and reacting in objective worlds, but these transactions are not automatic or blind. Experience is experimental and oriented towards the future, and subjects use concepts and theories as instruments to guide the process. Dewey viewed education and teaching as a means to support, through inquiry, the direction of experience. Figure 5.1 shows the two definitions of experience.

Transaction and thinking

The notion of interaction, and (later) the notion of transaction, refers to the mutual creation and formation of subjects at work with their worlds. The worlds, however, live their own lives and are subject to their own relations, which are what subjects experience. The mutual formation of subjects and worlds reaches beyond the given worlds, because subjects are capable of inquiring and looking at themselves as well as the situation and changing both what is experienced and how it is experienced through reinterpretations and reactions. To live is to be engaged in the transactions that comprise experience, and experience is a process of life that changes continuously and in which new uncertain situations are an invitation to respond, an incentive to inquire and an opportunity to critically and reflectively think and have new experiences. Education, in the scholastic definition of the term, is a specific form of experience. In education, the purpose is to guide the process of experience and to make it more rewarding than if the subject was left to him- or herself.

Development of experience happens when habitual actions and values are disrupted by encounters with difficult situations. This disruption can be a

Traditional concept of experience	Dewey's concept of experience
Experience as knowledge	Knowledge as a subset of experience
Experience as subjective	Experience as both subjective and objective
Experience as oriented to the past	Experience as future oriented (consequence)
Experience as isolated experiences	Experience as united experiences
Experience as action	Experience as encompassing theories and concepts and as such a foundation for knowledge

Figure 5.1 Comparison between a traditional concept of experience and Dewey's concept of experience.

trigger to a closer examination of the situation, to inquiry, and thus new experience can be had and new knowledge may be created. Not all experience, however, leads to knowledge. Some experiences never enter consciousness and communication, but remain emotional and subconscious. Dewey talks about the aesthetic and emotional experience, and about happiness and sorrow as also being experience. To become knowledgeable is just one way of having experience; there are many other kinds of experience.

It is possible to learn from experience, because experience can be used to create connections to the past and to the future. Dewey writes the following about experience that points to the past and the future:

> To 'learn from experience' is to make a backward and forward connection between what we do to things and what we enjoy or suffer from things in consequence. Under such conditions, doing becomes a trying; an experiment with the world to find out what it is like; the undergoing becomes instruction – discovery of the connection of things. Two conclusions important for education follow. (1) Experience is primarily an active–passive affair; it is not primarily cognitive. But (2) the *measure of the value* of an experience lies in the perception of relationships or continuities to which it leads up. It includes cognition in the degree in which it is cumulative or amounts to something, or has meaning.
>
> (Dewey, 1916 [1980]: 147)

The quote illustrates that Dewey's experience is a transaction ('an active–passive affair') between subject and worlds, and that 'we' as human beings anticipate the consequences of our actions. The quote, however, also shows that if learning is to be the outcome of experience, cognition is needed to create continuity in experience. Experience is had through experimenting with the world in which cognition is needed to create continuity in the experimental thinking and action. The dividing line between non-cognitive and cognitive experience fluctuates, but if experience is to become a learning experience in the sense that experience can inform future experience, experience has to get out of the bodily and non-discursive field and into the cognitive and conscious field of experience. In short, experience has to become reflective and communicated (with self and other) in order to later be used in an anticipatory way.

Subjects have experience because of how they live their lives and because of how they create relations to other subjects and worlds. It is impossible to avoid experience. Only through cognition and communication, however, can experience become learning experience. It is in this endeavour that education in its widest possible sense may be helpful, because a teacher or a more experienced person can open up avenues for hitherto unknown understandings and actions by introducing concepts and theories that were not otherwise accessible to the learner.

Inquiry is the process through which subjects become knowledgeable. It is through inquiry that experience is had and knowledge may be created. In this process, ideas and hypotheses, concepts and theories are a part. Different hypotheses can be formulated and a mixture of ideas and thoughts from former experiences activated. Concepts and theories are used instrumentally and experimentally both in thought actions ('imagination') and in bodily actions in which they can be tested. When a problem is resolved, a feeling of control may replace uncertainty for a period. Figure 5.2 is a graphical representation of Dewey's process of inquiry.

Dewey's concept of experience is, as mentioned, different from a traditional understanding of experience in that it is an ontological construct. Dewey's concept of experience is anchored in the natural and social worlds, because experience is had in the subject-world transaction. Dewey's concept of experience is directed towards the future; experience is had in the active process of living and life is lived with an eye to tomorrow. Experience is, according to Dewey,

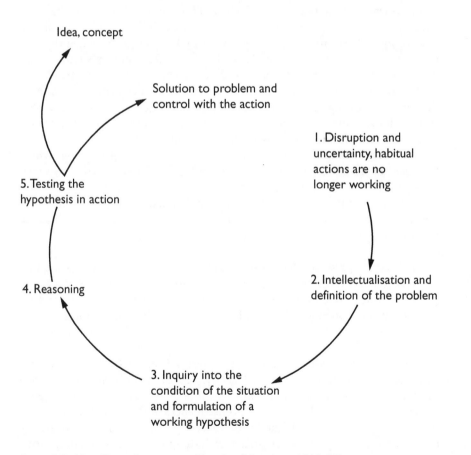

Figure 5.2 After Dewey's process of inquiry (Miettinen, 2000: 65).

a middle road between the total divide and constitutes a connection to the whole. It is out of experience (empirical data) that knowledge can be created, and it is through the subconscious experiences that thinking can be used to create connection to past and future and between action and consequence. Dewey's optimism lies in his belief in the value of developing individual and collective experience so that subjects can act increasingly 'intelligent' based on an increasingly informed empirical knowledge.

To use experience as defined above may cause some problems in educational research, because 'experience' is primarily used in the traditional sense, i.e. as an epistemological concept anchored in individuals' past and derived from bodily actions. David Kolb's definition of experience will be introduced to illustrate this alternate definition of experience (Kolb, 1984).

David Kolb's definition of experience

Kolb's learning cycle based on the notion of 'experience' is one of the most cited in educational research and deserves mention. Kolb's 'working definition' of learning is: 'Learning is the process whereby knowledge is created through the transformation of experience' (Kolb, 1984: 38). For Kolb, experience is not knowledge, but only a foundation for the creation of knowledge. Kolb says that he does not want to develop a third alternative to behaviourist and cognitive theories of learning, but 'rather to suggest through experiential learning theory a holistic integrative perspective on learning that combines experience, perception, cognition, and behavior' (Kolb, 1984: 20–21).

Kolb's theory is best known for its model of experiential learning, which he calls the 'Lewinian Experiential Learning Model'. Kolb constructs his own theory from this model. See Figure 5.3.

Kolb stressed two aspects in his learning cycle. First, concrete and immediate experiences are valuable for creating meaning in learning and for validating the learning process:

> Immediate personal experience is the focal point for learning, giving life, texture, and subjective personal meaning to abstract concepts and at the same time providing a concrete, publicly shared reference point for testing the implications and validity of ideas created during the learning process.
> (Kolb, 1984: 21)

Second, the model is based upon action research and laboratory teaching, which are both characterised by feedback processes. The information provided by feedback is the starting point of a continuous process consisting of goal-directed action and evaluation of the consequences of this action. Kolb writes that each stage in the model fits into different forms of adaptation to reality or different 'learning styles'. A particular individual ability or learning style corresponds with each individual stage in the model:

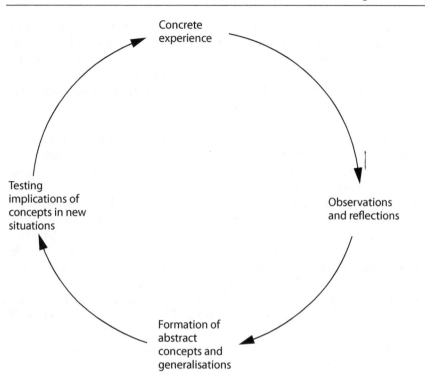

Figure 5.3 After Kolb's learning cycle (Kolb, 1984: 21).

> Learners, if they are to be effective, need four different kinds of abilities
> – concrete experience abilities, reflective observation abilities, abstract
> conceptualization abilities, and active experimentation abilities. That is,
> they must be able to involve themselves fully, openly, and without bias
> in new experiences. They must be able to reflect on and observe their
> experiences from many perspectives. They must be able to create concepts
> that integrate their observations into logically sound theories, and they
> must be able to use their theories to make decisions and solve problems.
>
> (Kolb, 1984: 30)

Thus, in spite of Kolb's use of a circle, it is possible to regard each element in
the circle with reference to a different individual ability. While Dewey talks
about integration of action and thinking, Kolb makes a distinction in his
learning cycle with reference to different abilities reflecting different learning
styles needed for effective action and thinking. The focus on experiences as
subjective and reaching backwards is, in Kolb's learning cycle, emphasised by
the correlation of the stages in the model with different individual learning
styles. This means that the stages in Kolb's learning cycle are not connected

with each other in an organic way. Kolb does not introduce a definition of experience that connects the stages, but he combines historical and theoretical elements in his model. He talks about a 'dialectic tension' between the experiential and the conceptual, but he resolves the tension by including both as separate stages in his model. The result being no dialectics, since dialectic logic would show how experience and conceptualisation are necessary for and condition each other (Miettinen, 2000).

When Kolb has won such a prominent position in many educational researchers' practice and research, I think it is because he says something that feels intuitively correct, namely that it is important to base teaching on participants' own experiences. This means taking the tacit knowledge derived from bodily actions into account. The idea being that it is by appealing to the participants' less articulated experiences that motivation for understanding the more abstract and general theories can be found. The problem is, however, that there are many different experiences in a classroom and that a teacher rarely is able to capture the attention of all the students by referring to their subjective experiences. From the vantage point of pragmatism and Dewey's definition of experience, Kolb distinguishes between action and thinking rather than seeing them as united, in spite of his stated outset in Dewey's concept of experience.

Dewey would probably have criticised Kolb's experiential definition of learning for focusing solely on individuals and their minds, just like he criticised Lewin for being 'mentalistically fashioned' (Dewey and Bentley, 1949 [1991]: 125, note 23). While Dewey's 'experience' connects subject and worlds, action and thinking, experiences for Kolb remain closed in a separation of the actions and thinking of subjects. Kolb wants to show that different learning styles are needed, and in order to do so he depicts learning as separate sequences in a closed circle. This happens at the expense of the integration of not only action and thinking, but also the mutual relation between subject and worlds. To Kolb, experience is an epistemological issue and not one of ontology, in spite of his view on learning styles. This also means that there is no room for emotion and aesthetics in Kolb's theory of learning (Vince, 1998).

Conclusion and discussion

I began this chapter by saying that contemporary societies need a learning theory that can respond creatively to difference and otherness. I discussed Dewey's definition of experience, which is grounded in transaction between subject and worlds as well as in the relation between thinking and action, being and knowing. Experience occurs when habitual action and thinking are disturbed and calls for inquiry. Inquiry begins in emotion, but may develop into cognition if verbal language is used to define and resolve the disruptive situation. The process of inquiry concerns the consequences of different ways of defining and resolving uncertainties. Inquiry is an experimental process in which ideas, hypotheses, concepts and theories are used instrumentally as 'tools to think with', and as such is a playful, creative and potentially innovative process. The result of inquiry, the new experience or 'warranted assertibilities' (knowledge), is therefore open-ended (fallible) and can be reinterpreted in light of new experiences.

The problem with using the term 'experience' is that it has several different connotations in educational research as illustrated by Kolb. Dewey knew that and suggested the term 'culture' to connote his more comprehensive understanding and use of 'experience'. Another problem with Dewey's understanding of experience is whether power and inequalities can be addressed. The term 'practice' may be a contemporary candidate to include power and at the same time to connote the content of Dewey's definition of experience.

One learning theory that has practice at its heart is described in the works of Jean Lave and Etienne Wenger and their understanding of learning as 'legitimate, peripheral participation in communities of practice' (Lave, 1993 [1996]; Lave and Wenger, 1991). The understanding of learning as participation in communities of practice took learning out of the clutches of individualism. Instead, Lave and Wenger's notion of learning is anchored in access to participation in communities of practice with the purpose of becoming competent practitioners. To take learning away from inside minds to social relations is also to move learning into an area of conflicts and power. The social structure of a practice, its power relations and its conditions for legitimacy, define the possibilities for learning (Gherardi *et al.*, 1998). The key issue is the relation between the institutional order and the participants' experience (Holland and Lave, 2001). This is another way to describe the relation between subjects and the worlds of which they are a part.

I, however, have some issues with practice-based learning. It is difficult to see learning as more than induction to a community, i.e. as adaptation and socialisation. This means that it is difficult to understand renewal of practice, i.e. to understand creativity and innovation. An understanding of learning as legitimate peripheral participation in communities of practice tends, in other words, to overlook conservatism, protectionism and the tendency to recycle knowledge rather than critically challenge and extend it. Furthermore, underlying contradictions and inequities that prevent growth may be hidden (Fenwick, 2001). The potentially constructive ambivalences and resistances in learning may not be captured when the concept of community is strongly emphasised (Wenger, 1998).

It is also difficult to see how thinking, concepts and theories can be part of learning in a practice-based understanding of learning. Action is central in Dewey's concept of learning – not just actions understood as bodily actions, but ideas about action (imagination, thought experiments) and 'speech acts' (language and communication) are also important actions in Dewey's definition of learning. Concepts and theories have an important pedagogical function, because they may guide the formation of new experience and new knowledge through a rigorous exploration of the past. This experience, in turn, can be used to inform the future. To paraphrase Dewey, a scientific mindset is, and should be, part of peoples' lives. This mindset is demonstrated by exerting still more informed inquiry and critical and reflective thinking. Learning is, however, not the same as transformation and change of conduct, because learning may result in a better understanding of a phenomenon, which cannot necessarily be observed as changed conduct.

Dewey's future-oriented and experimental concept of learning serves as a comprehensive and contemporary theory of learning that emphasises creativity and innovation. This leads to a greater need to educate for inquiry, for critical and reflective thinking into the uncertainties and the challenges of living in a global society with its constant demand of responsiveness to change. This means we must learn to live rather than to acquire a fixed curriculum. History is, obviously, not unimportant, but should not be transferred as a static 'body of knowledge' but as part of inquiry into contemporary challenges. We may, as educators, need to look for another term than 'experience' – a term that can be used today, and that captures the range of meaning that Dewey wanted with his 'experience' and later his interpretation of 'culture'. This means a term that captures the fact that learning is about living, and as such is 'lifelong'. The term 'practice' is a candidate, but it also comes with its own issues as indicated above.

References

Bernstein, R. J. (1966 [1967]). *John Dewey*. New York: Washington Square Press, Inc.

Biesta, G. J. J. (2006). *Beyond learning: Democratic education for a human future*. Boulder, CO: Paradigm Publishers.

Dewey, J. (1896 [1972]). The reflex arc concept in psychology. In J. A. Boydston (Ed.), *Early Works 5* (pp. 96–109). Carbondale, IL: Southern Illinois University Press.

Dewey, J. (1916 [1980]). Democracy and education: An introduction to the philosophy of education. In J. A. Boydston (Ed.), *Middle works 9*. Carbondale, IL: Southern Illinois University Press.

Dewey, J. (1917 [1980]). The need for a recovery of philosophy. In J. A. Boydston (Ed.), *Middle works 10* (pp. 3–48). Carbondale, IL: Southern Illinois University Press.

Dewey, J. (1933 [1986]). How we think: A restatement of the relation of reflective thinking to the educative process. In J. A. Boydston (Ed.), *Later works 8* (pp. 105–352). Carbondale, IL: Southern Illinois University Press.

Dewey, J. (1938 [1986]). Logic: The theory of inquiry. In J. A. Boydston (Ed.), *Later works 12*. Carbondale, IL: Southern Illinois University Press.

Dewey, J., and Bentley, A. F. (1949 [1991]). Knowing and the known. In J. A. Boydston (Ed.), *Later works 16* (pp. 1–294). Carbondale, IL: Southern Illinois University Press.

Elkjaer, B. (2000). The continuity of action and thinking in learning: Re-visiting John Dewey. *Outlines. Critical Social Studies*, 2, 85–101.

Fenwick, T. (2001). Tides of change: New themes and questions in workplace learning. *New Directions for Adult and Continuing Education*, 92, 3–17.

Gherardi, S., Nicolini, D., and Odella, F. (1998). Toward a social understanding of how people learn in organizations: The notion of situated curriculum. *Management Learning*, 29(3), 273–297.

Holland, D., and Lave, J. (2001). History in person: An introduction. In D. Holland and J. Lave (Eds.), *History in person: Enduring struggles, contentious practice, intimate identities* (pp. 3–33). Santa Fe and Oxford: School of American Research Press and James Currey.

Kolb, D. A. (1984). *Experiential learning: Experience as the source of learning and development.* Englewood Cliffs, NJ: Prentice-Hall.

Lave, J. (1993 [1996]). The practice of learning. In S. Chaiklin and J. Lave (Eds.), *Understanding practice: Perspectives on activity and context* (pp. 3–32). Cambridge, UK: Cambridge University Press.

Lave, J., and Wenger, E. (1991). *Situated learning: Legitimate peripheral participation.* Cambridge, UK: Cambridge University Press.

Miettinen, R. (2000). The concept of experiential learning and John Dewey's theory of reflective thought and action. *International Journal of Lifelong Education*, 19(1), 54–72.

Scheffler, I. (1974 [1986]). *Four pragmatists: A critical introduction to Peirce, James, Mead, and Dewey.* London and New York: Routledge and Paul.

Vince, R. (1998). Behind and beyond Kolb's learning cycle. *Journal of Management Education*, 22(3), 304–319.

Wenger, E. (1998). *Communities of practice: Learning, meaning, and identity.* Cambridge, UK: Cambridge University Press.

Chapter 6

An overview on transformative learning

Jack Mezirow

The concept of 'transformative learning' was launched in 1978 by Jack Mezirow, Professor of Adult Education at Teachers College, Columbia University, New York. For many years he had been an adult education consultant in various developing countries, inspired by Brazilian Paulo Freire and German Jürgen Habermas, among others. But it was in connection with women's adult education in the US that he discovered a wide-ranging kind of learning, reaching right into changes of the identity. Later, Mezirow elaborated on the concept of transformative learning in several writings and worked with it in practice, not least in the reputed Adult Education Guided Independent Study (AEGIS) doctoral programme. In the following chapter, which was first published in 2006 in Peter Sutherland and Jim Crowther (eds.) Lifelong Learning: Concepts and Contexts, *Mezirow recapitulates the history and main features of the concept of transformative learning and discusses various points of critique and suggestions for extension that have been put forward over the years. In this way, the chapter can be regarded as a final summing-up of his work.*

Introduction

The concept of transformative learning was introduced in the field of adult education in 1978 in an article that I entitled 'Perspective Transformation', published in the American journal *Adult Education Quarterly*. The article urged the recognition of a critical dimension of learning in adulthood that enables us to recognize and reassess the structure of assumptions and expectations which frame our thinking, feeling and acting. These structures of meaning constitute a 'meaning perspective' or frame of reference.

Influences in the development of this concept included Freire's 'consci-entization', Kuhn's 'paradigms', the concept of 'consciousness raising' in the women's movement, the writings and practice of psychiatrist Roger Gould, philosophers Jurgen Habermas, Harvey Siegal and Herbert Fingerette and my observation of the transformative experience of my wife, Edee, as an adult returning to complete her undergraduate degree at Sarah Lawrence College in New York.

The research base for the concept evolved out of a comprehensive national study of women returning to community colleges in the United States (Mezirow

1978). The study used grounded theory methodology to conduct intensive field study of students in 12 diverse college programmes, comprehensive analytical descriptions of an additional 24 programmes and responses to a mail inquiry by another 314.

A transformative learning movement subsequently developed in North American adult education, involving five international conferences, featuring over 300 paper presentations, the publication of many journal articles, over a dozen books and an estimated 150 doctoral dissertations on transformative learning in the fields of adult education, health and social welfare.

Foundations

Habermas (1981) makes a critically important distinction between instrumental and communicative learning. Instrumental learning pertains to learning involved in controlling or manipulating the environment, in improving performance or prediction. We validate by empirically testing contested beliefs regarding the truth of an assertion – that something is as it is purported to be. Instrumental learning is involved in learning to design automobiles, build bridges, diagnose diseases, fill teeth, forecast the weather and do accounting, and in scientific and mathematical inquiry. The developmental logic of instrumental learning is hypothetical-deductive.

Communicative learning pertains to understanding what someone means when they communicate with you – in conversation, or through a book, a poem, an artwork or a dance performance. To validate an understanding in communicative learning, one must assess not only the accuracy or truth of what is being communicated, but also the intent, qualifications, truthfulness and authenticity of the one communicating. Telling someone that you love them can have many meanings. We feel safer when a person prescribing medicine for us has training as a physician or pharmacist.

The purpose of communicative discourse is to arrive at the best judgement, not to assess a truth claim, as in instrumental learning. To do so one must access and understand, intellectually and empathetically, the frame of reference of the other and seek common ground with the widest range of relevant experience and points of view possible. Our effort must be directed at seeking a consensus among informed adults communicating, when this is possible, but, at least, to clearly understand the context of the assumptions of those disagreeing. The developmental logic of communicative learning is analogical-abductive.

For Habermas, discourse leading to a consensus can establish the validity of a belief. This is why our conclusions are always tentative: we may always encounter others with new evidence, arguments or perspectives. Thus diversity of experience and inclusion are essential to our understanding. It is important to recognize that the only alternatives to this dialectical method of inquiry for understanding the meaning of our experience is to rely on tradition, an authority or force.

In suggesting specific ideal conditions for human discourse, Habermas has provided us with an epistemological foundation defining optimal conditions for adult learning and education. The conditions also provide a foundation for a social commitment by adult educators to work toward a society that fosters these ideals. To freely and fully participate in discourse, learners must:

- have accurate and complete information;
- be free from coercion, distorting self-deception or immobilizing anxiety;
- be open to alternative points of view – empathic, caring about how others think and feel, withholding judgement;
- be able to understand, to weigh evidence and to assess arguments objectively;
- be able to become aware of the context of ideas and critically reflect on assumptions, including their own;
- have equal opportunity to participate in the various roles of discourse;
- have a test of validity until new perspectives, evidence or arguments are encountered and validated through discourse as yielding a better judgement.

Transformative learning theory

Transformative learning is defined as the process by which we transform problematic frames of reference (mindsets, habits of mind, meaning perspectives) – sets of assumption and expectation – to make them more inclusive, discriminating, open, reflective and emotionally able to change. Such frames are better because they are more likely to generate beliefs and opinions that will prove more true or justified to guide action.

Frames of reference are the structures of culture and language through which we construe meaning by attributing coherence and significance to our experience. They selectively shape and delimit our perception, cognition and feelings by predisposing our intentions, beliefs, expectations and purposes. These preconceptions set our 'line of action'. Once set or programmed, we automatically move from one specific mental or behavioural activity to another, and we have a strong tendency to reject ideas that fail to fit our preconceptions.

A frame of reference encompasses cognitive, conative and affective components, may operate within or outside awareness and is composed of two dimensions: a habit of mind and resulting points of view. Habits of mind are broad, abstract, orienting, habitual ways of thinking, feeling and acting, influenced by assumptions that constitute a set of codes. These codes or canon may be cultural, social, linguistic, educational, economic, political, psychological, religious, aesthetic and others. Habits of mind become articulated in a specific point of view – the constellation of belief, memory, value judgement, attitude and feeling that shapes a particular interpretation. Points of view are more accessible to awareness, to feedback from others. An example of a habit of mind is ethnocentrism, the predisposition to regard others outside one's own group as inferior, untrustworthy or otherwise less acceptable. A resulting point of view is the complex of negative feelings, beliefs, judgements and attitudes we may have regarding specific individuals or groups with characteristics different than our own. Having a positive experience with one of these groups may change an ethnocentric point of view but not necessarily one's ethnocentric habit of mind regarding other groups.

Transformative learning may occur in instrumental learning. This usually involves task-oriented learning. In communicative learning, as in the ethnocentric example, transformative learning usually involves critical self-reflection. However, elements of both task-oriented learning and critical self-reflection may be found in either type of learning. Habits of mind involve how one categorizes experience, beliefs, people, events and oneself. They may involve the structures, rules, criteria, codes, schemata, standards, values, personality traits and dispositions upon which our thoughts, feelings and action are based.

Meaning perspectives or habits of mind include the:

- *sociolinguistic* – involving cultural canon, social norms, customs, ideologies, paradigms, linguistic frames, language games, political orientations and secondary socialization (thinking like a teacher, doctor, policeman or an administrator), occupational or organizational cultures' habits of mind;
- *moral-ethical* – involving conscience, moral norms and values;
- *learning styles* – sensory preferences, focus on wholes or parts or on the concrete or abstract, working alone or together;
- *religious* – commitment to doctrine, spiritual or transcendental world views;
- *psychological* – theories, schema, scripts, self-concept, personality traits or types, repressed parental prohibitions, emotional response patterns, dispositions;
- *health* – ways of interpreting health problems, rehabilitation, near-death experience;
- *aesthetic* – values, taste, attitude, standards, judgements about beauty and the insight and authenticity of aesthetic expressions, such as the sublime, the ugly, the tragic, the humorous, the drab.

Transformative learning theory, as I have interpreted it, is a metacognitive epistemology of evidential (instrumental) and dialogical (communicative) reasoning. Reasoning is understood as the process of advancing and assessing a belief. Transformative learning is an adult dimension of reason assessment involving the validation and reformulation of meaning structures.

The process of transformative learning involves:

- reflecting critically on the source, nature and consequences of relevant assumptions – our own and those of others;
- in instrumental learning, determining that something is true (is as it is purported to be) by using empirical research methods;
- in communicative learning, arriving at more justified beliefs by participating freely and fully in an informed continuing discourse;
- taking action on our transformed perspective – we make a decision and live what we have come to believe until we encounter new evidence, argument or a perspective that renders this orientation problematic and requires reassessment;
- acquiring a disposition – to become more critically reflective of our own assumptions and those of others, to seek validation of our transformative insights through more freely and fully participating in discourse and to follow through on our decision to act upon a transformed insight.

Transformations may be *epochal* – sudden major reorientations in habit of mind, often associated with significant life crises – or *cumulative,* a progressive sequence of insights resulting in changes in point of view and leading to a transformation in habit of mind. Most transformative learning takes place outside of awareness; intuition substitutes for critical reflection of assumptions. Educators assist learners to bring this process into awareness and to improve the learner's ability and inclination to engage in transformative learning.

In our study of women returning to college, transformations often follow the following phases of meaning, becoming clarified:

- a disorienting dilemma;
- self-examination with feelings of fear, anger, guilt or shame;
- a critical assessment of assumptions;
- recognition that one's discontent and the process of transformation are shared;
- exploration of options for new roles, relationships and action;
- planning a course of action;
- acquiring knowledge and skills for implementing one's plans;
- provisional trying of new roles;
- building competence and self-confidence in new roles and relationships;
- a reintegration into one's life on the basis of conditions dictated by one's new perspective.

The two major elements of transformative learning are first, critical reflection or critical self-reflection on assumptions – critical assessment of the sources, nature and consequences of our habits of mind – and second, participating fully and freely in dialectical discourse to validate a best reflective judgement – what King and Kitchener define as that judgement involving 'the process an individual evokes to monitor the epistemic nature of problems and the truth value of alternative solutions' (1994: 12).

Issues

Emotion, intuition, imagination

Important questions have been raised by adult educators concerning trans-formation theory. One has to do with the need for more clarification and emphasis on the role played by emotions, intuition and imagination in the process of transformation. This criticism of the theory is justified. The process by which we tacitly construe our beliefs may involve taken-for-granted values, stereotyping, highly selective attention, limited comprehension, projection, rationalization, minimizing or denial. That is why we need to be able to critically assess and validate assumptions supporting our own beliefs and expectations and those of others.

Our experiences of persons, things and events become realities as we typify them. This process has much to do with how we come to associate them with our personal need for justification, validity and a convincing, real sense of self. Expectations may be of events or of beliefs pertaining to one's own involuntary reactions to events – how one subjectively expects to be able to cope. Our expectations powerfully affect how we construe experience; they tend to become self-fulfilling prophecies. We have a proclivity for categorical judgement.

Imagination of how things could be otherwise is central to the initiation of the transformative process. As the process of transformation is often a difficult, highly emotional passage, a great deal of additional insight into the role of imagination is needed and overdue. As many transformative experiences occur outside of awareness, I have suggested that, in these situations, intuition sub-stitutes for critical self-reflection. This is another judgement that needs further conceptual development.

I have attempted to differentiate between the adult educator's role in working with learners who are attempting to cope with transformations and that of the psychotherapist by suggesting that the difference in function pertains to the degree of anxiety generated by the transformative experience. More insight into the process of transformative learning that takes place outside of awareness is also in need of development.

Decontextualized learning

Another major criticism cites my emphasis on a concept of rationality that is considered an ahistorical and universal model leading to a 'decontextualized' view of learning – one that fails to deal directly with considerations and questions of context – ideology, culture, power and race-class-gender differences.

An epistemology of evidential and discursive rationality involves reasoning – advancing and assessing reasons for making a judgement. Central to this process is critical self-reflection on assumptions and critical–dialectical discourse. Of course, influences like power, ideology, race, class and gender differences and other interests often pertain and are important factors. However, these influences may be rationally assessed and social action taken appropriately when warranted.

Siegal (1988) explains that rationality is embodied in evolving traditions. As the tradition evolves, so do principles that define and assess reasons. Principles that define reasons and determine their force may change, but rationality remains the same: judgement and action in accord with reason. A critical thinker is one who is appropriately moved by reasons. Admittedly, this is an unfamiliar orientation. There are those who have always argued with great conviction that education – and indeed the very nature of learning and rationality itself – is and must be the handmaiden of a particular ideology, religion, psychological theory, system of power and influence, social action, culture, a form of government or economic system.

This familiar habit of mind dictates that learning, adult education and rationality must, by definition, be servants to these masters. A rational epistemology of adult learning holds the promise of saving adult education from becoming, like religion, prejudice and politics, the rationalization of a vested interest to give it the appearance of cause. Transformative learning is essentially a metacognitive process of *reassessing reasons* supporting our problematic meaning perspectives.

Social action

A major emphasis of critics of transformation theory, as I have conceptualized it, has been its de-emphasis of social action. Adult education holds that an important goal is to effect social change. Transformation theory also contends that adult education must be dedicated to effecting social change, to modifying oppressive practices, norms, institutions and socio-economic structures to allow everyone to participate more fully and freely in reflective discourse and to acquiring a critical disposition and reflective judgement. Transformative learning focuses on creating the foundation in insight and understanding essential for learning how to take effective social action in a democracy.

As Dana Villa notes in *Socratic Citizenship* (2001), one of our habitual frames of reference is to be disposed to view anything that is either cause-based, group-related or service-oriented as the core of 'good citizenship' and anything which simply dissents or says 'no' as of little value. Socrates' original contribution was the introduction of critical self-reflection and individualism as essential standards of justice and civic obligation in a democracy. Socrates undermined fellow citizens' taken-for-granted habits of mind pertaining to what justice and virtue require. He sought to distance thinking and moral reflection from the restraints of arbitrary political judgement and action – to move to a disposition of critical reflection on assumptions and the citizen's own moral self-formation as a condition of public life.

Habermas (1981) suggests that critical reflection on assumptions and critical discourse based on reflective judgement – the key dimensions of transformative learning – are characteristics of the highest level of adult morality.

Ideology critique

Adult educator Stephen Brookfield (1991) has challenged the breadth of transformative learning as I have conceptualized it. He writes:

> For something to count as a example of critical learning, critical analysis or critical reflection, I believe that the persons concerned must engage in some sort of power analysis of the situation or context in which the learning is happening. They must also try to identify assumptions they hold dear that are actually destroying their sense of well being and serving the interests of others: that is, hegemonic assumptions.
>
> (1991: 126)

For Brookfield, ideologies are pejorative 'sets of values, beliefs, myths, explanations and justifications that appear self-evidently true and are morally desirable' (1991: 129).

Brookfield is not suggesting a critique of all relevant ideologies, the point of view of transformation theory in adult education. He is quite specific that critical reflection as ideology critique 'focuses on helping people come to an awareness of how capitalism shapes belief systems and assumptions (i.e. ideologies) that justify and maintain economic and political inequity' (1991: 341). Issues raised here are echoed in critical pedagogy.

Critical pedagogy

Critical pedagogy, and its current form of popular education in Latin America, is an adult education programme evolving from the village-based literacy work of Paulo Freire that assigns priority to a guided analysis of how ideology, power and influence specifically impact upon and disadvantage the immediate lives of illiterate learners. The educator assists them to learn to read in the process of planning and taking an active role in collective social action to effect change. There is a praxis of transformative study and action.

For critical pedagogy, the critical learner, prototypically an illiterate rural peasant, not only comes to recognize injustice but, upon this recognition, is expected to actively participate in the specific political or social action required to change it. The process and problems involved in taking informed, collective, political action in a functioning democracy are seldom addressed in the literature of critical pedagogy.

Burbules and Burk (1999) note that in critical pedagogy everything is open to critical reflection except the premises and categories of critical pedagogy itself and comment that 'there is a givenness of what a "critical" understanding should look like that threatens to become its own kind of constraint' (1999: 54). 'From the perspective of critical thinking, critical pedagogy crosses a threshold between teaching critically and indoctrinating' (1999: 55). Transformation theory in adult education, on the other hand, involves how to think critically about one's assumptions supporting perspectives and to develop reflective judgement in discourse regarding beliefs, values, feelings and self-concept. It is not primarily to think politically; for ideology critique and critical pedagogy, this is a false assumption.

Cosmology

Cosmology is the study of the universe as a rational and orderly system. In the book *Expanding the Boundaries of Transformative Learning* (2002), Edmund O'Sullivan and his colleagues at the Ontario Institute for Studies in Education at the University of Toronto move far beyond critical pedagogy's sole concern with the political and social dimensions of capitalism to include environmental, spiritual and self-concept issues in what they call 'integral transformative learning':

> Transformative learning involves experiencing a deep structural shift in the basic premises of thought, feeling and action. It is a shift of consciousness that dramatically and permanently alters our being in the world. Such a shift involves our understanding of ourselves and our self-locations; our relationships with other humans and the natural world; our understanding of the relations of power in interlocking structures of class, race and gender; our body awareness; our visions of alternative approaches to living; and our sense of the possibilities for social justice and peace and personal joy.
>
> (2002: 11)

'Transformative criticism', as conceptualized from this perspective, posits a critique of the dominant culture's 'formative appropriateness' and provides a vision of an alternative form of culture and concrete indications of how to abandon inappropriate elements and to create more appropriate new cultural forms. They suggest that these elements should form a new type of integral education.

O'Sullivan *et al.*'s identification of transformative learning with movement toward the realization of a bold conception of a new cosmology moves well beyond the political focus of critical pedagogy. However, it shares the same limitation of not presenting or inviting a critical assessment of its core assumptions and categories. Such an assessment should consider the definition and validity of each of the five components designated in their definition of transformation, the assumptions regarding the role of education and adult education as the principal vehicle for effecting the broad multidimensional transformation they envision and how we are to understand the epistemology of transformative learning in adulthood, particularly the role of rationality, critical reflection on epistemic assumptions, and of discourse in the context of this theory.

Perspectives on transformative learning

Constructivist development

Constructivist developmental psychologists believe that development involves movement through a predictable sequence of 'forms' (frames of reference or meaning systems) culminating in the development of the adult capacity, and in some adult learners, the ability and disposition to engage in the transformative processes of critical self-reflection and reflective judgement through discourse.

Robert Kegan (2000) identifies five forms of meaning-making through the lifespan. These forms of mind include the perceptual/impulsive, the concrete/opinionated, the socialized, the self-authoring and the self-transforming mind that includes the capacity for self-reflection. He delineates the capabilities of adulthood: able to think abstractly, construct values and ideals, introspect, subordinate short-term interests to the welfare of a relationship and orient to and identify with expectations of groups and individual relationships of which one wishes to feel a part. It ordinarily takes two decades to develop these capacities and longer for some.

Mary Belenky and her associates (1986) identified six forms of knowing: silenced, received, subjective, separate, connected and constructed. The connected knower enters into the perspective of another and tries to see the world through his/her eyes. This is an essential dimension of transformative learning.

King and Kitchener (1994) have considerable evidence to support the assertion that it is only in adulthood that epistemic assumptions allow for true reflective thinking in a seven-stage movement. Stage seven involves understanding abstract concepts of knowledge as a system; knowledge is the outcome of the process of reasonable inquiry for constructing an informed understanding. This stage is comparable to the adult capacity to effectively participate in discourse in transformation theory.

Psychic distortion

Psychiatrist Roger Gould's 'epigenetic' theory of adult development (1978) holds that traumatic events in childhood may produce prohibitions that, though submerged from consciousness in adulthood, continue to generate anxiety feelings that inhibit adult action when there is a risk of violating them. This dynamic results in a lost function – the ability to take risks, feel sexual, finish a job – that must be regained if one is to become a fully functioning adult. The most significant adult learning occurs in connection with life transitions. As adulthood is a time for regaining lost functions, the learner should be assisted to identify the specific blocked action and the source and nature of stress in deciding to take action. The learner is helped to differentiate between the anxiety that is a function of the childhood trauma and the anxiety warranted by his or her immediate adult life situation.

Gould feels that learning to cope with ordinary existential psychological distortions can be facilitated by knowledgeable adult educators and adult counsellors as well as by therapists. He has developed an interactive, computerized programme of guided self-study for adult learners coping with life transitions. Educators and counsellors provide emotional support and help the learner think through the choices posed by the programme.

Schema therapy

As described by Bennett-Goleman (2001), schema therapy is an adaptation of cognitive psychotherapy that focuses on repairing emotional frames of reference, like maladaptive emotional habits, relentless perfectionism or the sense of emotional deprivation. Mindfulness, a Buddhist concept, defined here as a refined, meditative awareness, is combined by Bennett-Goleman with insights from cognitive neuroscience. Mindfulness may be applied by individuals to understand their patterns of emotional reactivity in workshops. Major schemas include:

> ... unloveability, the fear that people would reject us if they truly knew us; mistrust, the constant suspicion that those close to us will betray us; social exclusion, the feeling we don't belong; failure, the sense that we cannot succeed at what we do; subjugation, always giving in to other people's wants and demands; and entitlement, the sense that one is somehow special and so beyond ordinary rules and limits.
>
> (2001: 11)

> Mindfulness allows one to separate specific experience from the overlay of mental and emotional reaction to it. In that space there is room to examine whether we harbour distorted assumptions, ungrounded beliefs, or warped perceptions. We can see the ways our thoughts and feelings define us as they come and go – we can see our habitual lenses themselves
>
> (2001: 53)

As frames of reference, schemas are the way the mind organizes, retains and acts on a particular task, but they also selectively determine to what we will attend and what they deem irrelevant. When emotions intervene, schemas can determine what is admitted to awareness and can provide a plan of action in response. Schemas are mental models of experience.

Bennett-Goleman (2001) describes the process involved in challenging and changing schema thoughts:

- Become mindful of the feeling or typical thoughts associated with the schema. Focus on your thoughts, emotions and body sensations all – all due to which the schema has become activated. Test whether you are overreacting.
- Become aware of your schema thoughts as such and recognize they may be distortions.
- Challenge those thoughts. Recognize how you have learned through critical self-reflection that they embody false assumptions. Validate your transformative insights by getting involved in a discourse with another who has a more realistic understanding of the subject.
- Use empathic reframing to acknowledge the schema reality while you put into words a more accurate picture of things.

Individuation – Jungian psychology

Patricia Cranton (1994) interprets Jung's theory of psychological type to integrate his concepts with those of transformative learning theory in adult education. Learners' psychological predispositions form one kind of habit of mind. This involves two interrelated processes: to become more aware and to understand our own nature while, at the same time, individuating ourselves from the rest of humanity as we learn who we are.

Jung describes a continuum on which one may differentiate two ways of relating to the world and of making judgements: introverted and extraverted. We make judgements either logically or analytically – to assess a problem, weigh alternatives and make a decision – or rely upon deep-seated reactions of acceptance or rejection in which logic plays no part. This differentiation between perception and judgement is close to transformation theory's differentiation between learning outside awareness through intuition and learning within awareness through critical reflection on assumptions. Psychological preferences (thinking and feeling or sensing and intuition) are habits of mind.

John Dirkx (1997) also identifies the goal of Jung's concept of individuation as the development of an individual's personality. This development involves a dialogue between ego consciousness and the content of the unconscious. Transformation involves participating in dialogue with the unconscious aspects of the psyche. This frees one from obsessions, compulsions and complexes that can shape and distort our frame of reference. The symbolic process of individuation is expressed in the form of images. Through a dialogue between the conscious and unconscious, mediated through symbols and images, learners gain insight into aspects of themselves that are outside conscious awareness but influence their sense of self as well as their interpretations and actions. These symbols and images express emotions and feelings that arise in the learning process. 'Behind every emotion there is an image' (Dirkx 1997: 249).

The content or process of formal learning evokes images realized through dialogue. In the course of this interaction, 'both content and ourselves are potentially transformed. Individuation is an ongoing psychic process. When entered into consciously and imaginatively, it provides for a deepening of awareness of the self, an expansion of one's consciousness, and engendering of soul. We become more fully who we are and we are more fully able to enter into a community of humans. In Jungian terms, this is transformation – emergence of the self' (Dirkx 1997: 251).

Dean Elias (1997) has expanded the definition of transformative learning to explicitly include the unconscious: transformative learning is the expansion of consciousness through the transformation of basic world views and specific capacities of the self; transformative learning is facilitated through consciously directed processes such as appreciatively accessing and receiving the symbolic contents of the unconscious and critically analyzing underlying premises.

For additional insight into Jungian interpretations of transformative learning in the context of adult learning, see Robert Boyd (1991).

Facilitating transformation learning in graduate adult education

The first graduate programme in adult education designed to foster and facilitate the concept of transformative learning was established two decades ago at Teachers College, Columbia University, in New York. A highly selective doctoral programme, Adult Education Guided Independent Study, was designed for professionals with at least five years of experience in this field of practice. Students came on campus one weekend a month and attended intensive three-week summer sessions to satisfy course requirements in two years. Dialogue continued through the Internet. To practice and analyze the process of discourse, students collaborated on most problems with colleagues around tables of six. A major emphasis was placed on the creation of effective learning communities for collaborative inquiry.

Applicants were required to write a paper that described an issue in the field, present arguments on both sides, describe the point of view each represented and describe their own point of view and analyze their own assumptions. Faculty members, who placed emphasis on identifying additional missing assumptions, carefully reviewed the papers. Extensive revisions were requested. Revisions were often returned to the applicant with a faculty analysis of additional missed assumptions, and second and often third revisions were required. These exchanges were designed to force the applicants to critically examine their own habits of taken-for-granted ways of thinking and introduce the students to assumption analysis. Grading was limited to pass or incomplete. Academic standards were high. Three incompletes required that a student leave the programme.

Courses included assumption analysis, involving articles authored by adult educators, and life histories, involving comparative assessment of key turning points in the lives of students meeting in groups of three, designed to encourage them to recognize that there are alternative ways of interpreting common experience, as well as courses in ideologies, media analysis, the work of Paulo Freire and transformations through art and literature. Other courses, added over the years, focused on adult learning, research methods, adult literacy, community development and organizational development.

Methods found useful in fostering critical self-reflection of assumptions and discourse include using critical incidents, life histories, journal writing, media analysis, repertory grids, metaphor analysis, conceptual mapping, action learning, collaborative learning and John Peters' 'Action-Reason-Thematic Technique' – all described in Mezirow and Associates (1990).

Universal dimensions of adult knowing

There is a current debate over whether a learning theory must be dictated exclusively by contextual interests, as suggested by Brookfield, followers of critical pedagogy, other post-Marxist theorists and many postmodern critics.

Transformative learning theory, as I have conceptualized it, holds that cultures enable or inhibit the realization of common human interests – the ways adults realize common learning capabilities. Who learns what and the when, where and how of education are clearly functions of the culture. Transformative learning is a rational, metacognitive process of reassessing reasons that support problematic meaning perspectives or frames of reference, including those representing such contextual cultural factors as ideology, religion, politics, class, race, gender and others. It is the process by which adults learn how to think critically for themselves rather than take assumptions supporting a point of view for granted.

Universal dimensions of rationality and adult understanding upon which cultural or contextual influences impact – and may distort – include the following:

Adults

- seek the meaning of their experience – both mundane and transcendent;
- have a sense of self and others as agents capable of thoughtful and responsible action;
- engage in mindful efforts to learn;
- learn to become rational by advancing and assessing reasons;
- make meaning of their experience – both within and outside awareness – through acquired frames of reference – sets of orienting assumptions and expectations with cognitive, affective and conative dimensions that shape, delimit and sometimes distort their understanding;
- accept some others as agents with interpretations of their experience that may prove true or justified;
- rely upon beliefs and understandings that produce interpretations and opinions that will prove more true or justified than those based upon other beliefs and understandings;

- engage in reflective discourse to assess the reasons and assumptions supporting a belief to be able to arrive at a tentative best judgement – as a sometime alternative or supplement to resorting to traditional authority or force to validate a judgement;
- understand the meaning of what is communicated to them by taking into account the assumptions (intent, truthfulness, qualifications) of the person communicating as well as the truth, justification, appropriateness and authenticity of what is being communicated;
- imagine how things could be different;
- learn to transform their frames of reference through critical reflection on assumptions, self-reflection on assumptions and dialogic reasoning when the beliefs and understandings they generate become problematic.

These are generic dimensions of adult understanding that may be deliberately or unconsciously enhanced or discouraged through the process of adult education. Limiting the development of these qualitative dimensions of adult learning by exclusively focusing adult education on immediate contextual issues is self-defeating. It brings to mind the old Chinese saying, 'Give a man a fish and he can eat for a day; teach him to fish and he can eat for his lifetime'.

References

Belenky, M.F., Clinchy, B.M., Goldberger, N.R. and Tarule, J.M. (1986) *Women's Ways of Knowing: The Development of Self, Voice, and Mind*, New York: Basic Books.

Bennett-Goleman, T. (2001) *Emotional Alchemy: How the Mind Can Heal the Heart*, New York: Three Rivers Press.

Boyd, R. (1991) *Personal Transformations in Small Groups: A Jungian Perspective*, London: Routledge.

Brookfield, S. (1991) 'Transformative learning as ideology critique', in J. Mezirow (ed.) *Transformative Dimensions of Adult Learning*, San Francisco: Jossey-Bass.

Burbules, N. and Burk R. (1999) 'Critical thinking and critical pedagogy: relations, differences, and limits', in T. Popkewitz and L. Fendler (eds) *Critical Theories in Education: Changing Terrains of Knowledge and Politics*, New York: Routledge.

Cranton, P. (1994) *Understanding and Promoting Transformative Learning: A Guide for Educators of Adults*, San Francisco: Jossey-Bass.

Dirkx, J. (1997) 'Nurturing soul in adult learning', in P. Cranton (ed.) *Transformative Learning in Action: Insight from Practice*, San Francisco: Jossey-Bass.

Elias, D. (1997) 'It's time to change our minds', *ReVision*, 20(1), 1: 3–5.

Gould, R. (1978) *Transformations: Growth and Change in Adult Life*, New York: Simon & Schuster.

Habermas, J. (1981) *The Theory of Communicative Action*, vol. 1, Thomas McCarthy (trans.), Boston: Beacon Press.

Kegan, R. (2000) 'What "form" transforms?' in J. Mezirow and Associates *Learning as Transformation: Critical Perspectives on a Theory in Progress*, San Francisco: Jossey-Bass.

King, P. and Kitchener, K. (1994) *Developing Reflective Judgment*, San Francisco: Jossey-Bass.

Mezirow, J. (1978) *Education for Perspective Transformation: Women's Re-entry Programs in Community Colleges*, New York: Teachers College, Columbia University (available through ERIC system).

Mezirow, J. and Associates (1990) *Fostering Critical Reflection in Adulthood: A Guide to Transformative and Emancipatory Learning*, San Francisco: Jossey-Bass.

O'Sullivan, E., Morrell, A. and O'Connor, M. (2002) *Expanding the Boundaries of Transformative Learning: Essays on Theory and Praxis*, New York: Palgrave.

Siegal, H. (1988) *Educating Reason: Rationality, Critical Thinking, and Education*, New York: Routledge.

Villa, D. (2001) *Socratic Citizenship*, Princeton, NJ: Princeton University Press.

Chapter 7

Multiple approaches to understanding

Howard Gardner

Harvard professor Howard Gardner is known worldwide for his influential theory of "multiple intelligences," which was first put forward in 1983 and was later elaborated and expanded in several writings. As intelligence may be understood as the capacity or potential to learn in various connections, Gardner's work has also been an important contribution to learning theory and is therefore taken up in this volume – though Gardner is not primarily regarded as a learning theorist. The following text is the second half of a chapter which was originally published in C.M. Reigeluth (ed.) Instructional-Design Theories and Models: A New Paradigm of Instructional Theory, Volume 2 (pp. 69–89) *and is here reprinted with permission from Lawrence Erlbaum Associates. Gardner has himself chosen this text for the present book because it deals with his view and understanding on learning and education in extension of his work on multiple intelligences.*

Introduction

Let me introduce the core ideas of the educational approach that I embrace. I believe that every person ought to master a central body of curricular materials and approaches, though I am not thereby wedded to a specific canon. For this essay I have selected the examples of evolution and the Holocaust – though they are not without controversy – because I think that they lie comfortably within the ensemble of ideas that every educated person should have encountered, grappled with, and mastered. (In my book, *The Disciplined Mind* (1999), I have added to the true [evolution] and the evil [the Holocaust] an example of the beautiful [the music of Mozart].) I depart from traditional educators – and from their allies in psychology – in the assumption that such topics need to be taught or assessed in a single way.

Because of their biological and cultural backgrounds, personal histories, and idiosyncratic experiences, students do not arrive in school as blank slates, nor as individuals who can be aligned unidimensionally along a single axis of intellectual accomplishment. They possess different kinds of minds, with different strengths, interests, and modes of processing information. While this variation (a product of evolution!) initially complicates the job of the teacher, it can actually become an ally in effective teaching. For if the teacher is able to use different pedagogical approaches, there exists the possibility of reaching more students in more effective ways.

Differences among students can be described in innumerable ways and it is a simplification to prioritize any. For my purposes, I will speak of students as highlighting different intelligences. However, to follow this argument, one need not endorse my particular theory of intelligences. Any approach that recognizes and can somehow label or identify differences in intellectual proclivity or potential will suffice.

Assume that our educational goals include an enhanced understanding of the theory of evolution and the events called the Holocaust – topics drawn respectively from biology and from history. Specifically, we want students to appreciate that evolution, a process of random mutation in the genotype, is the driving force behind the variety of species that have existed historically and contemporaneously. The diverse phenotypes yielded by genetic variation result in organisms that are differentially able to survive in specific ecological contexts. Those that survive to reproduce in abundance have a competitive advantage over those that, for whatever reason, are less prone to adjust adequately to a given ecological niche. If these trends continue over the long run, the survivors prevail, while those that cannot compete successfully are doomed to extinction. The fossil record documents the course and fate of different species historically; one sees the gradual increase in variety of species, as well as the increasing complexity of certain lines of descent. It is possible to study the same processes contemporaneously, with relevant research ranging from the breeding of *Drosophila* of various strains to experimental investigations of the origin of genes.

Turning to the Holocaust, we want students to appreciate what happened to the Jewish people, and to certain other condemned minorities and political dissidents, during the Nazi Third Reich, from 1933 to 1945. Efforts to castigate and isolate the Jewish people began with simple verbal attacks and laws of exclusion, gradually evolved to more violent forms of abuse, and ultimately culminated in the devising of camps whose explicit goal was the extinction of European Jewry. The contours of anti-Semitism were laid out in Hitler's early speeches and writings; but the historical course from plans to actualities took several years and involved hundreds of thousands of individuals in various capacities. Genocide – the effort to eliminate a people in its entirety – is hardly a new phenomenon; it dates back to biblical times. Yet, the systematic way in which an allegedly civilized, modern nation proceeded to eradicate six million Jews is without precedent.

In brief form, these understandings would constitute a reasonable goal for a course or unit. Sheer memorization or faithful paraphrase of these paragraphs, of course, does not count for understanding. Rather, as noted above, students exhibit understanding to the extent that they can invoke these sets of ideas flexibly and appropriately to carry out specific analyses, interpretations, comparisons, and critiques. An "acid test" of such understanding is the student's ability to perform his understandings with respect to material that is new – perhaps as new as today's newspaper.

How to approach these formidable topics? From the vantage point of multiple intelligences, I propose three increasingly focused lines of attack.

A. *Entry points*   One begins by finding a way to engage the student and to place her centrally within the topic. I have identified at least six discrete entry points that can be roughly aligned with specific intelligences. In each case, I define the entry point and illustrate it with respect to our two topics:

1   *Narrative*   The narrative entry point addresses students who enjoy learning about topics through stories. Such vehicles – linguistic or filmic – feature protagonists, conflict, problems to be solved, goals to be achieved, tensions aroused and, often, allayed. Evolution invites treatment in terms of the story of Darwin's voyages (as it contrasts with the story of origins told in the Bible) or of the "course" of a particular species. The Holocaust can be introduced through a narrative account of a particular person or through a year-by-year chronicle of events in the Third Reich.

2   *Quantitative/numerical*   The quantitative entry point speaks to students who are intrigued by numbers, the patterns that they make, the various operations that can be performed, the insights into size, ratio, and change. From an evolutionary perspective, one can look at the incidence of different individuals or species in different ecological niches and how those aggregates change over time. With respect to the Holocaust, one can look at the movement of individuals to various camps, the survival rates at each, the comparisons of the fates of Jews and other victim groups in different cities and nations.

3   *Foundational/existential*   This entry point appeals to students who are attracted to fundamental "bottom line" kinds of questions. Nearly all youngsters raise such questions, usually through myths or art: the more philosophically oriented come to pose and argue about issues verbally. Evolution addresses the question of who we are and where we come from – and whence all living matter emanates. The Holocaust addresses the questions of what kinds of beings humans are, and what are the virtues and vices of which they/we are capable.

4   *Aesthetic*   Some individuals are inspired by works of art or by materials arranged in ways that feature balance, harmony, a carefully designed composition. The tree of evolution, with its many branches and interstices, may attract such individuals; Darwin himself was intrigued by the metaphor of the "tangled bank" of nature. Many efforts have been undertaken to portray the Holocaust in works of art, literature, film, and music, both by those who were killed and by those survivors and observers who have tried to capture its horror.

5   *Hands-on* Many individuals, particularly young persons, find it easiest
    to approach a topic through an activity in which they become actively
    engaged – one where they can build something, manipulate materials, carry
    out experiments. The chance to breed generations of fruit flies (*Drosophila*)
    gives one the opportunity to observe the incidence and fate of genetic
    mutations. Holocaust displays can provide a harrowing introduction to
    this event. When students receive an alternative "identity" upon their
    entrance to a Holocaust exhibit and later ascertain what happened to
    this person in the course of the Holocaust, the personal identification
    can be very powerful. Being a subject in a psychological experiment
    that documents the human proclivity to follow orders can be a jarring
    experience as well.

6   *Social* The entry points described thus far address the individual as a
    single person. Many individuals learn more effectively, however, in a
    group setting, where they have the opportunity to assume different roles,
    to observe others' perspectives, to interact regularly, to complement one
    another. A group of students can be given a problem to solve – for example,
    what happens to various species in a given environment following a
    dramatic change in climate; or how would the Germans have reacted had
    the Allies blown up the train tracks that led to a concentration camp. Or
    they can be asked to role-play different species in a shifting ecology, or
    different participants in a rebellion in a ghetto that is under siege.

B. *Telling analogies* An "entry point" perspective places students directly in the
center of a disciplinary topic, arousing their interests and securing cognitive
commitment for further exploration. The entry point, however, does not
necessarily inculcate specific forms or modes of understanding.

Here the teacher (or the student) is challenged to come up with instructive
analogies, drawn from material that is already understood, that can convey
important aspects of the less familiar topic. In the case of evolution, for
example, analogies can be drawn from history or from the arts. Societies change
over time, sometimes gradually, sometimes apocalyptically. The processes of
human social change can be compared with those of biological change within
and between species. Evolution can also be observed in works of art. Characters
change within the course of a book, and sometimes over a series of books. Themes
in a fugue evolve and develop in certain ways, and not (ordinarily) in others.

One may search for analogies to the Holocaust. The effort to annihilate a
people can be analogized to the eradication of traces of an event or even of an
entire civilization. Sometimes these efforts at eradication are deliberate, as
when the criminal seeks to hide all evidence of a crime. Sometimes these efforts
occur as a result of the passage of time, as happens when the traces of an ancient
city are virtually destroyed (absent relevant historical records, we do not know,
of course, about those cities whose vestiges have altogether disappeared as the
result of natural disaster or a vengeful enemy).

Analogies can be powerful, but they can also mislead. Analogies are an excellent way to convey important facets of a topic to individuals who have little familiarity with it. However, each analogy can also suggest parallels that do not hold – for example, the informing intelligence that constructs the theme of a fugue differs from the random nature of biological evolution; a murderer working in isolation differs from a large sector of society working secretly but in concert. The teacher is obligated to qualify each analogy as appropriate and to make sure that the misleading parts of the analogy are not allowed to distort or cripple the students' ultimate understanding.

C. *Approaching the core* Entry points open up the conversation; telling analogies convey revealing parts of the concept-in-question. Yet, the challenge to convey the central understandings still remains.

We come to the most vexing part of our analysis. Traditionally, educators have relied on two seemingly opposite approaches. Either they have provided quite explicit instructions – usually didactic – and assessed understanding in terms of linguistic mastery of materials ("Evolution is ..." or "The five central points about the Holocaust are ..."). Or they have supplied copious information to the student and hoped that, somehow, the student would forge his own synthesis ("On the basis of your reading, our trip to the museum, and various classroom exercises, what would you do if ..."). Some teachers have pursued both approaches, either simultaneously or successively.

Here we encounter the crucial educational question: Can one use knowledge about individual differences in strengths and modes of representations to create educational approaches that can convey the most important, the "core notions" of a topic in a reliable and thorough manner?

First off, one must acknowledge that there cannot be a formulaic approach. Every topic is different – just as every classroom context is different – and so each topic must be considered in terms of its own specific concepts, network of concepts, issues, problems, and susceptibilities to misconception.

A second step recognizes that topics do not exist in isolation – they come from and are, to some extent, defined by the ensemble of existing and emerging disciplines. Thus, a study of evolution occurs within the domain of biology and, more generally, within the realm of scientific explanation. As such, it involves the search for general principles and for models that will apply to all organisms under all kinds of circumstances (though some idiographically oriented scientists seek to explicate specific events like the disappearance of dinosaurs). In contrast, a study of the Holocaust occurs within history – and, sometimes, within literary or artistic efforts to render this historical event. Parts of the Holocaust may resemble other historical events, but a foundational notion about history is that it offers an account of specific events occurring in specific contexts. One can neither expect general principles to emerge nor build models that can be tested (though some scientifically oriented historians have attempted to construct and test such models).

The third step acknowledges commonly used ways of describing and explaining a concept. Thus evolution is typically described using certain examples (e.g. the disappearance of Neanderthal man, the branching tree of evolution), while the Holocaust is typically presented in terms of certain key events and documents (e.g. Hitler's *Mein Kampf*, the formulation of the Final Solution at the January 1942 Wannsee Conference, the records kept at Auschwitz, the reports by the first Allied soldiers to liberate the camps, the chilling photographs of the survivors). These familiar examples are not randomly chosen; rather, they have helped scholars to define these topics in the past, and they have proved effective pedagogically with at least a reasonable percentage of students.

But while these examples have their reasons, one must not infer that such examples are uniquely or permanently privileged. One can certainly feature these examples without ensuring understanding; and, by the same token, it is surely possible to enhance understanding of evolution or the Holocaust by using other examples, other materials, or differently formulated causal accounts. We know that this ensemble changes because there are new historical or scientific discoveries, as well as novel pedagogical approaches that proved effective. (Thus, for example, the opportunity to simulate evolutionary processes in a computer program, or to create virtual realities, spawns educational opportunities that could not have been anticipated a generation or two ago.)

The key step to approaching the core is the recognition that a concept can only be well understood – and can only give rise to convincing performances of understanding – if an individual is capable of representing that core in more than one way, indeed, in several ways. Moreover, it is desirable if the multiple modes of representing draw on a number of symbol systems, intelligences, schemas, and frames. Going beyond analogies – indeed proceeding in the opposite direction – representations seek to be as accurate and comprehensive as possible.

Several implications follow from this assertion. First of all, it is necessary to spend significant time on a topic. Second, it is necessary to portray the topic in a number of ways – both to illustrate its intricacies and to reach an ensemble of necessarily diverse students. Third, it is highly desirable if the multiple approaches explicitly call upon a range of intelligences, skills, and interests.

It may seem that I am simply calling for the "smorgasbord" approach to education – throw enough of the proverbial matter at students and some of it will hit the mind/brain and stick. Nor do I think that such an approach is without merit. However, the theory of multiple intelligences provides an opportunity, so to speak, to transcend mere variation and selection. It is possible to examine a topic in detail to determine *which* intelligences, *which* analogies, *which* examples are most likely *both* to capture important aspects of the topic *and* to reach a significant number of students. We must acknowledge here the cottage industry aspect of pedagogy – a craft that cannot now and may never be susceptible to an algorithmic approach. It may also constitute the enjoyable part of teaching – the opportunity continually to revisit one's topic and to consider fresh ways in which to convey its crucial components.

Educators and scholars may continue to believe that there is still an optimal mode for representing the core of a topic. I respond as follows. The history of disciplinary progress makes it inevitable that experts will think about a topic in terms of privileged considerations – perhaps genetic mutations and ecological niches in biology, perhaps human intentions and worldwide demographic and ecological forces in the case of history. Such consensual portrayal is reasonable. However, one should never lose sight of the fact that evolution did not occur in biology, and the Holocaust did not occur in history: they are processes and events that happened and became available for observers and scholars to describe, interpret, and explicate as best they could. New discoveries, as well as new disciplinary trends, gradually undermine today's orthodoxy; tomorrow's scholar might remake our understandings. Just as Darwin rewrote Lamarck's view of evolution, the believers in punctuated equilibrium aim to overthrow Darwinian gradualism (Gould, 1993). By the same token, Daniel Goldhagen's *Hitler's Willing Executioners* (1996) gives a far more "ordinary Germanic" cast to the Holocaust than had historians of earlier decades.

Generalizing the approach

Even if I have achieved some success in suggesting how best to approach two gritty topics of education, I evidently have left untouched the vast majority of the curriculum. My focus has been on a high school – perhaps a college – pair of topics; I have drawn from biology and European history, rather than from mathematics, music, or meteorology; and I have focused on topics or issues, rather than, say, specific chemical reactions, or metrical analyses, or geometric proofs.

I would be remiss were I to imply that the approach sketched here could be applied equivalently to every topic of the syllabus. Indeed, I deliberately selected two topics that are relatively rich and multifaceted, and that readily allow consideration from several perspectives. I suspect that no pedagogical approach is going to prove equally effective for the full range of topics and skills that need to be conveyed; teaching French verbs or the techniques of Impressionism is simply not commensurate with covering the Russian Revolution or explicating Newton's laws of mechanics.

Still, the approach sketched here can have wide utility. First of all, it raises the question of *why* one is teaching certain topics and what one hopes that students will retain at some time in the future. Much of what we teach recurs through habit; it makes sense to teach fewer topics and to treat them in greater depth. Such an approach allows one to relate materials to a few central themes – like evolution in biology, or the Holocaust in history (or energy in physics, or character in literature) – and to eliminate topics if they cannot be reasonably connected to some powerful themes or throughlines. After all, we cannot conceivably cover everything; we may as well strive to be coherent and comprehensive in what we do cover.

Having determined which topics require sustained attention, one can then exploit an ensemble of pedagogical approaches. To recapitulate: one begins by considering which entry points might succeed in attracting the interest and attention of diverse students. One then considers which kinds of examples, analogies, and metaphors might convey important parts of the topic in ways that are powerful and not misleading. Finally, one seeks to find a small family of literally appropriate representations that, taken together, provide a rich and differentiated set of representations of the topic under consideration. Such an ensemble conveys to students what it is like to be an expert. And to the extent that the family of representations involves a range of symbols and an array of schemes, it will prove far more robust and useful to students.

Presenting materials and fostering multiple representations is one component of effective teaching; the complementary component entails the provision of many opportunities for performance, which can reveal to the student and to interested observers the extent to which the material has been mastered. In stimulating revealing performances of understanding, teachers need to be imaginative and pluralistic. While it is easy to fall back on the tried-and-true – the short-answer test, the essay question – there is no imperative to do so. Performances can be as varied as the different facets of the topic and the diverse sets of skills of students. A variety of sanctioned performances not only provides more students with an opportunity to show what they have understood, but it also ensures that no single "take" on a topic exerts an inappropriate hegemony on students' (or test-makers'!) understandings of that topic.

With respect to our present examples, then, I encourage teachers to have students engage with one another in debates on the causes of the Holocaust or on the merits of Lamarckianism; carry out experiments that probe different aspects of the evolutionary process; interview individuals who have survived the Holocaust or various other global conflicts of our time; create works of art that commemorate heroes of the Resistance; or design a creature that can survive in an environment that has become highly toxic. Perhaps most challengingly, they might need to be asked to discuss the factors that permitted the Holocaust in terms of what we know about the evolution of behavior in that line called *Homo sapiens*. Hence, at last our two topics would be joined. Consultation of curricular guides and conversations with other teachers should stimulate the imagination with respect to other kinds of performances for other specimen curricula.

Just another call for projects, the sins of the Progressive Movement, as castigated by E. D. Hirsch (1996)? Quite the contrary. Student projects need to be considered critically in two respects: (1) adequacy as an example of a genre (Is it a coherent essay? Is it an effective monument? Does it qualify as a causal explanation?); and (2) adequacy as an occasion for performing one's understandings (Does the debater stick to the consensual facts or does she distort what is known? Does the newly designed species have a lifespan that allows reproduction and rearing of offspring?). Far from being a superficial measure of understanding, such projects and performances hold the students to high standards – the key features of the concept should be performed in vehicles that meet the test of cultural viability.

I have restricted myself until now almost entirely to the simplest forms of technology – books, pencils, and papers, perhaps a few art supplies, or a simple biochemical laboratory. This is appropriate – fundamental discussions of educational goals and means should not be dependent upon the latest technological advances. Yet, the approach outlined here promises to be enhanced significantly by current and future technologies. It is no easy matter for teachers to provide individualized curricula and pedagogy for a class of thirty elementary school students, let alone several high school classes totaling more than one hundred students. Similarly, it is challenging to have students provide a variety of performances and then provide meaningful feedback on this potpourri.

Happily, we have in our grasp today technology that will allow a quantum leap in the delivery of individualized services for both students and teachers. It is already possible to create software that addresses the different intelligences; that provides a range of entry points; that allows students to exhibit their own understandings in symbol systems (linguistic, numerical, musical, and graphic, just for starters); and that begins to allow teachers to examine student work flexibly and rapidly. Student work can even be examined from a distance, thanks to e-mail, video conferencing, and the like. The development of "intelligent computer systems" that will be able to evaluate student work and provide relevant feedback is no longer simply a chapter from science fiction.

In the past, it might have been possible to argue that individualized instruction – while desirable – was simply not possible. That argument is no longer tenable. Future reluctance will have to be justified on other grounds. My strong hunch is that such resistance is not likely to persuade students and parents who are not experiencing success "in the usual way" and who might benefit from alternative forms of delivery; neither will such resistance satisfy scholars who have arrived at new ways of conceptualizing materials, nor teachers who are themselves dedicated to a variety of pedagogies and assessments.

Educators have always tinkered with promising technologies, and much of the history of education chronicles the varying fates of paper, books, lecture halls, filmstrips, television, computers, and other human artifacts. Current technologies seem tailor-made to help bring into reality the kind of "MI approach" that I have endorsed here. Still, there are no guarantees. Many technologies have faded, and many others have been used superficially and unproductively. And we cannot forget that some of the horrible events of human history – such as the Holocaust – featured a perversion of existing technology.

That is why any consideration of education cannot remain merely instrumental. Not merely computers, we must ask – but computers for what? More broadly, education for what? I have taken here a strong position – that education must ultimately justify itself in terms of enhancing human understanding. But that understanding itself is up for grabs. After all, one can use knowledge of physics to build bridges or bombs; one can use knowledge of human beings to help or to enslave them.

I want my children to understand the world, but not just because the world is fascinating and the human mind is curious. I want them to understand it so that they will be positioned to make it a better place. Knowledge is not the same as morality, but we need to understand if we are to avoid past mistakes and move in productive directions.

An important part of that understanding is knowing who we are and what we can do. Part of that answer lies in biology – the roots and constraints of our species – and part of it lies in our history – what people have done in the past and what they are capable of doing. Many topics are important but I would argue that evolution and the Holocaust are especially important. They bear on the possibilities of our species – for good and for evil. A student needs to know about these topics not primarily because they may appear on an examination but rather because they help us to chart human possibilities. Ultimately, we must synthesize our understandings for ourselves. The performances of understanding that truly matter are the ones that we carry out as human beings in a world that is imperfect but one that we can affect – for good or for ill.

References

Gardner, Howard (1999): *The Disciplined Mind: What All Students Should Understand*. New York: Simon & Schuster.

Goldhagen, Daniel J. (1996): *Hitler's Willing Executioners: Ordinary Germans and the Holocaust*. New York: Alfred A. Knopf.

Gould, Stephen Jay (1993): *Wonderful Life: The Burgess Shale and the Nature of History*. New York: Norton.

Hirsch, E.D. (1996): *The Schools We Need and Why We Don't Have Them*. New York: Doubleday.

Reigeluth, Charles M. (ed.) (1999): *Instructional-Design Theories and Models: A New Paradigm of Instructional Theory*, Vol. 2. Mahwah, NJ: Lawrence Erlbaum.

Chapter 8

Biographical learning – within the new lifelong learning discourse

Peter Alheit

Biographical research is about how people's life courses develop through interaction between the individual subjectivity and the societal conditions. Learning is an important part of this interaction, and therefore biographical research of necessity includes a conception of learning. Conversely, important learning can only be understood concretely in relation to the biography of the learner. The German sociologist Peter Alheit, Professor at the University of Göttingen, is a core person in the development of European biographical research and theory, and in the following chapter, which is a further elaboration of earlier articles, he provides an overview of the theoretical understanding of learning in a biographical perspective.

Introduction

In the educational debate of the past 30 years – and especially during the most recent decade – the concept of lifelong learning has been sharpened strategically and functionally. In a certain sense, it stands for a new way of specifying the educational tasks in the societies of late modernity. In its programmatic and highly influential document on educational policy, the *Memorandum on Lifelong Learning*, the European Commission stated that '[l]ifelong learning is no longer just one aspect of education and training; it must become the guiding principle for provision and participation across the full continuum of learning contexts' (Commission of the European Communities, 2000, p. 3). Two decisive reasons are given for this assessment:

1 Europe has moved towards a knowledge-based society and economy. More than ever before, access to up-to-date information and knowledge, together with the motivation and skills to use these resources intelligently on behalf of oneself and the community as a whole, are becoming the key to strengthening Europe's competitiveness and improving the employability and adaptability of the workforce;

2 Today's Europeans live in a complex social and political world. More than ever before, individuals want to plan their own lives, are expected to contribute actively to society, and must learn to live positively with

cultural, ethnic and linguistic diversity. Education, in its broadest sense, is the key to learning and understanding how to meet these challenges. (Commission, 2000, p. 5)

This double rationale has narrowed the scope of the concept in a functionalistic manner, on the one hand, but on the other hand it also adds precision to its definition. The *Memorandum* explicitly states that lifelong learning relates to all meaningful learning activities:

- to the *formal* learning processes that take place in the classical education and training institutions and which usually lead to recognised diplomas and qualifications,
- to the *non-formal* learning processes that usually take place alongside the mainstream systems of education and training – at the workplace, in clubs and associations, in civil society initiatives and activities, in the pursuit of sports or musical interests – and
- to *informal* learning processes that are not necessarily intentional and which are a natural accompaniment to everyday life (Commission, 2000, p. 8).

The purpose behind this new understanding of the term 'learning' is the option of networking these different forms of learning in a synergistic way – learning should not only be systematically extended to cover the entire *lifespan*, but should also take place *'lifewide'*, i.e. learning environments should be engendered in which the various types of learning can complement each other organically. 'The "lifewide" dimension brings the complementarity of formal, non-formal and informal learning into sharper focus' (Commission, 2000, p. 9).

Lifelong, 'networked' learning thus seems to become an economic and social imperative of the first degree. The 'new' concept of lifelong learning betrays an ambition that John Field has termed *'the new educational order'* (Field, 2000, pp. 133ff.). Learning acquires a new meaning – for society as a whole, for education and training institutions and for individuals. The shift in connotation exposes an inner contradiction, however, in that this new learning is initially 'framed' by political and economic precepts. The goals are competitiveness, employment and adaptive competence on the part of the workforce. The intention is also, however, to strengthen freedom of biographical planning and the social involvement of individuals. Lifelong learning 'instrumentalises' and 'emancipates' at one and the same time.

The following analysis will focus on the curious tensions between these two perspectives. The first part looks at the social framework for lifelong learning – the *macro-perspective*, so to speak. In the second part, a particular theoretical view on 'education in the lifespan' will be put forward, namely the concept of *biographical learning* – the *micro-perspective*, if one wishes. A brief final section concentrates the findings in terms of relevant research questions, which will strengthen a development of the humanities *in relation to these issues*.

The macro-perspective: lifelong learning as reorganisation of the education system

To begin with, however, we must explain the astonishing fact that, at the end of the twentieth century, a global political consensus was generated on the concept of lifelong learning (Field, 2000, pp. 3ff.). The factors triggering this paradigm shift on an international scale in programmes for education and training are four trends in the post-industrial societies of the Western hemisphere, trends that mutually overlap and which led – in the words of John Field (2000, pp. 35ff.) – to a 'silent explosion' at the close of the twentieth century: the changing meaning of 'work', the new and totally transformed function of knowledge, the experience of increasing dysfunctionality on the part of mainstream education and training institutions and, in particular, challenges facing the social actors themselves that are characterised only roughly with labels such as 'individualisation' and 'reflexive modernisation' (Beck, 1992; Giddens, 1991).

The changing nature of 'work' in the societies of late modernity

The twentieth century has drastically modified the meaning and significance of employment. Most people spend much less of their lifetime in work than their great-grandparents ever did. As recently as 1906, an average working year in the UK comprised approximately 2,900 hours; in 1946, the figure had fallen to 2,440; and in 1988, to a mere 1,800 hours (see Hall, 1999, p. 427). Changes have also occurred to the 'inner structure' of work. The large-scale shift of jobs from the industrial sector to the services sector is merely a superficial symptom of the changes taking place. The more crucial aspect is that the notion of a consistent 'working life' is finally a thing of the past, even granting that women were traditionally excluded anyway. Average employment no longer means practising one and the same occupation over a substantial span of one's life, but now involves alternating phases of work and further training, voluntary and involuntary discontinuities of occupation, innovative career switching strategies and even self-chosen alternation between employment and family-centred phases (see Alheit, 1992).

This trend has not only *challenged* people's expectations regarding the classical life-course regime (Kohli, 1985) and made individual life planning a much riskier enterprise, but it also poses new problems for the institutions involved, in their capacity as 'structuring agents of the life course' – namely the agencies of the employment system and the labour market, the social and pension insurance institutions, but above all, the institutions of the education system. It is they who must compensate for the consequences of deregulation and flexibility in the labour market, provide support for unanticipated and risk-laden status passages and transitions to 'modernised' life courses and strike a new balance between the options held by individual actors, on the one hand,

and the functional imperatives of the institutional 'meso-level', on the other. As an innovative instrument for managing essential 'life politics', lifelong learning is the obvious answer.

The new function of knowledge

This idea of managing life politics seems all the more necessary the more diffuse its subject matter starts to become. The trivial, overriding consensus that, in the wake of the technological innovations engendered by the post-industrial information society, *knowledge* has become the key resource of the future conceals the perplexity over the actual function and character of this knowledge. The core issue, quite obviously, is not simply to disseminate and distribute a definable stock of knowledge as efficiently as possible, nor is it the fact that all areas of life are subjected to increasing scientification (Stehr, 2002), but rather it is a phenomenon that expands successively by virtue of the specific uses to which it is put, and which devalues itself again to a certain degree. Knowledge is no longer that 'cultural capital' that, according to Bourdieu, determines social structures and guarantees its astonishing persistence through ever-recurring reproduction (Bourdieu, 1984). Knowledge is a kind of 'grey capital' (Field, 2000, p. 1) that generates new, virtual economies. The stock market crash of the *New Economy* in 2000 is merely one dark side of the almost intangible quality of 'new knowledge'.

The communication and interaction networks of the IT age, which have long since permeated, extended and modified the realms of conventional industrial production and the character of classical services and administrations, remain dependent – more so than traditional forms of knowledge in the past – on the individual user. The latter's personal options in respect to the new, virtual markets – his/her contacts, productive inputs and consumer habits in the Internet – are what create the future forms of knowledge. The knowledge of the information society is *doing knowledge*, a kind of lifestyle that determines the structures of society far beyond the purely occupational domain and lends them a dynamic of ever-shorter cycles.

This very quality of 'new knowledge' now necessitates flexible feedback procedures, complex self-management checks and permanent quality management. In the process, the nature of education and learning is dramatically changed (Stehr, 2002). They no longer entail the communication and dissemination of fixed bodies of knowledge, values or skills, but rather a kind of 'knowledge osmosis' for ensuring what must now be a permanent and continuous exchange between individual knowledge production and organised knowledge management. The idea of lifelong learning, and especially self-managed learning, seems highly predestined for this process – as a framework concept at least.

The dysfunctionality of the established educational institutions

The conditions thus generated by a knowledge society in the making render classical teaching–learning settings problematic – above all, the idea that accompanied the 'first career' of the lifelong learning label in the early 1970s – the *human capital theory*. The latter concept measures, as it were, the capital invested in education and training according to the length of full-time schooling and assumes that extending its duration will have positive impacts on willingness to engage in lifelong learning (for a critique, see Schuller, 1998; Field, 2000, p. 135). A number of recent empirical studies, particularly in Great Britain (e.g. Tavistock Institute, 1999; Schuller and Field, 1999), provide evidence that the very opposite is the case – simply extending primary schooling, without drastic changes to the conditional framework and the quality of the learning process, led in the majority of those affected to a loss of motivation and to an instrumental attitude to learning that is in no way conducive to continued, self-managed learning in later phases of life, but which tends rather to suppress such learning (Schuller and Field, 1999).

Lifelong learning as it is now conceived requires a kind of *paradigm shift* in the organisation of learning – not in adulthood, but in the very first forms of schooling. The goals for orientation are no longer efficient learning, effective didactic strategies and consistent formal curricula, but rather the emphasis on the situation and the prerequisites on the part of *learners* (Bentley, 1998). This also means addressing non-formal and informal options for learning. The key educational question is no longer how certain material can be taught as successfully as possible, but which learning environments can best stimulate self-determined learning – in other words, how learning itself can be learned (Simons, 1992; Smith, 1992).

Of course, this perspective must also include the conveying of basic qualifications such as reading, writing, arithmetic or computer literacy, but even these *basic skills* must be linked to practical experience; the owners of cognitively acquired skills must be able to combine these with social and emotional competencies. Enabling such options demands a high degree of institutional 'self-reflexivity' on the part of education and training institutions in their classical form. They must accept that they, too, must become 'learning organisations'. The necessity of preparing their clientele for lifelong, self-determined learning implies a concept of lifewide learning, or 'holistic learning'.

Schools must network with the community to which they relate, with companies, associations, churches and organisations that are active in that district, and with the families of the schoolchildren in their care. They have to discover new locations for learning and invent other learning environments. Recent school development concepts, particularly those in which the separate institutions are granted substantial autonomy, are certainly providing for greater scope. What is valid for schools is equally valid, of course, for universities, adult education facilities and public administration academies. As John Field correctly points out, lifelong learning necessitates a *'new educational order'* (Field, 2000, pp. 133ff.) – a 'silent revolution' in education.

Individualisation and reflexive modernisation

This demand is neither absurd nor utopian when one looks at the situation faced by a growing group of society's members. The demands levelled at individuals in the second half of the twentieth century changed considerably. Economic factors are by no means the only ones responsible – social and cultural changes also play a critical role. Despite the continuation of social inequalities, the bonds to social milieus and classical mentalities have become looser (Beck, 1992). Patterns of orientation have become more localised and tend to relate more now to generational or gender-based experience, to the perception of one's own ethnicity or even to preferences for certain lifestyles (Alheit, 1999). Inflationary changes in the range of information and consumer products on offer have dramatically increased the number of options open to the members of society (Beck, 1992; Giddens, 1991). Life courses are therefore much less predictable than in the past. What is more, the compulsion to make decisions on a continual basis and to perform incessant changes of orientation *is* being devolved to the individuals themselves to an increasingly clear extent.

This visible trend towards individualisation of the life-course regime and the concomitant pressure to engage in continuous 'reflexivity' on one's own actions has led – as expressed in the prominent theses of Ulrich Beck or Anthony Giddens – to a different, *reflexive modernity*. Yet to be able to handle this different modernity (Beck, 1992), individuals need completely new and flexible structures of competence that can only be established and developed within lifelong learning processes (see Field, 2000, pp. 58ff.). And it demands fundamental changes in the entire educational system.

Contours of a new educational economy?

The astonishing consensus that appears to reign on these doubtlessly plausible and complementary analyses of the age we live in extends from representatives of the traditional business community, to protagonists of the New Economy, to education experts in the modernised left-wing parties. What makes that consensus problematic is its indifference to the social consequences that would be unleashed if such educational policies were implemented without a measure of distance. The delusion of a *lifelong learning society* does nothing whatsoever to eradicate the selection and exclusion mechanisms of the 'old' educational system. Indeed, it may conceal and exacerbate those mechanisms instead (see Field, 2000, pp. 103ff.).

It can already be shown with present empirical evidence that labour market segments requiring low skill levels are in chronic decline (OECD, 1997a). In other words, the expectations of the 'knowledge society' are raising the pressure on individuals to meet certain standards of skills and knowledge before they can be employed. The risks of exclusion for those who fail to meet those standards are more draconian than was ever the case in bygone industrial societies. Of course, the *logic* of exclusion is by no means new – class and gender remain the decisive indicators (Field, 2000, pp. 115ff.). As would be expected, age plays an increasingly significant role (Tuckett and Sargant, 1999). Anyone who never had the chance to learn how to learn will not make any effort to acquire new skills late in the life course.

The crude mechanisms of economic valuation prompt a sceptical view of any future scenario for the learning society – a small majority of 'winners', but with a 'life sentence' to learn, may close its borders to a growing minority of 'losers' who never had a chance, or who voluntarily liberated themselves from the straitjacket of having to perpetually acquire and market new knowledge. The OECD forecast, in any case, comes close enough to the scenario just painted:

> For those who have successful experience of education, and who see themselves as capable learners, continuing learning is an enriching experience, which increases their sense of control over their own lives and their society. For those who are excluded from this process, however, or who choose not to participate, the generalisation of lifelong learning may only have the effect of increasing their isolation from the world of the 'knowledge-rich'. The consequences are economic, in under-used human capacity and increased welfare expenditure, and social, in terms of alienation and decaying social infrastructure.
>
> (OECD, 1997b, p. 1)

Alternatives are therefore needed.

A reasonable consequence would be to realise that lifelong learning cannot be reduced to investment in short-lived, exploitable economic capital, but that it must also be an investment – of equal value – in social capital, in the way we treat those next to us: the family, the neighbour, the co-worker, the other club members, the people we meet in citizen's action groups or at the bar counter (see Field, 2000, pp. 145ff.). In this field of life, we are all lifelong learners. Nobody is excluded from the outset. Everyone is an expert. Shrinkage of this type of capital – declining trust, the moratorium on solidarity that Robert D. Putnam identified years ago not just in US society (Putnam, 1995) – is also economically counterproductive in the medium term. A balance between these two intractable types of capital, on the other hand, could lead to a new kind of 'educational economy' or, more correctly perhaps, to a *social ecology of learning* in modern, modernised societies. However, the precondition for such balance is that learning individuals be taken more seriously – which would also involve a *shift in analytic perspective*.

The micro-perspective: aspects of a phenomenology of biographical learning

So far we have talked about societal changes affecting the modern biography from a specific perspective, namely the *structural perspective*. And for good reason, since our lives are embedded in structures and cannot be extracted arbitrarily. Nevertheless, it would be theoretical foolishness to describe life and learning from this one perspective alone. If we view the problems that we typically encounter from the perspective of the subject, then 'structure' obtains an extraordinarily plastic character.

The 'hidden capacity' to lead our own lives

As biographical subjects we do indeed have the feeling of being the 'organisers' of our life course. Even when things do not run the way we hoped or expected they would, we perform corrections to our life plans under the impression that we do so with personal autonomy. In other words, the conscious disposition towards our biography can be understood as an *intentional action scheme*. The dominant attitude that we have to our own biography is one of planning. We are referring here to more than the 'big plans' that we cultivate for our lives – the dream job, the political career, house-building, finding a 'good match' – but also our plans for the weekend or the following afternoon, or what programmes we want to watch on TV. We decide, for example, to lose 10 pounds in weight or to give up smoking, and even succeed in doing so. All of this conveys to us the impression that we hold our own lives in our own hands and that we are the subjects of our biography. But this impression could be exceptionally problematic, and not only because fate could deal us a blow at any time, making us irrecoverably ill or unemployed, or making us lose a loved one or all that we possess. The point is rather that our supposed autonomy of action and autonomous planning is subordinated to 'processual structures' in our biography that we can influence to only a very marginal extent: institutional procedures like schooling or vocational training, trajectories like unemployment or a drug career, unconscious needs like a late coming-out as homosexual.

What is important is the finding that our basic feeling – that we can act relatively independently over our own biographies – does not necessarily conflict with the fact that the greater part of our biographical activities are either fixed to a large degree or require various 'supporters' to initiate them. It therefore appears plausible that the feeling is not actually an intentional action scheme at all, or a consciously desired biographical plan, but is instead a kind of hidden 'meaning' behind the alternating processual structures of our life course: the no-doubt ubiquitous, but strategically not always available intuition that for all the contradiction, we are still dealing with *our* lives. We entertain this unique 'background idea' of ourselves not in spite of, but precisely because of the structural limitations imposed by our social and ethnic origins, our gender and the era in which we are living. Structure and subjectivity form an important combination here, the dissolution of which can lead to crisis. Such crises obviously affect more than ourselves and our capacities. They also depend on structures. 'Life constructions' are generated between the twin poles of structure and subjectivity, and constructions only contain elements of reality if they also have a retroactive effect on underlying structures. This leads us to the final and most important idea relating to the consequences that the idea of biographical learning has for educational theory in the wider sense.

Learning processes within transition

Life constructions extend beyond what we narrate about our lives. They are hidden references to the structural conditions that are imposed on us. Bourdieu (1984) has provided convincing evidence of this fact, using his concept of habitus: the hidden way we express ourselves, the way we talk, think and eat, walk and dress. Our habitus shows us the limits of our social origins. But there is another side to life constructions: in the course of our lives we produce more meaning relating to ourselves and our social framework that we can actually have from the perspective of our reflexive biographical concern with self. We dispose of a biographical background knowledge with which we are able to fill out and utilise to the full the social space in which we move. None of us have all conceivable possibilities open to us. But within the framework of a restricted modification potential, we have more opportunities than we will ever put into practice. Our biography therefore contains a sizeable potential of *'unlived life'* (Weizsäcker, 1956). Intuitive knowledge about it is part of our 'practical consciousness' (Giddens, 1984). It is not accessible on a simple reflexive basis, but in a double sense it represents a very unusual resource for educational processes:

- Our prescriptive knowledge about life constructions which accompany us but which we have not implemented, or at least not yet, keeps the reflexively available reference to self fundamentally open and creates the preconditions for us to take a different attitude towards ourselves without having to revise this 'hidden' meaning. The processual structures of our life course, the dynamics of their emergence at the surface, suggest an extension or a restriction of autonomous biographical action. Conscious 'ratification' of them is our own responsibility as the subject of our own biography. We are, in a certain sense, 'autopoietic systems', to use an irritating and yet stimulating concept from Luhmann's systems theory. We possess the chance to identify the surplus meanings in our experience of life and to appropriate them for a conscious change in our self- and world-referentiality.

- Biographical background knowledge is at the same time, however, an emergent potential for changing structures. The modification of individual self- and world-referents – even in the limited context of specific life constructions – contains opportunities for the transformation of the institutional framework conditions of social existence. Substantial elements of these 'structures' are the unquestioned certainties functioning in the background to which social individuals relate intuitively when they act on the everyday plane, but also when they act biographically. As soon as such prescripts – or only parts of them – enter our awareness and become available, then structures begin to change. Unlived life does indeed possess socially explosive force.

The dynamics of this 'double educational resource' awaken associations with the enlightening option in classical psychoanalysis: *'Where Id was, Ego shall be'*. On closer inspection, however, it becomes clear that the important issue is not only the self-assured, strong ego dealing with a basic dynamic that is otherwise unchangeable, but is also the transition to a new quality of self- and world-referentiality – a process that leaves neither the learning subject nor the surrounding structural context unchanged. In other words, we are dealing here with learning processes within transitions (Alheit, 1993). Transitional learning processes are in a certain sense 'abductive'. They implement what is described in early American pragmatism, particularly by Charles Sanders Peirce, as the ability to network something that 'we would never previously have dreamed could be combined' (Peirce, 1991 [1903], p. 181).

This ability requires, of course, a social actor. Knowledge can only be genuinely transitional if it is *biographical knowledge*. Solely when specific individuals relate to their lifeworld in such a way that their self-reflexive activities begin to shape social contexts is contact established with that key qualification of modernity, what I have termed elsewhere *'biographicity'* (Alheit, 1992). Biographicity means that we can redesign again and again, from scratch, the contours of our life within the specific contexts in which we (have to) spend it, and that we experience these contexts as shapeable and designable. In our biographies, we do not possess all conceivable opportunities, but within the framework of the limits we are structurally set, we still have considerable scope open to us. The main issue is to decipher the 'surplus meanings' of our biographical knowledge, and that in turns means perceiving the potentiality of our unlived lives.

However, reflexive learning processes do not take place exclusively inside the individual, but depend on communication and interaction with others and relations to a social context. Biographical learning is embedded in lifeworlds that can be analysed under certain conditions as 'learning environments' or 'learning milieus' (see Lave and Wenger, 1991). Learning within and through one's life history is therefore interactive and socially structured, on the one hand, but it also follows its own individual logic that is generated by the specific, biographically layered structure of experience. The biographical structure does not determine the learning process, because it is an open structure that has to integrate the new experience it gains through interacting with the world, with others and with itself. On the other hand, it significantly affects the way in which new experience is formed and built into a biographical learning process. Biographical learning is both a *constructionist achievement* of the individual integrating new experiences into the self-referential 'architectonic' of particular personal past experiences and a *social process* which makes subjects competent and able to actively shape and change their social world (Alheit and Dausien, 2000).

New research questions on an international lifelong learning agenda

It seems, indeed, that any serious, analytical involvement with the complex phenomenon of lifelong learning will be contingent on a *paradigm shift* among educationalists:

*   at the social *macro*-level, in respect of a new policy for education and training that aims at striking a different balance between economic, cultural and social capital;
*   at the institutional *meso*-level, also in respect of a new self-reflexivity of organisations that should conceive of themselves as 'environments' and 'agencies' of complex learning and knowledge resources, and no longer as the administrators and conveyors of codified, dominant knowledge (Field, 2000);
*   at the individual *micro*-level, with regard to the increasingly complicated linkages and processing accomplished by the specific actors in the face of the social and media-related challenges of late modernity, which call for a new quality in the individual and collective construction of meanings (Alheit, 1999).

We still know too little, in fact, about the systemic balances between economic and social capital. We hardly know anything yet about that 'grey capital' of new knowledge (Field, 2000, p. 1) and its impacts on long-term learning processes. Of course, the comparison of different types of post-industrial society – e.g. the distinct differences between Danish or British or German strategies for arriving at a *learning society* – makes it worthwhile to carry out systematic international comparisons of educational economics.

Yet we have only scraps of information about the institutional prerequisites for the paradigm shift required:

> What pressures to change are operating on education and training institutions? [...] What concepts and measures are applied and accepted

as best practice in the fields of quality management, organisational development and personnel development? What theoretical and empirical conditions justify speaking of educational establishments as 'learning organisations'?

(*Forschungsmemorandum*, 2000, p. 13)

We are discovering more and more new, more complex and riskier status passages and transitions in modern life courses. We observe astonishing and creative (re-)constructions in individual biographies (Alheit, 1993; Dausien, 1996). However, we are still missing a systematically elaborated theory of *biographical and situated learning*: 'In which learning cultures and dependencies of supra-individual patterns, mentalities and milieus does individual learning develop? What implicit learning potentials and learning processes are shown in social milieus and groups (e.g. within families and between generations)?' (*Forschungsmemorandum*, 2000, p. 5)

These open research questions are raised by the 'new concept' of lifelong learning. They include the idea that social learning is obviously – more than ever before in history – an achievement of the *subjects* concerned. The *biographicity of learning* affects institutional and even societal macro-structures. Jacque Delors, in his famous UNESCO report (1996), called it *'The treasure within'*. We may add: it should be understood as an important social and cultural capital for the future development of civil societies.

References

Alheit, P. (1992) 'The biographical approach to adult education' in: Mader, W. (Ed.) *Adult Education in the Federal Republic of Germany: Scholarly Approaches and Professional Practice.* Vancouver: University of British Columbia, pp. 186–222.

Alheit, P. (1993) 'Transitorische Bildungsprozesse: Das "biographische Paradigma" in der Weiterbildung' [Transformative learning processes: The 'biographical paradigm' in adult education] in: Mader, W. (Ed.) *Weiterbildung und Gesellschaft. Grundlagen wissenschaftlicher und beruflicher Praxis in der Bundesrepublik Deutschland*, 2nd edition. Bremen: University of Bremen Press, pp. 343–418.

Alheit, P. (1999) 'On a contradictory way to the 'Learning Society': A critical approach,' *Studies in the Education of Adults* 31 (1), pp. 66–82.

Alheit, P. and Dausien, B. (2000) '"Biographicity" as a basic resource of lifelong learning' in: Alheit, P., Beck, J., Kammler, E., Salling Olesen, H. and Taylor, R. (Eds.) *Lifelong Learning Inside and Outside Schools*, Vol. 2. Roskilde: RUC, pp. 400–422.

Beck, U. (1992 [1986]) *Risk Society: Towards a New Modernity.* London: Sage.

Bentley, T. (1998) *Learning Beyond the Classroom: Education for a Changing World.* London: Routledge.

Bourdieu, P. (1984 [1979]) *Distinction: A Social Critique of the Judgement of Taste.* London: Routledge.

Commission of the European Communities (2000) *A Memorandum on Lifelong Learning.* Brussels: European Community.

Dausien, B. (1996) *Biographie und Geschlecht. Zur biographischen Konstruktion sozialer Wirklichkeit in Frauenlebensgeschichten* [Gender and Biography: Toward the Biographical Construction of Social Reality in Female Life Histories]. Bremen: Donat.

Delors, J. (1996) *Learning: The Treasure Within. Report to UNESCO of the International Commission on Education for the Twenty-First Century*. Paris: UNESCO.

Field, J. (2000) *Lifelong Learning and the New Educational Order*. Stoke-on-Trent, UK: Trentham Books.

Forschungsmemorandum für die Erwachsenen- und Weiterbildung (2000) Im Auftrag der Sektion Erwachsenenbildung der DGfE verfasst von Arnold, R., Faulstich, P., Mader, W., Nuissl von Rein, E., Schlutz, E. Frankfurt a.M. (Internet source: http://www.die-bonn. de/oear/forschungsmemorandum/forschungsmemorandum.htm download: 20.4.2008). [Research Memorandum of Adult and Continuing Education].

Giddens, A. (1984) *The Constitution of Society: Outline of the Theory of Structuration*. Cambridge, UK: Polity Press

Giddens, A. (1991) *Modernity and Self-Identity: Self and Society in the Late Modern Age*. Palo Alto, CA: Stanford University Press.

Hall, P. (1999) 'Social capital in Britain', *British Journal of Political Science* 29 (3), pp. 417–461.

Kohli, M. (1985) 'Die Institutionalisierung des Lebenslaufs. Historische Befunde und theoretische Argumente' [The Institutionalisation of the Life Course: Historical Facts and Theoretical Arguments], in: *Kölner Zeitschrift für Soziologie und Sozialpsychologie* 37, pp. 1–29.

Lave, J. and Wenger, E. (1991) *Situated Learning: Legitimate Peripheral Participation*. Cambridge, UK: Cambridge University Press.

OECD (1997a) *Literacy Skills for the Knowledge Society: Further Results of the International Adult Literacy Survey*. Paris: OECD.

OECD (1997b) *What Works in Innovation in Education: Combating Exclusion through Adult Learning*. Paris: OECD.

Peirce, Ch.S. (1991 [1903]) *Schriften zum Pragmatismus und Pragmatizismus* [Texts on Pragmatism and Pragmatizism] (edited by Karl-Otto Apel), Frankfurt a.M.: Suhrkamp.

Putnam, R.D. (1995) 'Bowling alone: America's declining social capital', *Journal of Democracy* 6, pp. 65–78.

Schuller, T. (1998) 'Human and social capital: Variations within a learning society' in: Alheit, P. and Kammler, E. (Eds.) *Lifelong Learning and Its Impact on Social and Regional Development*. Bremen: Donat, pp. 113–136.

Schuller, T. and Field, J. (1999) 'Is there divergence between initial and continuing education in Scotland and Northern Ireland?', *Scottish Journal of Adult Continuing Education* 5 (2), pp. 61–76.

Simons, P.R.J. (1992) 'Theories and principles of learning to learn' in: Tuijnman, A. and van der Kamp, M. (Eds.) *Learning Across the Lifespan: Theories, Research, Policies*. Oxford: Pergamon Press.

Smith, R.M. (1992) 'Implementing the learning to learn concept' in: Tuijnman, A. and van der Kamp, M. (Eds.) *Learning Across the Lifespan: Theories, Research, Policies*. Oxford: Pergamon Press.

Stehr, N. (2002) 'The social role of knowledge' in: Genov, N. (Ed.) *Advances in Sociological Knowledge: Over Half a Century*. Paris: ISSC, pp. 84–113.

Tavistock Institute (1999) *A Review of Thirty New Deal Partnerships. Research and Development Report ESR 32* Employment Service. Sheffield, UK: University of Warwick.

Tuckett, A. and Sargant, N. (1999) *Making Time: The NIACE Survey on Adult Participation in Learning 1999*. Leicester: NIACE.

Weizsäcker, V. von (1956) *Pathosophie* [Pathosophy]. Göttingen, Germany: Vandenhoeck & Ruprecht.

Chapter 9

Life cycles and learning cycles

John Heron

Briton John Heron is primarily known as the developer of the participatory research method in the social sciences called "co-operative inquiry". In the 1970s, Heron was the founder and director of the Human Potential Research Project at the University of Surrey. Later he worked with whole-person medicine in the British Postgraduate Medical Foundation at the University of London and was the director of the International Centre for Co-operative Inquiry in Volterra in Italy. Since 2000, he has been the director of the South Pacific Centre for Human Inquiry in Auckland, New Zealand. In 1992, he described the theoretical basis of his understanding in the book Feeling and Personhood: Psychology in Another Key. *In this book he used the area of learning as a case to illustrate his approach. The following chapter is made up of Chapter 11 and part of Chapter 12 of this book (in chapter 13 he goes on to formal learning, and in general a full understanding of his learning model implies a study of the preceding chapters).*

An overview

In this chapter, I present my understanding of the processes of living and learning as they can be derived from my theory of the person (Heron, 1992). This leads to a series of models and maps – structural conjectures – which the reader is invited to entertain as a set of lenses through which to view different aspects of living and learning. Because these lenses give a selective view, however much they may illuminate, they also constrain. They do not depict reality; they offer no more than possible ways of construing our experience. They focus on just one kind of story, among many other conceivable ones, about how we live and learn. But I believe the story is a useful one.

Many of the models are not only depictions of a process but also practical prescriptions about a possible way of managing some way of living and learning. Again, any such prescription is a tentative proposal, a working hypothesis, something it might be worth trying out in an experimental and critical way. It is a recommendation, not a solution; an invitation to inquiry, not a dogma; an exploratory project, not a panacea.

This chapter reflects the dynamic interplay of life and mind, which is the basic polarity of my theory of the person. It is about everyday living and everyday learning. The first of these is daily experience without any thought of learning from it; the second means the conscious intent to learn through such experience. I look at both these in terms of the four psychological modes – affective, imaginal, conceptual, practical – each including a basic polarity between an individuating function and a participatory one. They are conceived as a cycle, but with the up-hierarchy metaphor as the underlying rationale, i.e. that the later-mentioned mode is not controlled and ruled but branching and flowering out of the earlier-mentioned mode(s).

Everyday living cycles are called life cycles, and everyday learning cycles are called learning cycles. They may involve only the individuating modes, and then I call them cycles of the ego, since the ego is only busy with the individuating modes. Or they may engage the participatory modes as well, in which case I call them cycles of the person. Again, cycles of the ego or the person may be basic cycles or reversal cycles, in which the conceptual comes before the imaginal.

After discussing the life cycle and learning cycle of the ego, I explore some of the distressed states into which the ego can become locked. Then I move on to the life cycle and learning cycle of the person.

The cyclic process

The metaphor of a basic cycle portrays the ground process of the psyche, its flow of life through the four modes in a continuous rhythmic pulse. Derived from the up-hierarchy and its ground in affect, this cycle starts from the affective mode and proceeds through the imaginal, the conceptual and the practical to return to the affective, and so on. The individuating version of this basic cycle is depicted in Figure 9.1. It is the cycle of the ego, busy with the individuating modes – emotion, imagery, discrimination, action – that cluster round the claims of daily subsistence; the participatory functions are minimally or tacitly involved.

In this cycle the individuating modes exclude any conscious use of the participatory modes. In the basic cycle of the person, by contrast, conscious use of the participatory modes of feeling, intuition, reflection and intention includes the individuating modes, which are thus set within an extended awareness. Life is more considered: daily subsistence is realigned within an attunement to the wider scheme of things.

When I refer to a 'life cycle' I do not, of course, mean the course of a person's entire life, but simply the continuous cyclic succession of modes going on minute by minute and hour by hour in everyday living. The frequency of the rhythm will change a lot over any given day, with long and short cycles and overlapping cycles.

As well as the basic cycle, to do with the psyche's ground process, there is the reversal cycle when the psyche is reorganizing its ground process so that it functions with new content. I stress that the reversal cycle is only one form of reorganization: it just happens to be the one I choose to focus on in this chapter.

By using the model of the cycle, I can show the psychological modes involved with all three basic polarities: in the ego and person cycles the polarity between individuation and participation, in the basic and reversal cycles the polarity between ground process and reorganization, and in life cycles and learning cycles the polarity between life and mind. I don't cover all possible combinations of these, just some of the ones I am more familiar with.

The basic life cycle of the ego

This basic cycle involves the individuating modes of emotion, imagery, discrimination and action (with the participatory only subliminally involved). They are grounded in the overall emotional pattern which the person has acquired in the development of the ego and start from some immediate, active component of it. This egoic pattern is a systematic way of being fulfilled or frustrated in life. The emotional need felt now is an index of how the pattern seeks to influence behaviour in order to maintain itself. And the influence is first exerted through an image or selected percept. Once this image is launched the cycle is well under way: discrimination and action are simply means to the envisaged goal.

The ego is defined as a case of mistaken identity: the person unawarely identifies – at the expense of the whole person – with a compulsive pursuit of individuation so that it becomes distorted in the direction of separateness, alienation and rigidity of self. The life cycle here is not only conservative, it is defensively so: it is keeping the participatory modes at bay through the subject-object split; and it is also warding off the pain of primal wounding and the deep tensions of the human condition.

Figure 9.1 portrays the life cycle of the ego in the world of existence. 'Imagery' in this context basically means perception and memory. This is the cycle the ego continuously moves round in its everyday experience from hour to hour. The baseline of the cycle, and its starting point, is the individual's current emotional state, which is the felt fulfilment or frustration of its needs in the immediate world of existence. This influences perception of the present situation, within which the ego discriminates and makes relevant distinctions to service the actions that will satisfy its needs. Such actions will modify its emotional state, leading to the generation of a new cycle.

The four stages of the cycle can be very simply illustrated. Thus an individual (1) feels hungry; (2) looks around the kitchen to see what there is to eat; (3) selectively discriminates among the items to formulate a menu; and (4) cooks a meal and eats it. Next, the same person (1) feels the need to relax; (2) looks through the television programmes in the paper; (3) selectively discriminates among the programmes to make a viewing schedule; and (4) turns on the TV set and watches. And so on.

In terms of basic polarities, someone in this cycle is individuating only, is identified with a restricted ground process, and is living only – with learning reduced virtually to nil.

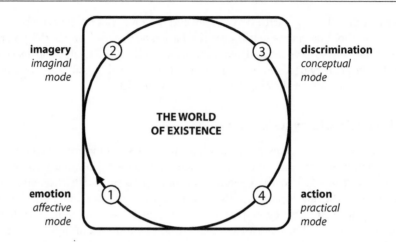

Figure 9.1 The basic life cycle of the ego.

The basic learning cycle of the ego

When its changing emotional state is relatively free from past afflictions, then the ego *can* choose to learn, by trial and error, and by social influence, what perceptions, discriminations and actions lead to felt fulfilment or frustration of its concerns. The life cycle then becomes a simple learning cycle utilizing feedback: the negative emotional outcomes of one cycle will be used to modify or change perception, discrimination or action in the next; and positive outcomes will reinforce those parts of the cycle that lead to them. Comments from others may aid this process. The individual learns through daily experience to get what he or she wants out of life.

In such ego learning, shown in Figure 9.2, the world is defined by deeds that satisfy one's needs and wants: it is the realm of everyday existence, its individual and socialized desires. The learning is mainly practical, that is, learning how to act in order to achieve these satisfactions. There is not much learning about the world as such going on, since the world is reduced by activism to those parameters that satisfy one's wants.

For the basic life cycle to become this simple everyday learning cycle, two qualities are needed as well as relative freedom from past affliction. First, a measure of mindfulness throughout the cycle, being aware of what is going on at each stage, and of how each stage influences the next. And second, a sufficient concentration of attention next time around the cycle to try out alternative ways of managing each of the stages. These are the twin signs that the mind is at work: some inclusive awareness and some focused awareness, both informed by the intention to grasp what is going on.

In Figure 9.2, mindfulness, the extra margin of awareness, is shown as an outer circle around the modes; and concentration is shown as a cross in the

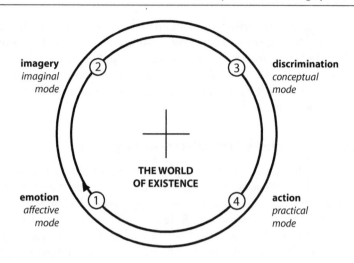

Figure 9.2 The basic learning cycle of the ego.

middle of the world of existence. In terms of basic polarities, someone involved with this cycle is individuating only, but with both intuition and reflection a little less tacitly involved; is identified with a restricted ground process; and is learning as well as living, although the learning is subordinate to a restricted kind of living.

Distressed egos

The ego's changing state is from time to time afflicted by repressed distress from the individual's past. This happens when the current situation echoes traumatic early life events which fixated the psyche on unmet needs and consequent pain. The ego then unawarely sees the situation in terms of these events: it reproduces in its present life a symbolic equivalent of the traumatic past, and its behaviour is compulsively distorted by the old buried longings and hurts. It is as if it is trying to create a current justification for feeling haunted by buried affliction and for being stuck with a strategy of surviving by identifying with frustration and hurt. It is also as if it is seeking to reproduce the problem until at last it can attract the attention of someone who can come forward, interrupt the whole production and break the old spell.

In this case the basic cycle will be a treadmill, with felt need, perception, discrimination and action being unawarely caught in reproducing the closed distorted loop of the past. Figure 9.3 portrays the predicament. So, for example, a person has a repressed frozen need for the love they never got as a child; they unconsciously project this longing on to someone who cannot assuage it; they rationalize all this as meeting their adult needs; and this launches them into compulsive symbolic re-enactment of their frustrating past.

Doing so displaces the frozen need and repressed pain while reinforcing them and keeping them in place. There is no possibility of learning from experience.

This pathological loop may overlap many cycles that characterize behaviour in more obvious and external terms. So however you fill out Figure 9.1 showing the basic life cycle of the ego, this distressed ego life cycle may be simultaneously involved.

Compulsive roles of the distressed ego

The classic roles of the afflicted ego, both in relation to itself and in relation with others, are those of the compulsive victim, the compulsive rescuer, the compulsive rebel and the compulsive oppressor. They correspond to the four stages of the distressed ego cycle, as if each stage can also turn into a subpersonality in its own disturbed right. The victim role represents the repressed distress and frozen needs. The rescuer role personifies the projection of frozen needs onto the current situation in the hope that they can be met. The rebel characterizes the defensive rationalization that refuses to acknowledge the truth of what is really going on. The oppressor portrays the compulsion to act in maladaptive and distorted ways.

Figure 9.4 shows the treadmill of compulsive ego roles. Applied within one ego on its own and not in interaction with anyone else, an individual (1) feels lowly, crushed and bad about him- or herself in some respect; (2) tries to do something about it in some inappropriate way; (3) gives this effort up with a rationalized refusal to acknowledge there is a problem; and then (4) punishes him- or herself with accusations of impotence and incompetence. He or she then (1) feels crushed and lowly and begins the cycle again. The point of the four-wheel treadmill is that each role propels the next. The victim runs the

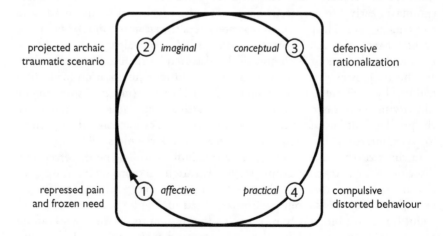

Figure 9.3 The distressed ego life cycle.

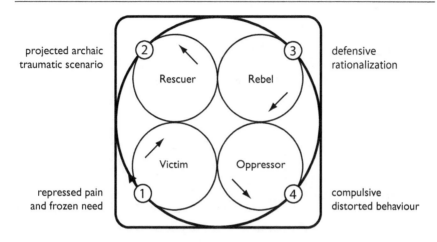

Figure 9.4 Compulsive roles of the distressed ego.

rescuer, who drives the rebel, who alerts the oppressor, who controls the victim.

If two interacting people are involved, then they share a two-person treadmill: when one is victim, the other is rescuer; when one is rescuer, the other is rebel; when one is rebel, the other is oppressor; and when one is oppressor the other is victim. So if you are compulsively down, and a partner inappropriately tries to help you, you rebel, the partner then accuses you, you irrationally sink again and so on.

There are many variations of this. You may be down, then *ask* for inappropriate help; when it is given, you reject it; your partner attacks you for this and you go down again and so on. Or you are driven to help your partner in some ill-conceived way; the partner rebels; you accuse him or her of ingratitude; he or she sinks in compulsive guilt and so on. So one person oscillates between victim and rebel, while the other is in a complementary swing between oppressor and rescuer, and at any point they may switch their allegiances, the one who was victim and rebel becoming oppressor and rescuer, and vice versa.

Whatever the variation, basically the two people are trading guilt and blame, passing it to and fro, because guilt and blame were imposed on them in early years, wounding their capacity for loving and congealing it in emotional pain. Thereafter the repressed pain of the wound is displaced into adult guilt and blame behaviours. The psychological colleagues of guilt and blame are collusion and denial. Two people locked into trading guilt and blame are colluding in acting out archaic scenarios, while at the same time denying to themselves and each other that it is going on.

Deeply irrational guilt makes a person identify and collude with a pathological relationship. The more collusion, the more the person has defensively to deny the pathology, leading to a build-up of repressed material which overflows into blaming behaviour, which flips the partner into their own rapid circuit of

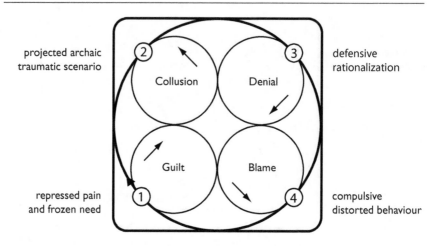

Figure 9.5 Guilt and blame of the distressed ego.

guilt, collusion, denial and counter-blame. Figure 9.5 shows this version of the cycle.

The reversal learning cycle of the ego

Here a person is interrupting the basic life cycle of the ego using the reversal cycle. So the ego's ground process is being reorganized for the purposes of learning how to live more effectively. Now I don't believe that all reversal cycles are necessarily learning cycles. For example, I think you can analyse the process of repression in terms of a subliminal reversal cycle, and that is to do with psychological survival: it is about negative living, not about learning. But here I am choosing a reversal cycle which does involve learning, not just living.

So this reversal learning cycle interrupts the first leg of the basic cycle (which moves promptly from emotion to imagery) and goes instead from emotion to discrimination. So as soon as the current, active component of the egoic emotional pattern arises, the individual discriminates its nature and its propensity to generate a certain kind of image and replaces this with a different kind of image, which leads directly to a different kind of action and outcome. The reversal cycle goes from emotion to discrimination to imagery to action, instead of the basic route from emotion to imagery to discrimination to action.

This goes against the grain of the basic life cycle. It is 'unnatural', revisionary, a reversal of the established, conservative scheme of things. It interrupts the normal order and coherence of the psyche, so it requires alert inward discrimination and motivation to get it going.

The cycle will be used until there is a shift in the underlying emotional pattern and its associated imagery, so that the basic cycle is re-established at a different level and in different terms. The individual is learning how to live in a way that frees behaviour from unwanted habits or the distorting effects of an afflicted past. This is a more sophisticated kind of everyday learning compared to the basic learning cycle of the ego, which simply involves learning how to act in order to achieve ego satisfactions. But note that both of them are concerned mainly with practical learning.

Figure 9.6 illustrates the reversal cycle in arrows and the old, interrupted basic cycle as a circle. To give an example: anxiety (1) about an impending appointment is about to launch the image of an oppressive encounter. But this image propensity doesn't get off the ground, because the aware individual spots it (2), substitutes the image (3) of a challenging meeting, follows this through into action (4) and reaps its emotional rewards (1). This way there is the possibility of establishing a new kind of basic cycle with a different underlying pattern, in which the emotion of excitement generates an image of a challenging encounter.

What this sort of reversal learning cycle proposes is that innovation in individuated behaviour involves a discriminating substitution of imagery. 'Substitution' is perhaps hardly the word: what is involved is the insertion of an image to banish an image propensity. And while these are not symbolized in the figure, the use of the cycle presupposes mindfulness and concentration informed by the learning intention. In terms of basic polarities, someone using this cycle is individuating primarily, but with both intuition and reflection more noticeably involved; is reorganizing a restricted ground process; and is learning through living, with the learning here widening out the living. So this is work on opening up the ego.

A classic use of this reversal cycle in everyday life is to interrupt restimulated old hurt so that it does not drive the distressed cycle of the ego and is not acted out in compulsive behaviour. For repressed pain can be activated by those features

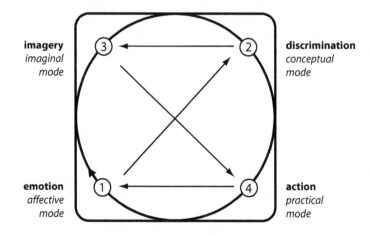

Figure 9.6 The reversal learning cycle of the ego.

of the current situation that are unconsciously seen as symbolic equivalents of troubled events of the past. Once aroused, it strains at the repressive barrier, generating images of driven displacement.

So the reversal cycle starts with this restimulated distress. Stage 2 is the discrimination of it, and this can have various features. It can be a simple noticing and identifying. It can develop into cognitive restructuring, construing the situation in a positive light that replaces the old negative projected template.

The third stage is image insertion, a picture of alternative behaviour to the trigger-happy acting-out tendency. Attention is now switched off the agitated emotion and on to a vision of a different kind of immediate future. This is taken into action in stage 4. The revised action may entirely deactivate the restimulated distress, replacing it, at stage 1 of the next cycle, with a different emotional state, in which case a new, wholesome kind of basic cycle has been launched, instead of the old distressed one. If the distress charge is reduced but still twitching, then the reversal cycle is continued until a reshaped basic cycle takes over in full swing.

Figure 9.7 shows the reversal cycle at work, interrupting a distress-driven basic cycle, which is indicated by the faint circle. Of course, it can be used to interrupt and change any kind of basic cycle, not just a distress-driven one: any life-cycle habit that is due for a shift. But remember, the use of the reversal cycle is 'unnatural', revisionary, a reversal of the established order in the psyche, so it requires inner alertness to launch it.

Given this alertness, the revisionary cycle is for use in the thick of daily egoic life. To give an example: George has an irrational impulse (1) to blame his partner. He immediately notices this (2), and instead of seeing the other as the bad parent of the past, sees (3) his partner as the one loved now, and then acts accordingly (4).

How effective this cycle is in relation to restimulated distress depends on several factors: the intensity of the restimulation; how much practice a person has had in using the cycle like this; and whether the person also has access to co-counselling or other therapy outlets for healing old traumatic memories by releasing their distress charge. I don't think it can be reliably effective without some back-up of this last kind. Given this back-up, it can be applied to dismantle many of the more gross confusions of egoic behaviour.

Everything depends on inner alertness at the point of discrimination. This is a combination of mindfulness and concentration: one needs to be aware of one's process and ready to focus thought. The person has to be immediately ready to conceptualize the irrational storm gathering on the emotional threshold *as* restimulated distress. The more it can be construed in terms of historical psychodynamics, the less its tendency to afflict the present.

A co-counselling co-operative inquiry in which I was engaged looked at a wide range of different methods for dealing with restimulated distress in everyday life. It did not explicitly identify this reversal cycle; nevertheless

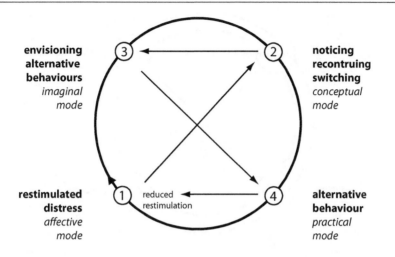

envisioning
alternative
behaviours
*imaginal
mode*

③ ← → ②

noticing
recontruing
switching
*conceptual
mode*

restimulated
distress
*affective
mode*

① reduced ← ④
restimulation

alternative
behaviour
*practical
mode*

Figure 9.7 Reversal learning cycle of the ego applied to restimulated distress.

the inquiry findings can be seen as full of practical psychological devices for making it effective (Reason and Heron, 1982).

They made an important distinction between tactics and strategies: the former are practical methods for use in the particular situation; the latter are *policies to adopt* some preferred tactic or set of tactics. So strategies mean a greater readiness at stage 1 of the reversal cycle:

> They present a higher order approach to life management, rising above the purely tactical, ad hoc response to particular situations. The tactical approach is simply crisis-management: the restimulation is already upon you and you choose whatever tactic will best enable you to handle it. The strategic approach is more comprehensive: it anticipates and educates before the event.
>
> (Reason and Heron, 1982: 17)

Figure 9.8 shows the three stages of change when using the reversal cycle. The inner circle is the old basic cycle, changed into the new basic cycle of the outer circle by the figure-of-eight arrows of the reversal cycle.

The basic life cycle of the person

The more limited, preoccupied life cycle of the ego, shown in Figure 9.1, takes it around the individuating modes of emotion, imagery, discrimination and action. It is preoccupied with its needs and interests in the world of existence. The participatory modes remain latent, working in a tacit way, the ego feeding off their subliminal presence for its own ends, and ignoring some of their impulses.

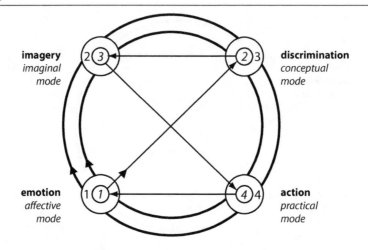

Figure 9.8 The three stages of change using the reversal learning cycle.

The person, by contrast, is functioning awarely in these wider modes, including the individuating modes within them. The basic life cycle of the person, the ground process, takes into account the participatory modes of feeling, intuition, reflection and intention, as well as emotion, imagery, discrimination and action.

It is shown in Figure 9.9 as four rotating larger wheels – the participatory modes – which touch and turn each other; and within each of these is a smaller wheel – the corresponding individuating mode – influenced by the movement of the larger wheel that contains it. Each mode is shown as generating the relevant worldview of which it is the primary parent.

The cycle starts with a person feeling in empathic resonance with their total situation. Out of this felt participation, the person exercises an intuitive awareness of the entire pattern of what is appearing, seeing this perhaps in terms of some metaphor, story or myth that opens up life with expansive possibilities. This in turn gives rise to reflection, taking hold of the practical issues involved in relating to the situation. And this leads to some intention to act in a way that takes account of both the possibilities and the practicalities. With such action, the situation changes and a new cycle commences.

At each stage, the individuating modes are subsumed and modified. Felt participation at stage 1 will influence and may alter the person's primary need and its degree of satisfaction and hence their current emotional state. At stage 2, intuitive grasp of the total pattern of the situation will affect the imagery of what is perceived, remembered and anticipated. At stage 3, discrimination will be in the service of a reflective grasp of relevant practical issues. And at stage 4, action is the expression of wider purposes and intentions. What might otherwise be the more limited address of the ego at all four stages becomes transformed within a wider ambience.

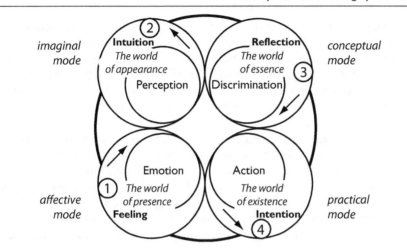

Figure 9.9 The basic life cycle of the person.

As an illustration of this cycle, let us take a holistic medical practitioner relating to a client. (1) The practitioner attunes empathically to the total being of the client, realigning her own emotional needs and interests accordingly. (2) Then, as she questions, talks with and examines the client, she grasps intuitively the total imagery of spoken and bodily cues and the story revealed by the client and explores these imaginatively in terms of analogy and metaphor. (3) At the back of her mind, she reflects on all this imaginal data, while discriminating among them, and formulates a range of possible diagnoses. (4) Finally, she selects one of these as primary, makes a diagnosis and puts forward a plan of practical therapy.

Since she is a holistic practitioner, working with the participatory cycle of the person, she will want to include the client – wherever appropriate and possible – in mutuality of attunement in stage 1, in shared discussion in stages 2 and 3 and in co-operative problem solving and planning in stage 4 (Heron, 1978).

In terms of the three basic polarities of the psyche, the person here is being participative, including the individuating modes; is involved with an expanded ground process; and is primarily living, the learning being minimal. So here is a person being consciously participative through feeling, intuition and reflection, who has an open ego and is living through the apertures but is not learning to any significant degree.

The basic learning cycle of the person

As with the ego, the life cycle of the person can become a learning cycle if, once again, the person is mindful throughout it and concentrates with the intention of grasping what is going on. Mindfulness and concentration are symbolized by the outermost circle and the central cross in Figure 9.10. In this figure,

I use the stages followed by the holistic medical practitioner, as outlined in the previous section. So the practitioner in this figure may be learning about empathizing more fully, or intuiting a wider pattern of cues, or reflecting rapidly on alternative hypotheses, or administering therapy. The learning takes place by a simple feedback loop: what is noticed in one cycle is used to confirm or alter what is done in the next cycle. And what is noticed may be what goes on within a stage or the effect of one stage on another.

Whereas the ego is learning through everyday experience how to become more effective in satisfying its individual needs, the person is learning how to become more effective in participating actively in wider and more inclusive fields of endeavour. In terms of the three basic polarities, the person here is being participative, including the individuating modes; is involved with an expanded ground process; and is learning through living, with the learning deepening the living. The person has an open ego and is living and learning through the apertures.

The co-operative reversal learning cycle of the person

The basic learning cycle of the person, just considered, can benefit from being included within a wider circle of co-operative learning, in which people meet to share their experience and reflect together on its meaning and practical implications. This is a higher-order cycle, which includes at one of its stages the whole of a lower-order cycle. Again, its effective use presupposes both mindfulness and concentration.

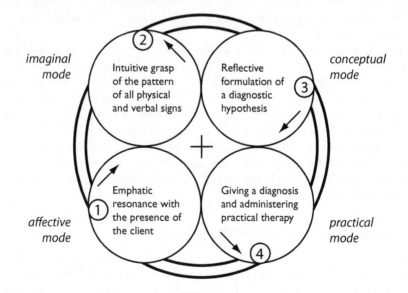

Figure 9.10 The basic learning cycle of the person.

The model I propose for this is a co-operative reversal learning cycle. It is a reversal cycle to interrupt the social ground process that gets established when people meet together informally. Let us suppose it involves a peer professional development group of holistic medical practitioners. It is shown in Figure 9.11.

Stage 1 is the opening, affective stage. In the emotional mode, it is a time for celebration and positive encounter, and for dealing with any unresolved tensions between members of the group and with any anxiety that any aspect of the impending process provokes. In the feeling mode, it is a time of group communion, a meditation in which members ground themselves in their mutual compresence. This nourishes the whole enterprise.

At stage 2, they share data from case histories and reflect on this together, discriminating the main issues, to get a deeper understanding of the therapeutic process, with implications for revised practice. At stage 3, practitioners reformulate their image of their therapeutic practice in the light of their prior deliberations. This is a conscious exercise of active imagination, in which practitioners see themselves – each one on their own terms and in their own way – going about their business in the future in ways which take account of whatever it is they wish to incorporate into their practice from the sharing of stage 2.

This active imagination can be verbalized, working in pairs or small groups. It can be elaborated through graphics, allegory or story, or demonstrated in projected rehearsal through role-play. The group then disbands, and each person takes their image into action at stage 4, which is daily professional

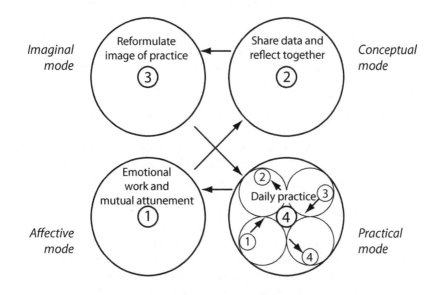

Figure 9.11 The co-operative reversal learning cycle of the person.

practice and consists of the basic learning cycle of the person, as described in the previous section, undertaken with many clients. After an appropriate period of daily practice, they meet again to start a second co-operative cycle.

So this is a co-operative reversal learning cycle, a higher-order cycle, which includes within it an individual basic learning cycle at stage 4. The co-operative cycle can be used by any group of people, from two to two dozen, who wish to enhance, and support each other in, their learning through living. In terms of the three basic polarities, the persons involved being participative in their way of relating, including the individuating modes, are reorganizing social ground process; and are learning co-operatively to deepen their individual living. They have open egos and are living and learning through the apertures.

Autonomy and holism

In ordinary usage, 'learning' refers to the acquisition of knowledge or skills from experience, study or teaching. It involves interest and commitment: we only really learn what we are interested in and follow through with some degree of earnestness. Then too it supposes understanding and retention: we have learnt something if we understand it or understand how to do it (in the case of a skill) and can retain that understanding for some significant period of time.

Learning is necessarily self-directed: no one else can do it for you. Interest, commitment, understanding and retention are all autonomous, self-generated and self-sustaining. Learning also involves the whole person, either by inclusion or by default. Either all of us is explicitly involved in the learning process or only part of us is explicitly involved and what is excluded can be negatively influential, undermining either the content or the process.

These are the two poles of the learning process, autonomy and holism. In living-as-learning, they are necessarily interdependent, to the extent, at any rate, that your living involves all four psychological modes. In educational institutions and formal courses, they can be developed in relative isolation from each other. A course can involve lots of autonomy, with student self-direction in course design, project work and assessment, yet have a rather restricted, unholistic intellectual focus.

Conversely, there can be a programme which involves all aspects of the students' psyches but which is entirely decided and managed by the staff, the students only being self-directing within set exercises. There is thus an interesting creative tension between autonomy in learning and holism in learning which educationalists are only just beginning to address, and which I believe is one of the major challenges for the next decades.

There are four levels of student autonomy. The first and minimal level is the student being self-directing only within teacher-prescribed learning activities: the teacher alone makes all the decisions about the programme of learning and its assessment. The second and more significant level is the student participating with the teacher in negotiated programme planning and assessment. The third level involves a small or large amount of exclusive student self-direction in programme planning and assessment. The fourth level, the most sophisticated, refers to student involvement in decisions with staff about whether students or staff or both shall be involved in decision-making about this or that aspect of programme planning and assessment. I have discussed all this in detail elsewhere (Heron, 1989).

Likewise there are four levels of student holism. The first involves only the four individuating modes of emotion, imagery, discrimination and action: this is limited holism at the egoic level. The second level combines the individuating and participatory modes in particular creative classroom activities where the focus is on the content of some subject matter. The third level involves the individuating and participatory modes in more person-centred concerns: personal development, interpersonal skills, professional work, group and team work, organizational structures and wider social, ecological and planetary commitments. The fourth level includes the second and third levels, integrated with development in psychic and spiritual dimensions.

Kinds of learning

In terms of the theory of this book (J. Heron: *Feeling and Personhood*) there are four kinds of learning – experiential, presentational, propositional and practical. Experiential learning is acquiring knowledge of being and beings through empathic resonance, felt participation. Imaginal learning is acquiring knowledge of the patterning of experience through the exercise of intuition, imagination and perception. Propositional learning is acquiring knowledge stated in propositions through the exercise of the intellect. And practical learning is acquiring knowledge of how to do something through the practice of the particular skill in question.

If Howard Gardner (1983) now believes in eight kinds of intelligence, then some *very* rough and ready correspondences can be set up with them as follows. Experiential learning: intrapersonal, interpersonal, intuitive/spiritual intelligences. Presentational learning: visual/spatial, musical/auditory intelligences. Propositional learning: linguistic, mathematical/logical intelligences. Practical learning: kinaesthetic intelligence.

However, leaving aside Gardner's scheme, I prefer to think that each of the eight modes represents a basic kind of intelligence. Experiential learning: empathic, emotional intelligences. Presentational learning: intuitive, imaging intelligences. Propositional learning: reflective, discriminatory intelligences. Practical learning: intentional, action intelligences. Which is all just another way of making the same basic point: intelligence, learning, knowing – each of these are of several different kinds, are One-Many, and need to be exercised as such.

Learning, inquiry and living

If learning is acquiring knowledge that is already established in the culture, it is simply learning. But if it is acquiring new knowledge that no one else has, then it becomes inquiry or research. Learning as inquiry overlaps with learning what is known, but extends beyond it with a more sophisticated methodology.

Living-as-learning means that daily life, or some significant aspect of it, is consciously undertaken as a learning process, and I have already explored some models for this. This involves all four kinds of learning brought to a focus in practical learning, which in this case, and in very broad terms, means learning how to live, whether from the perspective of the ego or the person. It is ambiguous as to whether it is simple learning or learning as inquiry, since it is difficult to know what other people have or have not established as knowledge of how to live. Many people just live, as distinct from living-as-learning. And living-as-learning may be too individualistic, episodic and unfocused to count as establishing any kind of solid practical knowledge. However, if it is undertaken co-operatively with other people in some systematic way, especially from the perspective of the whole person, the enterprise is so original that it is almost certain to lead to learning as inquiry (see Figure 9.11).

A special case of living-as-learning is working-as-learning. Here daily work is the exclusive focus of conscious learning. At an earlier stage in working life, working-as-learning can also mean learning the job on the job, through some kind of apprenticeship or work placement or work under supervision system.

References

Gardner, H. (1983) *Frames of Mind: The Theory of Multiple Intelligences.* New York: Basic Books.

Heron, J. (1978) *Humanistic Medicine.* London: British Postgraduate Medical Federation.

Heron, J. (1989) *The Facilitators' Handbook.* London: Kogan Page. Revised and enlarged (1999) as *The Complete Facilitators' Handbook.*

Heron, J. (1992) *Feeling and Personhood: Psychology in Another Key.* London: Sage.

Reason, P. and Heron, J. (1982) *Co-counselling: An Experiential Inquiry (2).* Guildford, UK: University of Surrey.

Chapter 10

Lifelong learning as a technology of the self

Mark Tennant

Mark Tennant is Professor of Adult Education at the University of Technology in Sydney, which for many years has been a leading research centre in this area. Tennant is internationally known for his book Psychology and Adult Learning, *which was published for the first time in 1988 and later in new editions in 1997 and 2005. For many years Tennant has had a special interest in the development of personal identity and the self, especially in adult education and in relation to postmodern and social constructivist approaches. The following chapter is a slightly abridged version of an article first published in 1998 in the* International Journal of Lifelong Education, *which discusses the postmodern tendencies of instability and fragmentation of the self and how this challenges traditional aims of adult education to develop the self-understanding, self-esteem and self-confidence of the students.*

Introduction

Adult education has a long history of interest in the development and trans-formation of the self. As such it is useful to consider a range of adult education programmes as belonging to and extending the lineage of technologies of the self identified by Foucault (1988). In all such programmes, even the most individualistic, there are implicit or explicit theorizations concerning the nature of the self and the way the self relates to others or to society more generally. The purpose of this chapter is to explore the postmodern critique of the dominant theorizations of the self in adult education – the psychological/humanistic and the sociological/critical – and to comment on the 'solution' proffered by a postmodern theorization. The postmodern critique is valuable in drawing attention to the difficulties of theorizing some kind of originary, core, true, stable, or ahistorical self. Nevertheless it is important to acknowledge that in many of the sites in which adult educators work, the pursuit of a coherent, continuous self is indispensable to transformative (and thereby resistant) adult education practice.

The title of this chapter is taken from Foucault's essay 'Technologies of the Self', which appears in an edited book of the same title (Martin *et al.*, 1988). In this essay Foucault traces the development of technologies of the self in

Greco-Roman philosophy and in early Christianity. Technologies of the self (which stand alongside and interact with technologies of production, sign systems, and power):

> permit individuals to effect by their own means or with the help of others a certain number of operations on their own bodies and souls, thoughts, conduct and way of being, so as to transform themselves in order to attain a certain state of happiness, purity, wisdom, perfection or immortality.
>
> (1988: 18)

I have commenced with this reference to Foucault because it is useful to consider adult education as belonging to and extending this lineage of technologies of the self. Indeed, adult education has a long history of interest in the development and transformation of the self. A range of programmes exist: from those which aim to promote self-development as an end in itself (e.g. programmes which improve self-esteem or self-concept or which help people to be more in touch with their 'authentic' self) to those programmes in which changes to the self are seen as being a necessary component of broader social change (e.g. programmes aimed at consciousness-raising for those who have suffered from or perhaps even perpetrated discrimination, and public education campaigns in areas such as health, the environment, civics, and domestic violence). In between these extremes are a host of programmes where self-change is important in its own right, but where the 'other' is implicated in different degrees (e.g. programmes for AIDS patients, those addicted to drugs, diabetes sufferers, recent migrants, soon-to-be parents, or domestic violence and sexual assault offenders). All such programmes include implicit or explicit theorizations about the self and how it relates to others. Such theorizations are a necessary part of our conceptions of the possibility of self-change and the associated technologies deployed for the purpose of change. Different theoretical perspectives pose essentially different questions and cast the problematic in different ways. However, a common problem across all perspectives concerns the way in which we participate in our own self-formation and the extent to which the social is constituted in or is constitutive of the self. Foucault offers a theoretical perspective on the formation of the self, and the relationship between self and society, which is quite different from the theoretical perspectives which have hitherto informed adult education practice. Because of this association (albeit by others) with postmodernism, it is worth exploring the postmodern perspective more broadly, both for what it has to say about existing adult education technologies and for its potential to create alternative technologies.

The postmodern critique

There are a number of reviews of the traditions of learning in adult education, but Usher *et al.* (1997) provide perhaps the most useful postmodern account of how these traditions conceive of the self. Usher and colleagues, following Boud (1989), comment on four traditions: the training and efficiency tradition (with its classical scientific self, a kind of self-contained mechanistic learning machine); the self-direction or andragogical tradition (where the self is conceived as individualistic and unitary, capable of rational reflection on experience, and conferring meaning on experience); the learner-centred or humanistic tradition (with the notion of an innate or authentic self which is in a process of 'becoming' in a holistic integration of thinking, feeling, and acting); and the critical pedagogy and social action tradition (with its exploited self of 'false consciousness', an inauthentic self which is socially formed and distorted by ideology and oppressive social structures). The problem with the first three of the above is that they accept as given or neutral that which is highly problematic: for example, knowledge and skills are assumed to be neutral rather than socially and culturally constructed; or experience is seen as given, the source of authentic knowledge, and not in any way problematic; or there is assumed to be a true self which exists independently of the social realm. In the andragogical and humanistic traditions in particular, the social is something which is cast as oppressive and to be overcome or transcended through technologies which promote self-control, self-direction, self-management, self-knowledge, autonomy, or self-realization – technologies which are aimed at empowering the individual learner. In this scenario social change is a matter of individuals acting authentically and autonomously: being truly themselves. Now this view of the self, which is largely informed by psychology, has been criticized as being overly individualistic: of portraying social problems as largely individual problems with individual solutions, of accepting as given the social world in which the self resides. This version of self-empowerment through the fostering of personal autonomy is seen by critics as illusory, largely because social structures and forces remain unchallenged. Ultimately, and ironically, the technologies which enhance autonomy are said to serve the interests of existing social structures and forces. This view is well expressed by Usher *et al.*:

> These traditions make much of empowering the individual learner, yet they have shown themselves to be wide open to hijacking by an individual and instrumental ethic. The psychologism and individualism of humanistic discourse presented as a concern for the 'person' can lead ultimately and paradoxically to a dehumanisation through the substitution of covert for overt regulation under the guise of 'being human', enabling learners to 'open up', and provide access to their 'inner world'. This is an infiltration of power by subjectivity and a complementary infiltration of subjectivity by power.

> (1997: 98)

Such a position is not new in social theory. Indeed, critical pedagogy, and its associated technologies, is based upon a view of the self as socially constituted. Now there are very different versions of how the social becomes a constitutive part of the self: how the 'outside' gets 'inside' so to speak, and how social processes interpenetrate the psyche. Nevertheless they all have in common the notion that the self participates in its own subjugation and domination, whether it is through 'false consciousness' produced by membership of a particular social group or the internalization of social 'oppression' through individual 'repression' (in the psychoanalytic sense). But Usher *et al.*, from their postmodernist stance, regard critical pedagogy as reifying the social as a monolithic 'other' which serves to oppress and crush, and they warn that it is a mistake to adopt an oversocialized and overdetermined view of the person:

> There is a tendency in the critical tradition to end up with a conception of the self which is, on the one hand, oversocialised and overdetermined and on the other, patronising in so far as selves have to be seen as normally in a state of false consciousness. In stressing the negative and overwhelming effects of social relations and social structures, persons are made into social 'victims', dupes and puppets, manipulated by ideology and deprived of agency.
>
> (1997: 99)

The technology of the self in critical pedagogy is one based on ideology critique, whereby the aim is to analyze and uncover one's ideological positioning, to understand how this positioning operates in the interests of oppression, and through dialogue and action, free oneself of 'false consciousness'. From a postmodern point of view the problem with this is that it theorizes a self which is capable of moving from 'false' to 'true' consciousness: that is, a rational and unified self which is capable of freeing itself from its social situatedness. It is this which links critical pedagogy with the andragogical and humanistic traditions, traditions which it opposes for their individualistic approach.

Postmodern theory holds that in the social sciences, and the educational technologies they foster, the problematic of the social within the self is traditionally framed in terms of a binary opposition or dualism between the 'individual' and 'society'. It is as if the two poles 'individual' and 'society' are antithetical and separate, and pull in opposite directions. Moreover, theoretical positions which pose an ongoing dialectical interaction between 'individual' and 'society' have hitherto been unable to escape the dualism and invariably privilege one term over the other. For example, there have been a number of attempts in psychology to theorize the social component of psychological functioning, particularly in social and developmental psychology. Concepts such as 'internalization', 'interaction', 'intersubjectivity', 'accommodation', 'shaping', 'role', and 'modelling' are recognizable as part of the vernacular adopted by psychology to explain how the 'outside' gets 'inside', so to speak.

From a postmodern point of view, they all fail because they are based on an acceptance of the individual–society dualism. Theories which stress 'shaping' and 'modelling', for example, assume a totally passive individual who is moulded by external forces. Theories which employ the concepts of 'interaction', 'internalization', 'accommodation', 'role', and 'intersubjectivity' ultimately rely on the existence of a unitary, rational, pre-given individual subject.

A unique aspect of postmodernism has been its development of a way of theorizing subjectivity which is not reliant on this individual–society dualism. It does so by reconceptualizing and renaming the terms of the dualism, so that 'individual' and 'society' are replaced by the concepts of 'the subject' and 'the social', which are understood as *produced* rather than as pre-given and then interacting. Thus postmodernism problematizes at the outset the concepts of individual and society as effects which are produced rather than accepted as pre-given entities. For example, the idea of the unitary, coherent, and rational subject as agent is 'deconstructed' by postmodern analysis as being a historical product, best seen as a discourse embedded in everyday practices and as part of the productive work of, say, psychology and its associated educational technologies. Replacing this view of the individual is the idea of the subject as a position within a discourse. Moreover, because there are a number of discourses, a number of subject positions are produced, and because discourses are not necessarily coherent or devoid of contradiction, subjectivity is regarded as multiple, not purely rational, and potentially contradictory. Usher *et al.* portray the postmodern 'story' of the self as:

> that of a decentred self, subjectivity without a centre of origin, caught in meanings, positioned in the language and narratives of culture. The self cannot know itself independently of the significations in which it is enmeshed. There is no self-present subjectivity, hence no ultimate transcendental meaning of the self. Meanings are always 'in play' and the self, caught up in this play, is an ever changing self, caught up in the narratives and meanings through which it leads its life.
>
> (1997: 103)

This is the self of the postmodern condition, in which there is a decentring of the self away from the notion of a coherent 'authentic' self and towards the notion of 'multiple subjectivities', 'multiple lifeworlds', or 'multiple layers' to everyone's identity.

To summarize the postmodern critique: traditional theorizations of adult education practice invariably privilege one of the two poles of the individual–society dualism: the psychological/humanistic pole which stresses the agency of the subject and the sociological/critical theory pole which stresses how the subject is wholly determined. The dilemma for the adult educator is that neither pole offers a satisfactory perspective on practice: the former seems too naive in failing to acknowledge the power of social forces, and the latter is too pessimistic and leaves no scope for education to have a meaningful role, and there is certainly no role for the autonomous learner. Postmodernism offers a way out of this dilemma by collapsing the binary opposition on which it is built and treating the 'subject' and the 'social' as jointly produced through discursive practices. What is required, then, is a shift in the theories upon which adult education draws: from theories of the knowing subject to theories of discursive practices.

An alternative reading

The postmodernist view has been contested on a number of grounds: that it leads to nihilism and a politics of despair, that it underestimates the extent to which people's lives are shaped by economic and political forces, that it is a Eurocentric master narrative which delegitimizes black expressive culture and undermines feminist discourse, that the claim about social fragmentation is overstated, and that ultimately it is a view which is politically disabling because it directs people's attention away from collective struggle (Foley 1993: 83; McLaren 1995: 206). I don't wish to pursue these broad criticisms here, but would like to take up some issues concerning the postmodern view of the subject. The first is that the various theorizations about how such a subject comes into being do not convincingly escape the notion of an untheorized originary subject. What is this 'something' which, through a process of recognition, becomes a subject? As Hirst observes of Althusser's notion of 'interpellation' (which, as Hall (1997) points out, continues to be used in a general way for describing the 'summoning into place' of the subject):

> Recognition, the crucial moment of the constitution (activation) of the subject, presupposes a point of cognition prior to the recognition. Something must recognise that which it is to be ... The social function of ideology is to constitute concrete individuals (not-yet-subjects) as subjects. The concrete individual is 'abstract' – it is not yet the subject it will be. It is, however, *already* a subject in the sense of the subject which supports the process of recognition. Thus something which is not a subject must have the faculties necessary to support the *recognition* which will constitute it as a subject. It must have a *cognitive* capacity as a prior condition of its place in the process of recognition. Hence the necessity of the distinction of the concrete individual and the concrete subject.
>
> (1979: 65)

Hall (1997) argues that Foucault comes up against the same difficulty (especially in his 'archaeological' works *Madness and Civilization, The Birth of the Clinic, The Order of Things,* and *The Archaeology of Knowledge)* where, he claims, 'Discursive subject positions become *a priori* categories which individuals seem to occupy in an unproblematic fashion' (10). That this continues to be problematic is significant because it subjects postmodernism to its own forceful critique of the 'originary' self presupposed in the social sciences.

The second issue concerns the theorization of resistance within a postmodern view. Once again, Hall, with reference to Foucault's *Discipline and Punish* and *The History of Sexuality*, observes that:

> the entirely self-policing conception of the subject which emerges from the disciplinary, confessional and pastoral modalities of power discussed there, and the absence of any attention to what may in any way interrupt, prevent or disturb the smooth insertion of individuals into the subject positions constructed by these discourses.
>
> (1997: 11)

I will try to illustrate this second issue initially through examining Usher and Edwards's (1995) analysis of the guidance and counselling of adult learners. They argue that in the contemporary period there has been a shift from disciplinary power (the gaze from the tower) to pastoral power (the gaze from within). This is particularly apparent in the emergence of technologies of self-management in guidance and counselling (e.g. learning contracts, self-evaluation, portfolio development) which encourage people to document their lives in every detail, and to take responsibility for life planning, self-development, and self-realization. Usher and Edwards argue that constituting the self as an object of knowledge, in order to discover the 'truth' about oneself with the aid of a guide or counsellor, is a form of confessional practice which is ultimately disempowering:

> [T]his process has spread and has now become central in the governance of modern society, where externally imposed discipline has given way to the self-discipline of an autonomous subjectivity. With the spread of confession, its purpose shifts from one of salvation to self-regulation, self-improvement and self-development. In other words, confession actively constitutes a productive and autonomous subject already governed and thereby not requiring externally imposed discipline and regulation ... [W]hile confession plays an important role in displacing canonical knowledge by valorising individual experience, this simply extends the range of pastoral power embedded in the confessional regime of truth.
>
> (1995: 12–13)

I want to emphasize that, for Usher and Edwards, it is enough that counselling is directed towards finding a stable, autonomous identity to declare it disempowering: it is not a question of some counselling practices producing identities which are empowering and others disempowering. This constitutes quite a challenge to those adult education technologies which invite self-examination and self-transformation, either collectively or individually, in order to oppose and resist domination and domestication. Irrespective of whether these technologies have an essentialist or constructivist view of the self, most adhere to the modernist project of developing a self with a semblance of stability, unity, coherence, and continuity – however multiple or subject to change. Should this be abandoned in favour of celebrating the ever-changing, multiple, fragmented, and unstable self of postmodernity? Or, on the contrary, should the postmodern self be resisted as a potential form of domination? As a way of addressing these questions I would like to explore further the counselling as confessional practice theme.

Now it is clearly possible to have alternative readings of counselling and confessional practices. One can think of contemporary forms of confession where the link between disclosure and renunciation is broken, for example, where the confessional disclosure is a move to obtain a reciprocal confession from the 'other', in order to solicit mutual support. In this way the confession, far from disciplining the subject, serves to maintain the transgression.

Contrary to the postmodern view, it is possible to argue that some level of continuity and coherence to the self, however contingent, is a necessary condition for resistance to domination and oppression. Indeed it is for good reason that adult education has a tradition of empowerment based upon the modern subject, especially when it is addressing the concerns of those whose sense of self has been dislocated and fragmented through a history of domination and oppression.

In many of the sites in which adult educators work, the pursuit of a coherent, continuous self is indispensable to empowerment. Far from inducing an incredulous attitude towards any newly 'discovered' self, adult educators should properly work against incredulity and, where disbelief is the tendency, encourage the suspension of disbelief.

While it is undoubtedly true that many of the technologies in counselling and adult education serve to disempower in the name of individual liberation, the source of disempowerment is to be found in the production of particular types of coherent subjectivities and not in the pursuit of coherence itself. The postmodern subject can be seen in one sense as untouchable, and in another, as infinitely malleable with respect to these technologies. While it is true that it is difficult to recruit the postmodern subject into the process of self-government because of a refusal to be self-disciplined, this refusal is accompanied by an openness to externally imposed discipline. Notwithstanding the above, the postmodern subject *can* be enticed into self-discipline with the clever manipulation of taste and opinion. The modern self, with its sense of coherence and continuity, potentially offers resistance to both self-discipline and externally imposed discipline. In struggles which involve contestations of identity, it is those who have a strong sense of their own identity who offer the best potential for resistance.

A postmodern technology of the self?

In the above I have distinguished between the 'postmodern self' and the 'modern self', as if they are entities, for heuristic purposes only. I have no desire to argue for the existence of any kind of originary, core, true, stable, or ahistorical self. Rather I am concerned with avoiding an 'essential' view of the self, but at the same time developing a concept of the self which is compatible with transformative (and thereby resistant) adult education practice. In referring to the importance of 'continuity' and 'coherence' of the self, I am referring to a constructed closure, not one which is natural or essential, but one which nevertheless connects an individual's subject positions.

Accepting the merits of persisting with this version of a coherent and continuous 'self', how does the postmodern critique guide the reformation of technologies of the self in adult education? Certainly postmodernism retains the idea of the critical subject, and Foucault, for one, regarded a permanent critique of ourselves, and the relation of self to self, as central to the practice of liberty. Perhaps the most powerful notion here is the situated self: the self as part of the text of the world, which opens up the possibility of refusing the way one has been inscribed and exploring alternative discourses about oneself as a means of resisting domination and oppression. To return to Usher:

> We can only be the agents of our experience by engaging in a hermeneutic dialogue with the confused and often contradictory text of our experience of the world and of ourselves. The dialogue is one where formation in intersubjectivity and language, location in discourses and practical involvement in the world is a condition for the achievement of autonomy rather than a barrier to its discovery. Language, for example, does not merely constrain subjectivity but offers the possibility for constructing a critical self and social awareness through which subjectivity can be changed.
>
> (1992: 210)

Thus it is not the true or authentic self which is discovered through reflection on experience; instead, experience is viewed as a text which can be reinterpreted and reassessed. In effect we learn to read the text into which our self has been inscribed, and we discover that there are alternative readings and therefore there is an alternative self to be constructed. This doesn't mean we can ascribe any meaning to our experiences or that we can create any self we choose. We need to give a plausible reading to our experience, one which can legitimately contest, say, dominant meanings. Also the self remains situated in history and culture and continually open to reinscription and reformulation. Hall expresses the project clearly:

> [I]dentities are about questions of using the resources of history, language and culture in the process of becoming rather than being: not 'who we

are' or 'where we came from', so much as what we might become, how we have been represented and how that bears on how we might represent ourselves.

(Hall 1997: 4)

This is the approach taken by Michael White, a key figure in the narrative therapy movement. I will briefly describe his therapeutic technique to give the reader a sense of the kind of transformative educational intervention implied by a situated perspective on the 'self'.

Michael White is a family therapist who consciously draws on Foucault (and others) as a means of shaping his therapeutic technique. Remembering that he is a therapist who directs his energies towards the problems of clients, his basic technique is to externalize these problems. The problem is treated as an external entity, separate from the person or relationship ascribed to the problem. For example, if a person has a compulsion to wash their hands every three minutes, it is usual for family members to define this problem as internal to the person, together with a 'problem saturated' description of the family's inability to solve it. One technique is to talk of the problem as though it were a separate entity, for example, giving it a name such as 'Squeaky Clean'. This is followed by the plotting of experiences or events into stories or 'self-narratives' around the problem. Firstly, he invites persons, through careful questioning, to review the effects of the problem in their lives and relationships – this leads to a mapping of the influence of the problem. Once the problem's sphere of influence has been mapped, questions are introduced to map the persons' influence in the life of the problem. This leads to the identification of new information which shows the agency of persons in resisting the problem, acts of defiance or refusal of the problem that have been written out of the dominant story. New stories are then built around these experiences:

> I introduced questions that encouraged them to perform meaning in relation to these examples, so that they might 're-author' their lives and relationships. How had they managed to be effective against the problem in this way? How did this reflect on them as people and on their relationships? What personal and relationship attributes were they relying on in making these achievements ? Did success give them any ideas about further steps that they might take to reclaim their lives from the problem?
>
> (White 1989: 11)

White regards the process of externalizing as a counter-practice to cultural practices which objectify persons and their bodies. It enables people to separate from the dominant stories that have been shaping their lives and relationships, and it opens spaces for people to re-author themselves. He avoids individualizing the problem, while retaining the notion of responsibility through improving the capacity for personal agency in the pursuit of new possibilities.

A great deal of attention is paid to defining the problem to be externalized. For example, it would be inappropriate to externalize problems like violence and sexual abuse: in such cases the therapist:

> would be more inclined to encourage the externalisation of the attitudes and beliefs that appear to compel the violence, and those strategies that maintain persons in their subjugation: for example, the enforcement of secrecy and isolation.
>
> (White 1989: 12)

In such cases the technique would still involve the twin steps of asking the persons involved to tell their story, say, about men's aggression in general and the circumstances leading to particular instances of violence; and then to introduce a new account or reading of the problem, say, patriarchal ideology and how it is supported through various cultural 'instructions', with the invitation to challenge such instructions. In other instances, the 'problem' is already external, such as when people who are trying to re-author their lives find it difficult to do so because of the circulation of dominant and disqualifying stories that others have about them and their relationships. In such instances White suggests exploring ways of ensuring that one's preferred stories are circulated.

The approach of narrative therapy has much in common with existing practices in adult education, especially those associated with reflection on experience. Such technologies certainly offer scope for the opening up of alternative discourse about oneself, but they can be equally oppressive, depending on how they are practised. A 'test' of whether such practices are liberatory is the extent to which they expose the social and cultural embeddedness and taken-for-granted assumptions in which the self is located; explore the interests served by the continuation of the self thus positioned; incite a refusal to be positioned in this way when the interests served are those of domination and oppression; and encourage alternative readings of the text of experience. Of course, as McLaren (1995) points out, the reinvention of the self must be linked to the remaking of the social, which implies a shared vision (however contingent or provisional) of democratic community and an engagement with language of social change, emancipatory practice, and transformative politics. In this way, learners:

> are able to call into question the political assumptions and relations of determination upon which social truths are founded in both the communities in which they work and the larger society of which they are a part.
>
> (McLaren 1995: 227)

Taking into account the postmodern critique, Jarvis (1997), for one, goes a long way towards identifying the ethical basis of such a shared vision (i.e. concern for the Other as the only universal moral good). I don't wish to pursue this here, except to signal that any project aimed at reconstructing the self needs to address the broader issue of the 'just society'.

To conclude, the postmodern critique is valuable in drawing attention to the way in which selves can participate in their own subjugation and how existing adult education technologies, in the name of promoting autonomy and freedom, can be accomplices in the process of subjugation. As such it is important to 'deconstruct' such technologies and the selves produced by them. But what of the reconstruction of selves? In this regard, the postmodern focus on the self as text offers new possibilities for 'self-work', but these possibilities can only be realized if this text has some degree of closure and continuity, and if this (rather than fragmentation and discontinuity) is seen as a cause for celebration.

References

Boud, D. (1989) Some competing traditions in experiential learning. In S. Weil and I. McGill (eds) *Making Sense of Experiential Learning: Diversity in Theory and Practice* (Milton Keynes, UK: Open University Press).

Foley, G. (1993) Postmodernism, adult education and the 'emancipatory' project. *Convergence*, 26 (4), 79–88.

Foucault, M. (1988) Technologies of the self. In L. Martin, H. Gutman and P. Hutton (eds), *Technologies of the Self: A Seminar with Michel Foucault* (Amherst: University of Massachusetts Press), 16–49.

Hall, S. (1997) Who needs identity? In S. Hall and P. du Gay (eds), *Questions of Cultural Identity* (London: Sage), 1–17.

Hirst, P. (1979) *On Law and Ideology* (London: Macmillan).

Jarvis, P. (1997) *Ethics and Education for Adults in a Late Modern Society* (Leicester, UK: National Institute for Adult and Continuing Education).

Martin, L., Gutman. H. and Hutton, P. (eds) (1988) *Technologies of the Self: A Seminar with Michel Foucault* (Amherst: University of Massachusetts Press).

McLaren, P. (1995) *Critical Pedagogy and Predatory Culture: Oppositional Politics in a Postmodern Era* (London: Routledge).

Usher, R. (1992) Experience in adult education: A post-modern critique. *Journal of Philosophy of Education*, 26, 201–214.

Usher, R. and Edwards, R. (1995) Confessing all? A 'postmodern guide' to the guidance and counselling of adult learners. *Studies in the Education of Adults*, 27 (1), 9–23.

Usher, R. Bryant, I. and Johnston, R. (1997) *Adult Education and the Postmodern Challenge* (London: Routledge).

White, M. (1989) *Selected Papers* (Adelaide, Australia: Dulwich Centre Publications).

Chapter 11

Culture, mind, and education

Jerome Bruner

Jerome Bruner rightly occupies a position as "the grand old man" of American learning and cognitive research and theory. For more than half a century he has been active as a researcher, developer, and debater of learning and education. In the late 1940s, he made detailed studies on perception and thinking. During the 1950s, his studies of cognition were an important basis for what was later termed "cognitive science." After the so-called "Sputnik-shock" in 1957, when Russia sent up the first satellite, Bruner was appointed chairman of the scientific commission which was set up to fundamentally reconstruct the American school system, and his books The Process of Education, Toward a Theory of Instruction *and* The Relevance of Education *laid the groundwork for the concept of science-centered curriculum. Later he scrutinized the concepts of "mind" and "meaning," and as late as 1996, at the age of 82, he published* The Culture of Education, *which summarizes the broad understanding of learning and education as cultural processes he gradually developed. This chapter is made up of the two first programmatic sections of that book, which probably will stand as the most durable work of his vast production.*

Computationalism and culturalism

The essays in [*The Culture of Education*] are all products of the 1990s, expressions of the fundamental changes that have been altering conceptions about the nature of the human mind in the decades since the cognitive revolution. These changes, it now seems clear in retrospect, grew out of two strikingly divergent conceptions about how mind works. The first of these was the hypothesis that mind could be conceived as a computational device. This was not a new idea, but it had been powerfully reconceived in the newly advanced computational sciences. The other was the proposal that mind is both constituted by and realized in the use of human culture. The two views led to very different conceptions of the nature of mind itself and of how mind should be cultivated. Each led its adherents to follow distinctively different strategies of inquiry about how mind functions and about how it might be improved through "education."

The first or *computational* view is concerned with *information processing*: how finite, coded, unambiguous information about the world is inscribed, sorted, stored, collated, retrieved, and generally managed by a computational device. It takes information as its given, as something already settled in relation to some preexisting, rule-bound code that maps onto states of the world. This so-called "well-formedness" is both its strength and its shortcoming, as we shall see. For the process of knowing is often messier and more fraught with ambiguity than such a view allows.

Computational science makes interesting general claims about the conduct of education (Segal *et al.* 1985, Bruer 1993, Chi *et al.* 1988), though it is still unclear what specific lessons it has to teach the educator. There is a widespread and not unreasonable belief that we *should* be able to discover something about how to teach human beings more effectively from knowing how to program computers effectively. One can scarcely doubt, for example, that computers provide a learner with powerful aids in mastering bodies of knowledge, particularly if the knowledge in question is well defined. A well-programed computer is especially useful for taking over tasks that, at last, can be declared "unfit for human production." For computers are faster, more orderly, less fitful in remembering, and do not get bored. And of course, it is revealing of our own minds and our human situation to ask what things we do better or worse than our servant computer.

It is considerably more uncertain whether, in any deep sense, the tasks of a teacher can be "handed over" to a computer, even the most "responsive" one that can be theoretically envisioned. Which is not to say that a suitably programmed computer cannot lighten a teacher's load by taking over some of the routines that clutter the process of instruction. But that is not the issue. After all, books came to serve such a function after Gutenberg's discovery made them widely available (Ong 1991, Olson 1994).

The issue, rather, is whether the computational view of mind itself offers an adequate enough view about how mind works to guide our efforts in trying to "educate" it. It is a subtle question. For in certain respects, "how the mind works" is itself dependent on the tools at its disposal. "How the *hand* works," for example, cannot be fully appreciated unless one also takes into account whether it is equipped with a screwdriver, a pair of scissors, or a laser-beam gun. And by the same token, the systematic historian's "mind" works differently from the mind of the classic "teller of tales" with his stock of combinable myth-like modules. So, in a sense, the mere existence of computational devices (and a theory of computation about their mode of operating) can (and doubtless will) change our minds about how "mind" works, just as the book did (Olson 1994).

This brings us directly to the second approach to the nature of mind – call it *culturalism*. It takes its inspiration from the evolutionary fact that mind could not exist save for culture. For the evolution of the hominid mind is linked to the development of a way of life where "reality" is represented by a symbolism shared by members of a cultural community in which a technical-social way of life is both organized and construed in terms of that symbolism. This symbolic mode is not only shared by a community, but conserved, elaborated, and passed on to succeeding generations who, by virtue of this transmission, continue to maintain the culture's identity and way of life.

Culture in this sense is *superorganic* (Kroeber 1917). But it shapes the minds of individuals as well. Its individual expression inheres in *meaning making*, assigning meanings to things in different settings on particular occasions. Meaning making involves situating encounters with the world in their appropriate cultural contexts in order to know "what they are about." Although meanings are "in the mind," they have their origins and their significance in the culture in which they are created. It is this cultural situatedness of meanings that assures their negotiability and, ultimately, their communicability. Whether "private meanings" exist is not the point; what is important is that meanings provide a basis for cultural exchange. On this view, knowing and communicating are in their nature highly interdependent, indeed virtually inseparable: however much the individual may seem to operate on his or her own in carrying out the quest for meanings, nobody can do it unaided by the culture's symbolic systems. It is culture that provides the tools for organizing and understanding our worlds in communicable ways. The distinctive feature of human evolution is that mind evolved in a fashion that enables human beings to utilize the tools of culture. Without those tools, whether symbolic or material, man is not a "naked ape" but an empty abstraction.

Culture, then, though itself man-made, both forms and makes possible the workings of a distinctively human mind. On this view, learning and thinking are always *situated* in a cultural setting and always dependent upon the utilization of cultural resources (see e.g. Bruner 1990). Even individual variation in the nature and use of mind can be attributed to the varied opportunities that different cultural settings provide, though these are not the only source of variation in mental functioning.

Like its computational cousin, culturalism seeks to bring together insights from psychology, anthropology, linguistics, and the human sciences generally, in order to reformulate a model of mind. But the two do so for radically different purposes. Computationalism, to its great credit, is interested in any and all ways in which information is organized and used – information in the well-formed and finite sense mentioned earlier, regardless of the guise in which information processing is realized. In this broad sense, it recognizes no disciplinary boundaries, not even the boundary between human and non-human functioning. Culturalism, on the other hand, concentrates exclusively on how human beings in cultural communities create and transform meanings.

I want to set forth in this chapter some principal motifs of the cultural approach and explore how these relate to education. But before turning to that formidable task, I need first to dispel the shibboleth of a necessary contradiction between culturalism and computationalism. For I think the apparent contradiction is based on a misunderstanding, one that leads to gross and needless overdramatization. Obviously the approaches are very different, and their ideological overspill may indeed overwhelm us if we do not take care to distinguish them clearly. For it surely matters ideologically what kind of "model" of the human mind one embraces (Brinton 1965). Indeed, the model of mind to which one adheres even shapes the "folk pedagogy" of schoolroom practice. Mind as equated to the power of association and habit formation privileges "drill" as the true pedagogy, while mind taken as the capacity for reflection and discourse on the nature of necessary truths favors the Socratic dialogue. And each of these is linked to our conception of the ideal society and the ideal citizen.

Yet in fact, neither computationalism nor culturalism is so linked to particular models of mind as to be shackled in particular pedagogies. Their difference is of quite a different kind. Let me try to sketch it.

The objective of computationalism is to devise a formal redescription of *any* and *all* functioning systems that manage the flow of well-formed information. It seeks to do so in a way that produces foreseeable, systematic outcomes. One such system is the human mind. But thoughtful computationalism does *not* propose that mind is like some particular "computer" that needs to be "programmed" in a particular way in order to operate systematically or "efficiently." What it argues, rather, is that any and all systems that process information must be governed by specifiable "rules" or procedures that govern what to do with inputs. It matters not whether it is a nervous system, or the genetic apparatus that takes instruction from DNA and then reproduces later generations, or whatever. This is the ideal of artificial intelligence (AI), so-called. "Real minds" are describable in terms of the same AI generalization – systems governed by specifiable rules for managing the flow of coded information.

But, as already noted, the rules common to all information systems do not cover the messy, ambiguous, and context-sensitive processes of meaning making, a form of activity in which the construction of highly "fuzzy" and metaphoric category systems is just as notable as the use of specifiable categories for sorting inputs in a way to yield comprehensible outputs. Some computationalists, convinced a priori that even meaning making can be reduced to AI specifications, are perpetually at work trying to prove that the messiness of meaning making is not beyond their reach (McClelland 1990, Schank 1990). The complex "universal models" they propose are sometimes half-jokingly referred to by them as "TOEs," an acronym for "theories of everything" (Mitchell 1995). But though they have not even come near to succeeding and, as many believe, will probably never in principle succeed, their efforts nonetheless are interesting for the light they shed on the divide between meaning making and information processing.

The difficulty these computationalists encounter inheres in the kinds of "rules" or operations that are possible in computation. All of them, as we know, must be specifiable in advance, must be free of ambiguity, and so on. They must, in their ensemble, also be computationally consistent, which means that while operations may alter with feedback from prior results, the alterations must also adhere to a consistent, prearranged systematicity. Computational rules may be contingent, but they cannot encompass unforeseeable contingencies. Thus Hamlet cannot (in AI) tease Polonius with ambiguous banter about "yonder cloud shaped like a camel, nay 'tis backed like a weasel," in the hope that his banter might evoke guilt and some telltale knowledge about the death of Hamlet's father.

It is precisely this clarity, this prefixedness of categories, that imposes the most severe limit on computationalism as a medium in which to frame a model of mind. But once this limitation is recognized, the alleged death struggle between culturalism and computationalism evaporates. For the meaning making of the culturalist, unlike the information processing of the computationalist, is in principle interpretive, fraught with ambiguity, sensitive to the occasion, and often after the fact. Its "ill-formed procedures" are like "maxims" rather than like fully specifiable rules (Sperber and Wilson 1986, Grice 1989). But they are hardly unprincipled. Rather, they are the stuff of *hermeneutics*, an intellectual pursuit no less disciplined for its failure to produce the click-clear outputs of a computational exercise. Its model case is text interpretation. In interpreting a text, the meaning of a part depends upon a hypothesis about the meanings of the whole, whose meaning in turn is based upon one's judgment of meanings of the parts that compose it. But a wide swath of the human cultural enterprise depends upon it. Nor is it clear that the infamous "hermeneutic circle" deserves the knocks it gets from those in search of clarity and certainty. After all, it lies at the heart of meaning making.

Hermeneutic meaning making and well-formed information processing are incommensurate. Their incommensurability can be made evident even in a simple example. Any input to a computational system must, of course, be encoded in a specifiable way that leaves no room for ambiguity. What happens, then, if (as in human meaning making) an input needs to be encoded according to the context in which it is encountered? Let me give a homely example involving language, since so much of meaning making involves language. Say the input into the system is the word *cloud*. Shall it be taken in its "meteorological" sense, its "mental condition" sense, or in some other way? Now, it is easy (indeed necessary) to provide a computational device with a "look-up" lexicon that provides alternative senses of *cloud*. Any dictionary can do it. But to determine *which* sense is appropriate for a particular context, the computational device would also need a way of encoding and interpreting all contexts in which the word *cloud* might appear. That would then require the computer to have a look-up list for all possible contexts, a "contexticon." But while there are a finite number of words, there are an infinite number of contexts in which particular words might appear. Encoding the context of Hamlet's little riddle about "yonder cloud" would almost certainly escape the powers of the best "contexticon" one could imagine!

There is no decision procedure known that could resolve the question whether the incommensurability between culturalism's meaning making and computationalism's information processing could ever be overcome. Yet, for all that, the two have a kinship that is difficult to ignore. For once meanings are established, it is their formalization into a well-formed category system that *can* be managed by computational rules. Obviously one loses the subtlety of context dependency and metaphor in doing so: *clouds* would have to pass tests of truth functionality to get into the play. But then again, "formalization" in science consists of just such maneuvers: treating an array of formalized and operationalized meanings as if they were fit for computation. Eventually we come to believe that scientific terms actually were born and grew that way: decontextualized, disambiguated, totally "look-uppable."

There is equally puzzling commerce in the other direction. For we are often forced to interpret the output of a computation in order to "make some sense" of it – that is, to figure out what it "means." This "search for the meaning" of final outputs has always been customary in statistical procedures such as factor analysis where the association between different "variables," discovered by statistical manipulation, needed to be interpreted hermeneutically in order to "make sense." The same problem is encountered when investigators use the computational option of parallel processing to discover the association between a set of coded inputs. The final output of such parallel processing similarly needs interpretation to be rendered meaningful. So there is plainly some complementary relationship between what the computationalist is trying to explain and what the culturalist is trying to interpret, a relationship that has long puzzled students of epistemology (von Wright 1971, Bruner 1985).

In an undertaking as inherently reflexive and complicated as characterizing "how our minds work" or how they might be made to work better, there is surely room for two perspectives on the nature of knowing (von Wright 1971). Nor is there any demonstrable reason to suppose that without a single and legitimately "true" way of knowing the world, we could only slide helplessly down the slippery slope that leads to relativism. It is surely as "true" to say that Euclid's theorems are computable as to say, with the poet, that "Euclid alone has looked on beauty bare."

A theory of mind

To begin with, if a theory of mind is to be interesting educationally, it should contain some specifications for (or at least implications bearing on) how its functioning can be improved or altered in some significant way. All-or-none and once-for-all theories of mind are not educationally interesting. More specifically, educationally interesting theories of mind contain specifications of some kind about the "resources" required for a mind to operate effectively. These include not only instrumental resources (like mental "tools"), but also settings or conditions required for effective operations – anything from feedback within certain time limits to, say, freedom from stress or from excessive uniformity. Without specification of resources and settings required, a theory of mind is all "inside-out" and of limited applicability to education. It becomes interesting only when it becomes more "outside-in," indicating the kind of world needed to make it possible to use mind (or heart!) effectively – what kinds of symbol systems, what kinds of accounts of the past, what arts and sciences, and so on. The approach of computationalism to education tends to be inside-out – though it smuggles the world into the mind by inscribing bits of it in memory, as with our earlier dictionary example, and then relies on "look-up" routines. Culturalism is much more outside-in, and although it may contain specifications about mental operations *eo ipso*, as it were, they are not as binding as, say, the formal requirement of computability. For the approach of the computationalist to education is indeed bound by the constraint of computability – that is, whatever aids are offered to mind must be operable by a computational device.

When one actually examines how computationalism has approached educational issues, there seem to be three different styles. The first of these consists in "restating" classical theories of teaching or learning in a computable form. But while some clarity is gained in so doing (for example, in locating ambiguities), not much is gained by way of power. Old wine does not improve much for being poured into differently shaped bottles, even if the glass is clearer. The classic reply, of course, is that a computable reformulation yields "surplus insight." Yet "association theory," for example, has gone through successive translations from Aristotle to Locke to Pavlov to Clark Hull without much surplus yield. So one is justifiably impatient with new claims for veiled versions of the same as with many so-called parallel distributed processing (PDP) "learning models" (Rumelhart and McClelland 1986).

But in fact, computationalism can and does do better than that. Its second approach begins with a rich description or protocol of what actually transpires when somebody sets out to solve a particular problem or master a particular body of knowledge. It then seeks to redescribe what has been observed in strict computational terms. In what order, for example, does a subject ask for information, what confuses him, what kinds of hypotheses does he entertain? This approach then asks what might be going on computationally in devices that operate that way, for instance, like the subject's "mind." From this it seeks to reformulate a plan about how a learner of this kind might be helped – again within the limits of computability. John Bruer's interesting book *Schools for Thought* (1993) is a nice example of what can be gained from this fresh approach.

But there is an even more interesting third route that computationalists sometimes follow. The work of Annette Karmiloff-Smith (1979, 1992) provides an example if taken in conjunction with some abstract computational ideas. All complex "adaptive" computational programs involve redescribing the output of prior operations in order both to reduce their complexity and to improve their "fit" to an adaptation criterion. That is what "adaptive" means: reducing prior complexities to achieve greater "fitness" to a criterion (Mitchell 1995, Crutchfield and Mitchell 1994). An example will help. Karmiloff-Smith notes that when we go about solving particular problems, say language acquisition, we characteristically "turn around" on the results of a procedure that has worked locally and try to redescribe it in more general, simplified terms. We say, for example, "I've put an *s* at the end of that noun to pluralize it; how about doing the same for *all* nouns?" When the new rule fails to pluralize *woman*, the learner may generate some additional ones. Eventually, he ends up with a more or less adequate rule for pluralizing, with only a few odd "exceptions" left over to be handled by rote. Note that in each step of this process that Karmiloff-Smith calls "redescription," the learner "goes meta," considering how he is thinking as well as what he is thinking about. This is the hallmark of "metacognition," a topic of passionate interest among psychologists – but also among computational scientists.

That is to say, the rule of redescription is a feature of *all* complex "adaptive" computation, but in the present instance, it is also a genuinely interesting *psychological* phenomenon. This is the rare music of an overlap between different fields of inquiry – if the overlap turns out to be fertile. So, REDESCRIBE, a TOE-like rule for adaptive computational systems that also happens to be a good rule in human problem solving, may turn out to be a "new frontier." And the new frontier may turn out to be next-door to educational practice.

So the computationalist's approach to education seems to take three forms as noted. The first reformulates old theories of learning (or teaching, or whatever) in computable form in the hope that the reformulation will yield surplus power. The second analyzes rich protocols and applies the apparatus of computational theory to them to better discern what might be going on computationally. Then it tries to figure out how the process can be helped. This, in effect, is what Newell, Shaw, and Simon did in their work on the General Problem Solver, and what is currently being done in studies of how "novices" become "experts" (Chipman and Meyrowitz 1993). Finally there is the happy fortuity where a central computational idea, like "redescription," seems to map directly onto a central idea in cognitive theory, like "metacognition."

The culturalist approaches education in a very different way. Culturalism takes as its first premise that education is not an island, but part of the continent of culture. It asks first what function "education" serves in the culture and what role it plays in the lives of those who operate within it. Its next question might be why education is situated in the culture as it is and how this placement reflects the distribution of power, status, and other benefits. Inevitably, and virtually from the start, culturalism also asks about the enabling resources made available to people to cope and what portion of those resources is made available through "education," institutionally conceived. And it will constantly be concerned with constraints imposed on the process of education – external ones like the organization of schools and classrooms or the recruitment of teachers and internal ones like the natural or imposed distribution of native endowment, for native endowment may be as much affected by the accessibility of symbolic systems as by the distribution of genes.

Culturalism's task is a double one. On the "macro" side, it looks at the culture as a system of values, rights, exchanges, obligations, opportunities, and power. On the "micro" side, it examines how the demands of a cultural system affect those who must operate within it. In that latter spirit, it concentrates on how individual human beings construct "realities" and meanings that adapt them to the system, at what personal cost, with what expected outcomes. While culturalism implies no particular view concerning inherent psycho-biological constraints that affect human functioning, particularly meaning making, it usually takes such constraints for granted and considers how they are managed by the culture and its instituted educational system.

Although culturalism is far from computationalism and its constraints, it has no difficulty incorporating its insights – with one exception. It obviously cannot rule out processes relating to human meaning making, however much they do not meet the test of computability. As a corollary, it cannot and does not rule out subjectivity and its role in culture. Indeed, as we shall see, it is much concerned with mtersubjectivity – how humans come to know "each other's minds." In both these senses, culturalism is to be counted among the "sciences of the subjective." And, in consequence, I shall often refer to it as the "cultural psychological" approach, or simply as "cultural psychology." For all that it embraces the subjective in its purview and refers often to the "construction of reality," cultural psychology surely does not rule out "reality" in any ontological sense. It argues (on epistemological grounds) that "external" or "objective" reality can only be known by the properties of mind and the symbol systems on which mind relies (Goodman 1978).

A final point relates to the place of emotion and feeling. It is often said that all "cognitive psychology," even its cultural version, neglects or even ignores the place of these in the life of mind. But it is neither necessary that this be so nor, at least in my view, is it so. Why should an interest in cognition preclude feeling and emotion (see e.g. Oatley 1992)? Surely emotions and feelings are represented in the processes of meaning making and in our constructions of reality. Whether one adopts the Zajonc view that emotion is a direct and unmediated response to the world with subsequent cognitive consequences or the Lazarus view that emotion requires prior cognitive inference, it is still "there," still to be reckoned with (Zajonc 1980, 1984, Lazarus 1981, 1982, 1984). And as we shall see, particularly in dealing with the role of schools in "self construction," it is very much a part of education.

References

Brinton, C. (1965): *The Anatomy of Revolution*. New York: Vintage Books.

Bruer, J.T. (1993): *Schools for Thought: A Science of Learning in the Classroom*. Cambridge, MA: MIT Press.

Bruner, J. (1985): "Narrative and Pragmatic Modes of Thought." In E. Eisner (ed.): *Learning and Teaching the Ways of Knowing: Eighty-Fourth Yearbook of the National Society for the Study of Education*. Chicago: Chicago University Press, pp. 97–115.

Bruner, J. (1990): *Acts of Meaning*. Cambridge, MA: Harvard University Press.

Chi, M.T.H. – Glaser, R. – Farr, M.J. (eds.) (1988): *The Nature of Expertise*. Hillsdale, NJ: Lawrence Erlbaum.

Chipman, S. – Meyrowitz, A.L. (1993): *Foundations of Knowledge Acquisition: Cognitive Models of Complex Learning*, vols. 1 and 2. Boston: Kluwer Academic Publishers.

Crutchfield, J.P. – Mitchell, M. (1994): *The Evolution of Emergent Computation*. Santa Fe Institute Technical Report 94–03–012, Santa Fe, NM: Santa Fe Institute.

Goodman, N. (1978): *Ways of Worldmaking*. Indianapolis, IN: Hackett.

Grice, H.P. (1989): *Studies in the Way of Words*. Cambridge, MA: Harvard University Press.

Karmiloff-Smith, A. (1979): *A Functional Approach to Child Language: A Study of Determiners and Reference*. Cambridge, UK: Cambridge University Press.

Karmiloff-Smith, A. (1992): *Beyond Modularity: A Developmental Perspective on Cognitive Science*. Cambridge, MA: MIT Press.

Kroeber, A.L. (1917): "The Superorganic." *American Anthropologist*, 19 (2), pp. 163–213.

Lazarus, R.S. (1981): "A Cognitivist's Reply to Zajonc on Emotion and Cognition." *American Psychologist*, 36, pp. 222–223.

Lazarus, R.S. (1982): "Thoughts on the Relations between Emotion and Cognition." *American Psychologist*, 37 (9), pp. 1019–1024.

Lazarus, R.S. (1984): "On the Primacy of Cognition." *American Psychologist*, 39 (2), pp. 124–129.

McClelland, J.L. (1990): "The Programmable Blackboard Model of Reading." In D.E. Rumelhart and J.L. McClelland: *Parallel Distributed Processing: Psychological and Biological Models*, vol. 2. Cambridge, MA: MIT Press, pp. 122–169.

Mitchell, M. (1995): "What Can Complex System Approaches Offer the Cognitive Sciences?" Paper presented at the Annual Meeting of the Society for Philosophy and Psychology, State University of New York at Stony Brook, June 10.

Oatley, K. (1992): *Best Laid Schemes: The Psychology of Emotions*. Cambridge, UK: Cambridge University Press.

Olson, D.R. (1994): *The World on Paper: The Conceptual and Cognitive Implications of Writing and Reading*. Cambridge, UK: Cambridge University Press.

Ong, W.J. (1991): *Orality and Literacy: The Technologizing of the Word*. London: Routledge.

Rumelhart, D.E. – McClelland, J.L. (eds.) (1986): *Parallel Distributed Processing: Explanations in the Microstructure of Cognition*, vols. 1 and 2. Cambridge, MA: MIT Press.

Schank, R.C. (1990): *Tell Me a Story: A New Look at Real and Artificial Memory*. New York: Scribner.

Segal, J.W. – Chipman, S.F. – Glaser, R. (1985): *Thinking and Learning Skills: Volume 2, Relating Instruction to Research*. Hillsdale, NJ: Lawrence Erlbaum.

Sperber, D. – Wilson, D. (1986): *Relevance: Communication and Cognition*. Cambridge, MA: Harvard University Press.

Von Wright, G.H. (1971): *Explanation and Understanding*. Ithaca, NY: Cornell University Press.

Zajonc, R.B. (1980): "Feeling and Thinking: Preferences Need No Inferences." *American Psychologist*, 35 (2), pp. 151–175.

Zajonc, R.B. (1984): "On the Primacy of Affect." *American Psychologist*, 39 (2), pp. 117–123.

Chapter 12

Experience, pedagogy, and social practices

Robin Usher

In international learning and educational theory, British-Australian philosopher and educator Robin Usher has a clear position as the first spokesman of the postmodern approach, strongly inspired by Michel Foucault and other French postmodernists. Since the late 1990s, Usher has been the Research Director of the Royal Melbourne Institute of Technology. Before that he was a Reader at the University of Southampton, and in 1997, together with his colleagues Ian Bryant and Rennie Johnston, he published what may be regarded as his most significant book, entitled Adult Education and the Postmodern Challenge: Learning Beyond the Limits. *The following chapter, of which Usher is the main author, is an abridged version of the last part of chapter 5 of that book, describing what Usher and his co-authors understand as the four postmodern modes of learning and practice as seen in relation to adult education.*

Experience, pedagogy, and social practices

In adult education discourse, experience has mainly signified freedom from regulation in the service of personal autonomy and/or social empowerment. Autonomy, empowerment, self-expression and self-realisation are key signifiers. Other hitherto more submerged signifiers such as 'application' and 'adaptation' now also have a key significance. The meaning of experience will vary according to different discursive practices, as too will the particular significance given to learning derived from experience. Although experiential learning has become central to the theory and practice of education in the postmodern moment, as a pedagogy it is inherently ambivalent and capable of many significations. There is a need to stop seeing experiential learning in purely logocentric terms, as a natural characteristic of the individual learner or as a pedagogical technique, and more in terms of the contexts – socio-cultural and institutional – in which it functions and from which it derives its significations. In itself, therefore, it has no unequivocal or 'given' meaning – it is inherently neither emancipatory nor oppressive, neither domesticating nor transformative. Rather, its meaning is constantly shifting between and across these polarities. It is perhaps most usefully seen as having a potential for emancipation and oppression, domestication and transformation, where at any one time and according to

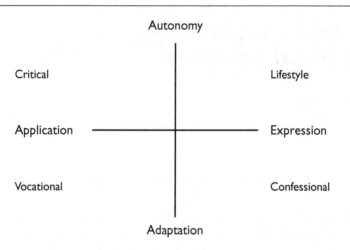

Figure 12.1 A 'map' of experiential learning in the social practices of postmodernity.

context both tendencies can be present and in conflict with one another. Accordingly, it offers a contestable and ambiguous terrain where different socio-economic and cultural assumptions and strategies can be differentially articulated. As a field of tension, it can be exploited by different groups, each emphasising certain dimensions over others.

Experiential learning can, for example, be deployed as a pedagogical strategy both in a disciplines-based curriculum and within a competences-based curriculum. Equally, it can be deployed as part of a continued questioning of and resistance to the forms of power that situate us as subjects. But at the same time, even here, experiential teaming can function as both a more effective means of disciplining the 'whole' subject rather than simply the reasoning part and as a strategy to subvert the dominance of an oppressive universalistic reason by giving 'voice' to difference. What this implies, then, is that experience is always a site of struggle, a terrain where the meaning and significance of the experience to be cultivated in learning contexts is fought over. Central to this struggle is the reconfiguration of emancipation and oppression in the postmodern moment.

The schema or 'map' of experiential learning shown in Figure 12.1 attempts to depict the various possibilities. It is structured around two continua: Autonomy–Adaptation and Expression–Application. The resulting four quadrants represent four discursive/material practices, here referred to as Lifestyle, Confessional, Vocational and Critical. In effect, what is being depicted here is that application/expression/autonomy/adaptation are the continua around which the pedagogy of experiential learning is differentially structured within different discursive/material practices. What these signify will differ relatively to the different discursive practices and the pedagogic and epistemological relationships within each practice. The schema enables an exploration of the contexts and meanings of experience, and hence the location of learning from experience, both between and within the quadrants.

Lifestyle practices

Today lifestyle practices have significant implications for a reconfiguring of the theory and practice of adult education. In the postmodern, the educational is recast as the cultivation of desire through experience, both conditional upon and responsive to contemporary socio-economic and cultural fragmentation. Learning does not simplistically derive from experience; rather, experience and learning are mutually positioned in an interactive dynamic. Learning becomes the experience gained through consumption and novelty, which then produces new experience. Consequently, the boundaries defining 'acceptable' learning break down – in lifestyle practices learning can be found anywhere in a multiplicity of sites of learning. The predominant concern is with an ever-changing identity through the consumption of experience and of a learning stance towards life as a means of expressing identity. Pedagogically, experiential learning, sitting comfortably within the postmodern, gains an increasingly privileged place as the means by which desire is cultivated and identity formed.

Lifestyle practices centre on the achievement of autonomy through individuality and self-expression, particularly in taste and sense of style. Within a general stylisation of life, the mark of autonomy is a stylistic self-consciousness inscribed in the body, in clothes, in ways of speaking, in leisure pursuits, in holidays and the like. A lifestyle is adopted and cultivated but in a reflexive and self-referential way – lifestyle is never practised 'blindly' and un-self-consciously.

Lifestyle practices are firmly located within the play of difference that is characteristic of consumer culture. Unlike the mass consumption of modernity, consumption in the postmodern is based on choice as difference and difference as choice. In the postmodern, a lifestyle revolves around difference, the acquisition of the distinctive and the different within a signifying culture (Featherstone 1991) that summons up dreams, desires and fantasies in developing a life-project of self and where there is a continual construction (and reconstruction) of identity and a trying-on of relationships.

Empowerment through autonomy and self-actualisation (self-expression) becomes important but assumes a range of very different meanings, from the crumbling of hierarchy in new post-Fordist management to social and cultural empowerment in new social movements, e.g. the women's movement and movements for ethnic and sexual awareness. One effect of this is that intellectuals, and indeed educators, are forced to assume the role of commentators and interpreters rather than legislators and 'enlightened' pedagogues. Educational practitioners, rather than being the source/producers of knowledge/taste, become facilitators helping to interpret everybody's knowledge and helping to open up possibilities for further experience. They become part of the 'culture' industry, vendors in the educational hypermarket. In a reversal of modernist education, the consumer (the learner) rather than the producer (educator) is articulated as having greater significance and power.

On the other hand, consumerism knows no boundaries nor does it respect existing markers. Image, style and design take over from modernist meta-narratives in conferring meaning. The 'culture' industry, advertising and the media both 'educate' the consumer and, through the bombardment of images with which people must experientially identify and interpret, make consumption necessary and compulsive.

It is the promotion of lifestyle practices – the obligation to shape a life through choices in a world of self-referenced objects and images – that influences the self in postmodernity. Autonomy becomes a matter of expressing identity through the consumption of signifying choices. The project of self, rather than being unidirectional and governed by instrumental rationality, becomes one of the possession of desired goods and the pursuit of a lifestyle governed by the incitement of desire. Pleasure, once the enemy, is now considered indispensable. Rather than life being seen as a search for coherent and lasting meaning, it is construed as the pleasure of experiencing – from the immersion in images, from the flow of images in consumption and leisure and their combination in postmodern pursuits such as shopping. Here, experiences are valued as experiences – for example, one does not shop for the sake of satisfying 'real' needs (since needs are defined by the demands of lifestyle practices, there are no 'real' or 'underlying' needs), let alone for the utility of the goods purchased. When consumption is a matter of consuming signs, it is the experience itself that counts, i.e. that signifies and defines.

Selves become constructed through 'media-ted' experience. Consumption requires each individual to choose from a variety of products in response to a repertoire of wants that may be shaped and legitimised by advertising but must be experienced and justified as personal desires. However constrained by external or internal factors, economic or psychological, the postmodern self is required to construct a life through the exercise of choice amongst alternatives. Every aspect of life, like every commodity, is imbued with a self-referential meaning; every choice we make is an emblem of our identity, a mark of our individuality; each is a message to ourselves and others as to the sort of person we are; each casts back a glow illuminating the self who consumes.

Lifestyle is not confined to any one particular social or age group, nor is it purely a matter of economic determination. Economic capital is important but so too is cultural capital – both play a part in influencing the capacity of individuals to be more or less active in their exercise of lifestyle choices. The social group that is most readily associated with lifestyle practices, the so-called new middle class, demonstrates this. Their involvement in lifestyle practices cannot be explained simply as a function of income or ideology. I will argue rather that the key to their postmodern sensibility is the adoption of a learning mode towards life. Their habitus – their unconscious dispositions, classificatory schemes, taken-for-granted preferences – is evident in their sense of the appropriateness and validity of their taste for cultural goods and practices. They are the bearers of explicit notions of lifelong learning which are integral to their sensibility, values, assumptions and the aspirations of their cultural stance. They adopt a learning mode towards life – the conscious and reflexive education of self in the field of taste and style. They express their opposition to the established order by giving priority to experience as the mediator through which meaning is constructed, and to the demand for new experiences and new meanings. Thus, an emphasis is given to experiential learning which, for them, is invested with the significance of autonomy and self-expression in the pursuit of lifestyle practices. Coupled with this is a general tendency towards the relativisation of knowledge with knowledges generated from a number of local sources, including everyday life. Here, experience is not pre-given but constantly reconstructed. Meaning is constructed through experience rather than simply being conveyed by it. Experiential learning is established as a legitimate ground for education but with contestation over its meaning and significance.

Within lifestyle practices, the relationship between experience, knowledge and pedagogy is articulated in a particular way. Experience is something to get immersed in, valued as a means of defining a lifestyle rather than something whose value lies in its potential for knowledge. It is consumed because it signifies in relation to a lifestyle. Knowledge is multiple, based on multiple realities and the multiplicity of experience. It is neither canonical nor hierarchical. There is no notion of intrinsically 'worthwhile' knowledge other than in terms of taste and style. Pedagogy does not seek to transmit a canon of knowledge or a single ordered view of the world. It is not concerned with Enlightenment 'messages'. Given this, therefore, the learner is positioned within a multiplicity of experience whose meanings are located within a consumerist market-led culture. Experience is the means by which a lifestyle is created and 're-created'.

In one sense, therefore, learners are positioned by lifestyle practices as active subjects, creating themselves, free from constraining traditions and ideologies. But they are also positioned as passive subjects, since lifestyle is socially defined, culturally legitimised, economically influenced and prey to consumerism and media-generated images. Flexible accumulation and the techno-scientific revolution have changed processes of production and reduced the need for manual work (hence creating active 'power-ful' subjects) but at the same time have invaded people's lives with a flood of commodities, seductive images and signifying rivalries. All of this can be seen as liberating but also as a seduction that constitutes a new form of social control and which, in the process, creates 'subjectified' power-less subjects. Furthermore, seduction goes hand-in-hand with repression (Bauman 1992), as those who are excluded from the realms of choice yet who are nonetheless affected by the global reach of consumer society find themselves increasingly subjected to the repression of poverty and marginalisation.

Vocational practices

Postmodernity is a global condition where both dispersal and fragmentation coexist. Flexible accumulation and post-Fordism bring more volatile labour markets, faster switches from one product to another, niche marketing and a greater consumer orientation. Post-Fordism involves changes in production and consumption – from mass-production, mass-market, machine-paced systems to the production of specialist, niche and luxury goods, and to production systems based on the application of information technology (IT). These fundamental changes in production – 'flexible specialisation' – have reduced the need for manual work and led to the development of a new form of social labour. At the same time, contemporary education is characterised by its increasing transformation into a market form, a transformation which is best understood as a postmodern phenomenon. Education appears to gain increasing autonomy from central and local government control but also loses autonomy through the emphasis on privatisation, marketisation and vocationalism. As nonmarket relations are redefined according to the logic of the market, education, unable to insulate itself from these developments, assumes a market/consumer orientation.

Vocational practices are constructed through the market form where multi-skilling and personal motivation are privileged. Here, learning signifies 'application', with pedagogy structured around problem solving and project-based activities. The learner is required to be highly motivated in the direction of a personal change linked to 'reading' the market and continually adapting to the needs of the socio-economic environment. This reflects the post-Fordist organisation of work, marked by informal and networked social relations and flat/lateral hierarchies. Vocationalist discourse, therefore, personalises economic competitiveness by stressing the need for motivation and for becoming skilled. At the same time, it offers a formula for economic recovery, based on a reconfiguration of human capital theory, and a metonymic of blame ('If only you were trained and motivated, we wouldn't be where we are today!' – Ball 1993: 74). Education is cast as turning out the product which industry consumes. Changes in industry and changes in the processes of schooling go hand in hand, with educational institutions being expected to produce enterprising, consumption-oriented individuals with the attitudes and competencies, the flexibility and predisposition to change appropriate to the post-Fordist economy and ready to take their place in the market.

Vocationalism then is designed to produce flexible competencies and a predisposition to change. This is allied to a critique of the dominant liberal-humanist academic curriculum and draws upon some aspects of progressivist theories of motivation and learning (process-orientation, cooperation, problem solving, open-ended investigation). It argues, first, that the 'real' world (by which is meant the world of post-Fordism and flexible specialisation) is not subsumable under academic subject divisions, and hence the academic curriculum provides an 'irrelevant' education and preparation for this world, and second, that the didacticism and teacher-centredness of this curriculum does not provide the appropriate attitudes and capabilities. These curricular changes, intended to enhance learning experiences and increase motivation, are implicated with the technological changes affecting the labour process and modes of production. New attitudes and competences are required from employees, and hence the relationship between pedagogy, knowledge and the labour process changes. What is foregrounded is the need for flexibility and continuous learning, social skills and flexible competences, rather than subject-based knowledge.

As a pedagogy, experiential learning has the capacity to unsettle the established order and hence has a transformative potential. In vocational practices, experiential learning holds out the promise of breaking the stranglehold of a selective and elitist higher education. It challenges the notion that knowledge is only to be found within educational institutions and through a subject-based curriculum. It challenges also the prerogative of self-selecting and unaccountable academic professionals in controlling and defining what is to count as knowledge. Experiential learning, therefore, becomes the key to broadening access to higher education and to 'democratising' the curriculum.

At the same time, however, vocationalist pedagogy creates a context where learning means proceeding to the correct answer in the most efficient way. Here, adaptation and application have no room for experimentation, open-endedness or unforeseen outcomes. Hence, the experience and knowledge of learners and knowledge arising from it becomes a mere device, a means for best achieving a pre-defined end. Learners are manipulated pedagogically to access already-existing forms of knowledge either in the form of disciplines or, more usually, in the form of sets of behavioural objectives. Learner experience appears to be valued, but its use is instrumental, selective and at best illustrative. It is only accorded significance if it contributes to the learning of the pre-defined knowledge or skills; if not, it is discounted. This is then a 'techni-cised' pedagogy, where experience has no inherent value but functions merely as a tool for enhancing motivation. Experience becomes assimilated to behavioural competences.

Experiential learning is itself a pedagogy constructed through vocational practices; thus, it is both socially constructed and contested. Different social groups give it their own meanings, represent it in different ways. Thus, as we have seen, the new middle class invest it with a signification of autonomy and expression. For those groups associated with the New Right, it means adaptation to a pre-defined world and learning applicable and relevant to that world. Experience represents relevance, usefulness, self-discipline and market effectiveness. Paradoxically, however, and this is where there are resonances with contemporary lifestyle practices, experiential learning is the means by which the cultural and educational establishment can be resisted and subverted – for example, through challenging the power of the academy to define 'worthwhile' knowledge and by presenting alternatives to curricula based on disciplinary knowledge. Of course, this challenge has to be related to rapid economic and social change – flexible capital accumulation, specialisation, the rise of core and periphery workforces coupled with the growth of an underclass, fear of inflation and the loss of confidence in government's ability to manage the economy. The resulting uncertainty and breakdown of established patterns of work and life lead to the possibility of deviance, delinquency and disorder.

For government, instability must be managed either directly through the law and order system or indirectly through education. One way of managing instability through education is by normalising discipline and, more importantly, self-discipline. In the post-compulsory sector this poses some difficulty since students are there by choice. Yet the need for self-discipline is not diminished nor is self-discipline easily attained. Rather than taking control of what happens in the post-school arena, government divests itself of control – directly by giving more power to employers, indirectly by encouraging opportunities for people to learn outside educational institutions and to have it accredited outside of the educational system. Hence, young adults are 'educated' into and by the self-discipline of labour. The focus is on an employability that somehow reinvents and captures the work ethic yet does not necessarily lead to paid work. Here then, we see experiential learning circumscribed by employers' needs for particular kinds of labour and particular kinds of consumers and by government's need for a means of social control through self-discipline.

Thus, a pedagogy of experiential learning can also have a domesticating potential. In vocational practices, experiential learning can be the means to control change – at the same time that it unsettles the established order, it also functions to ensure that the unsettling remains within established parameters of social order. Thus, for example, assessment and accreditation procedures ensure that only certain forms of experience are valued. Furthermore, the regulation of experience is taken out of the control of educational practitioners and placed instead in centrally formulated anticipated outcomes. Within vocational practices, what we see happening is the commodification of experiences – experience becomes a commodity to be exchanged in the marketplace of educational credit.

In vocational practices the relationship between experience, knowledge and pedagogy is articulated in such a way that experience functions to provide a personal motivation and a feet-on-the-ground pragmatism. Learning becomes a matter of applying knowledge where knowledge itself is narrowly defined, a heuristic, 'factual' knowledge which enables the learner to adapt to a taken-for-granted, pre-defined 'real world'. Pedagogy is the link between personal motivation and the learning of pre-defined outcomes in the form of adaptive skills. In this context, the learner is positioned as a subject in need of skills in the post-Fordist marketplace. Skills are empowering – through them one becomes more competent and 'employable'. Learning is a matter of applying what is learnt so that one can become better adapted and adaptable to the perceived needs of the economy. Experiential learning is open and closed in the same moment.

Confessional practices

'Selves' are not natural givens in the world and to have knowledge of them is not simply a matter of discovering or uncovering their reality. Conceptions of the self have significatory power and selves are constructed through these conceptions and their associated discursive practices. A pastoral power which works by enabling people to actively and committedly participate in disciplinary regimes seems to have a contemporary significance. In effect, people are educated to govern themselves through bringing their inner lives into the domain of power. Pastoral power works, not through imposition or coercion but through people investing their identity, subjectivity and desires with those ascribed to them through certain 'knowledgeable' or expert discourses.

In this process, people's self-regulating capacities become allied with social and economic objectives. To know one's inner self is for that inner self to be known, and being known becomes the condition for a more effective regulation in the service of contemporary political rationalities which foreground the individual and the market. The private, in effect, becomes public and becomes a support for enterprise culture and the market. In other words, to realise oneself, to find out the truth about oneself, to accept responsibility for oneself, becomes both personally desirable and economically functional.

Contemporary governmentality works in terms of the affective and effective governing of persons where positioning and investment in a subject position is a crucial factor. What is involved here is a 'bringing forth of one's self' as an object of knowledge through a pedagogy which functions to open up for intervention those aspects of a person which have hitherto remained unspoken. The self is constituted as an object of knowledge through discovering the 'truth' about itself. However, in confessing, subjects have already accepted the legitimacy and truth of confessional practices and the particular meanings and investments that these invoke. Adults, for example, accept themselves as 'learners' in need of 'learning' provided by professional adult educators for their future development. In doing so, they align their subjectivities with these educational discourses and meanings they invoke. They become enfolded within a discursive matrix of practices which constitute their felt needs and paths of self-development.

In contemporary society externally imposed discipline gives way to the self-discipline of an autonomous subjectivity. With confession, the emphasis is on self-improvement, self-development and self-regulation. It displaces canonical knowledge by valorising individual experience but, at the same time, rather than displacing power as such it extends the range of pastoral power embedded in the confessional regime of truth and self-knowledge. Confessional practices therefore create productive and empowered subjects who are, however, already governed (by themselves). Thus, externally imposed discipline and regulation is not required. There is regulation through self-regulation, discipline through self-discipline, a process which is pleasurable and even empowering, but only within a matrix from which power is never absent (Usher and Edwards 1995).

In confessional practices, psychotherapeutic expertise in a variety of forms from the academic to the 'popular' plays a key role in presenting a morality of freedom, fulfilment and empowerment. It offers the means by which the regulation of selves by others and by the self is made consonant with the current situation. Thus, in confessional practices, autonomy becomes adaptation, an autonomy enhanced through the application of expertise. Empowerment is psychological and individualistic. Political, social and institutional goals are realigned with individual pleasures and desires, with self-expression, the happiness and fulfilment of the self. Pedagogic practices, such as assertiveness training and educational guidance, illustrate this very clearly. They emphasise the 'liberation' of the self but only within the confines and limitations of understood and unchallenged contexts and systems.

Knowledge/expertise of the self stimulates subjectivity, promotes self-knowledge and seeks to maximise capacities. Persons are cast as active citizens, ardent consumers, enthusiastic employees and loving parents – and all of this as if they were seeking to realise their own most fundamental desires and innermost needs. At the same time, however, by enhancing subjectivity (creating active subjects), subjectivity is connected to power by means of new languages (psychotherapeutic expertise) for speaking about subjectivity. However, confessional practices are not recognised as powerful because they are cloaked in an esoteric yet seemingly objective expertise and a humanistic discourse of helping and empowerment. Thus, an active, autonomous and productive subjectivity is brought forth in confessional practices even as it remains subject to the power/knowledge formations which bring forth this form of subjectivity and invest it with significance.

In confessional practices, the relationship between experience, knowledge and pedagogy is articulated in terms of a representation of experience as enabling access to knowledge and the innermost truths of self. Pedagogy involves the deployment of psychodynamic expertise to facilitate this process. Given this relationship, the learner is positioned to discover the meaning of his/her experience by becoming an active subject within a network of confession. The meaning of experience is bound up with finding the truth about self in order to enhance capacities and become adapted and well adjusted, but this active subject in control of self is at the same time subjectified within a network of pastoral power. Experiential learning becomes a matter of self-expression in the interests of adaptation.

Critical practices

Critical practices work through particular meanings given to autonomy and application. Autonomy in critical practices has a different signification to the autonomy of lifestyle practices. In the latter, it is oriented towards expression through the cultivation of desire and the display of difference through consumption. In the former, it is oriented towards application, which again is not the same as the 'application' of vocational practices. It is not the application of learning in the service of adaptation to the existing techno-social order but rather an application of learning in the cause of self and social transformation. It is in changing particular contexts rather than adapting to them that autonomy is ultimately to be found.

In critical practices, there is more of a recognition that meaning is discursively produced and that experience, therefore, is never simply an 'innocent' or basic given. Experience and the way it is represented are the stakes in the struggle to find 'voice', to exercise control and power. The key question, then, becomes how representations of experience are discursively produced and how subjects both position themselves and are positioned discursively. This opens up issues of power, given that discourses serve the interests of particular groups. Thus a pedagogy that assumes experience is innocent is challenged because it must inevitably be uncritically supportive of the status quo. The refusal to accept that the representation of experience is political means that the power relations embedded in discourses and the interests of particular groups served by particular discourses remain unseen and unquestioned.

In critical practices, therefore, pedagogy becomes a political practice. Allied to this is an emphasis on the cultural, a recognition that culture is a lived ongoing process as important as the material and the economic and as much a terrain of struggle. Pedagogy is not seen as a technical matter directed to imparting a canon of knowledge but as vitally implicated in a politics of representation (how people present and understand or are presented and understood) in the cultural processes that shape the meanings and understanding of experience and the formation of identity.

The relationship between experience, knowledge and pedagogy is articulated in terms of a self-conscious questioning of the representation(s) of experience. There is an explicit recognition that experience 'signifies' and that the significations of experience are imbued with power and are influential in the shaping of identity. The relationship between experience and knowledge is not taken as either given or unproblematic, nor is it seen as purely a matter of deploying methodical will or eradicating false consciousness. There is an acknowledging of the place of desire in how people are positioning vis-à-vis their experience, the investments that tie people to particular positions and identities and the multiple and ambiguous positioning that people find themselves in.

Critical practices have a clear and explicit transformative potential, but this resides in localised contexts and operates through the deployment of specific knowledge. In their pedagogical aspects (and in a sense they are almost exclusively pedagogic), they reject the conventional domesticating effects of pedagogy. Experiential learning becomes a strategy designed to privilege 'voice' in the service of self and social empowerment and transformation. At the same time, however, it is this very emphasis which can give critical practices a regulatory dimension. The 'critical' easily becomes a norm, a final truth which is just as heavy in its regulation as any openly oppressive discourse – as, for example, in the worst excesses of political correctness. Indeed, in some ways this regulation may be even more difficult to resist, speaking as it does in the name of empowerment and transformation. As Gore (1993) argues, critical pedagogy, whilst rhetorically opposing 'regimes of truth', can itself easily become one. She refers to this as the difference between the pedagogy argued for and the pedagogy of the argument – in the case of critical pedagogy, the former liberatory and transformative, the latter totalising and regulative.

New forms of critical practice have been associated with what some commentators have referred to as 'postmodern' social movements. They are characterised by a cultural activism and an emphasis on experience as an intense 'here and now'. Whilst seeking personal and social transformation, they do so in a non-totalising and non-teleological way and outside the comforting rationales of the grand narratives of modernity. Although pedagogic, they deploy a pedagogy of performance, often transgressive and sometimes 'outrageous' to bourgeois sensibilities. In critical practices, experience is not regarded as something that leads to knowledge but as knowledge. Knowledge, however, is in the service of action, an activity, a practice which does things.

Rethinking experience in the context of contemporary adult learning

At this point it might be useful to relate these quadrants and the practices they represent to the well-known 'villages' of experiential learning as identified originally by Weil and McGill (1989a). To some extent they are representative of the mainstream discourse of experiential learning within adult education. These 'villages' have served a useful purpose as a heuristic device for conceptualising and categorising the various forms of experiential learning and for examining the assumptions, influences and purposes within and between these forms. Indeed, the very concept of 'village' was formulated in order to avoid creating exclusive distinctions and divisions between various forms and practices of experiential learning and as a means of encouraging dialogue between them.

The exploration and development of the quadrants may help to complement and expand upon the impact of the villages. Indeed, meaningful distinctions and connections can be made between these categorisations in terms of their emphases, their dynamics and their complexity. Within the quadrants as they have been formulated here, the emphasis is as much on problematising and understanding experience in relation to different contexts and discourses as it is on focusing on the learning process contingent on experience. This wider emphasis may serve to avoid the danger of 'locking onto' a particular village because of its association with a specific ideological tradition or institutionalised educational practice. Equally, it may make it less likely that existing social relations are left unquestioned within a preoccupation with experiential techniques and methods.

The significance of the interrelationship of application/expression/autonomy/ adaptation within and between the different quadrants is that it allows greater fluidity in representing the dynamic interconnections between experience, knowledge and pedagogy in relation to different and changing discursive practices. By this means, it is possible to move away from the tendency of the villages concept to be overdescriptive and overschematic and to counter the very real possibility of reifying the different villages. It also allows a more complex and flexible understanding of experience and experiential learning, which can take account of context, theory and practice, enabling a move from what Wildemeersch (1992: 25) calls an essentially 'narrative type of conversation' to a more challenging 'discursive type of conversation' about education and learning. This can help show the way towards the paradigm shift aspired to by Weil and McGill which looks to 'push the boundaries of our visions and our villages to acknowledge the inter-connectedness of the whole' (Weil and McGill 1989b: 269). In this wider context we can better understand the potential within the various discursive practices for experiential learning to be both domesticating and transformative.

I have argued that experience is not unproblematic, that it needs to be understood and interpreted in relation to differing contexts and the influence of a variety of discourses. It can function both to empower and control, to create both powerful and powerless selves. What, then, are the implications for educational practice?

In focusing on student experience, I suggest that educators need to help students to problematise and interrogate experience as much as to access and validate it. Complementary to the acknowledgement that experiential learning is a holistic process, that it is socially and culturally constructed and that it is influenced by the socio-emotional context in which it occurs (Boud *et al.* 1993) must be a similar understanding about the nature, construction and context of experience itself. First, educators need to be wary of basing their practice on the proposition that experiential learning involves a 'direct encounter' with experience (Weil and McGill 1989b: 248). Whereas experience can provide new and useful insights into a wide range of issues and problems and can clearly be used to access, supplement, complement, critique and challenge understandings of the world derived from disciplinary knowledge, I agree with Wildemeersch (1992: 22) that the creation of a specific 'opposition between experiential and theoretical knowledge is unfruitful and even false'.

A learning focus on experience certainly has the potential to be 'liberating' in its concern for the 'neglected learner' and its opposition to 'banking' education, in that it highlights and confers meaning on knowledge, skills and attitudes previously undervalued and motivates students to extend their learning and pursuit of knowledge. Yet it can also be domesticating, in that learners can become unreflexive prisoners of their experience or have their experiences colonised and reduced, on the one hand, by oppressive educational institutions and, on the other hand, by totalising 'radical' discourses. Such approaches run the risk of selling learners short on culturally valued knowledge and, at worst, lock them into second-best knowledge and, through uncritical and unrigorous approaches to recognising and accrediting prior learning from experience, even into second-best qualifications. At the same time, by continuing to see experience as the 'raw material' of knowledge, we are unable to create situations where we can examine how, as selves, we move back and forth between our own particular stories through which we construct our identities and the social production that is knowledge. In the process, we fail to challenge dominant knowledge taxonomies and the relations of power in which they are implicated.

Educators need to move beyond practice based on overly simplistic observations that 'you can always learn from experience' etc. and look more carefully at the necessary preconditions for experiential learning. Part of this might involve, rather than an unsophisticated, untheorised and potentially threatening delving into student experience, working towards building the necessary psychological climate and infrastructure from which experience can both be explored and problematised. This might mean creating sufficient student security and self-confidence, 'the right emotional tone under which authentic discourse can occur' (Brookfield 1993: 27), and at least an outline theoretical framework from which to examine and understand student experience. It might mean acknowledging more explicitly, honestly and sensitively the possibility of limiting or oppressive experience – for example, the experience of personal unemployment, bereavement or loss – as well as the difficulties involved in transferring learning from one experiential and cultural context to another – for example, the problematic connection between domestic management skills and knowledge and those in a more regulated, hierarchical and gendered workplace (Butler 1993).

A more productive approach to knowledge might be to engage in the process of 're-view' (Usher 1992; Brookfield 1993), exploring how and why we theorise experience and critically examining the influence on experience of contexts, cultures and discourses in the past and for the future. Such a procedure avoids the pitfalls of a naive and even potentially manipulative pedagogical approach to learner experience where educator theories are present but unacknowledged and learner experience is foregrounded but inadequately framed or contextualised.

Equally, it may be necessary to reformulate Weil and McGill's location of experience in individuals who give personal meaning to different ways of knowing so that more account can be taken of selves as meaning-takers as well as meaning-givers. With this in mind, in reconfiguring a pedagogy of experiential learning, it may be insufficient to rely exclusively either on psychologistic models to uncover, diagnose, categorise or sequence individual experience or on the artificial creation of shared experience through gaming, role-play and simulations. An alternative approach to experiential learning might be, rather, to attempt to triangulate experience through an investigation of personal meanings alongside the meanings of engaged others and the presence and influence of different contexts and different discourses. Here, the quadrants could themselves function as a useful heuristic device. This might help learners to see their experience more as 'text' than as 'raw material', thus leaving open the possibility of a variety of interpretations and assessments of experience, including the possibility that experiential learning might be both 'liberating' and 'domesticating', according to its contextual and discursive location.

References

Ball, S.J. (1993) 'Self-Doubt and Soft Data: Social and Technical Trajectories in Ethnographic Fieldwork', in M. Hammersley (ed.), *Educational Research: Current Issues*, London: Open University/Chapman.

Bauman, Z. (1992) *Intimations of Postmodernity*, London: Routledge.

Boud, D., Cohen, R. and Walker, D. (1993) 'Introduction: Understanding Learning from Experience', in D. Boud, R. Cohen and D. Walker (eds), *Using Experience for Learning*, Milton Keynes, UK: SRHE/Open University Press.

Brookfield, S. (1993) 'Through the Lens of Learning: How the Visceral Experience of Learning Reframes Teaching', in D. Boud, R. Cohen and D. Walker (eds), *Using Experience for Learning*, Milton Keynes, UK: SRHE/Open University Press.

Butler, L. (1993) 'Unpaid Work in the Home and Accreditation', in M. Thorpe, R. Edwards and A. Hanson (eds), *Culture and Processes of Adult Learning*, London: Routledge.

Featherstone, M. (1991) *Consumer Culture and Postmodernism*, London: Sage.

Gore, J. (1993) *The Struggle for Pedagogies: Critical and Feminist Discourses as Regimes of Truth*, London: Routledge.

Usher, R. (1992) 'Experience in Adult Education: A Postmodern Critique', *Journal of Philosophy of Education* 26, 2: 201–213.

Usher, R. and Edwards, R. (1995) 'Confessing All? A "Postmodern" Guide to the Guidance and Counselling of Adult Learners', *Studies in the Education of Adults* 27, 1: 9–23.

Weil, S. and McGill, I. (1989a) 'A Framework for Making Sense of Experiential Learning', in S. Weil and I. McGill (eds), *Making Sense of Experiential Learning: Diversity in Theory and Practice*, Milton Keynes, UK: SRHE/Open University Press.

Weil, S. and McGill, I. (1989b) 'Continuing the Dialogue: New Possibilities for Experiential Learning', in S. Weil and I. McGill (eds), *Making Sense of Experiential Learning: Diversity in Theory and Practice*, Milton Keynes, UK: SHRE/Open University Press.

Wildemeersch, D. (1992) 'Ambiguities of Experiential Learning and Critical Pedagogy', in D. Wildemeersch and T. Jansen (eds), *Adult Education, Experiential Learning, and Social Change: The Postmodern Challenge*, The Hague: VUGA.

Chapter 13

'Normal learning problems' in youth

In the context of underlying cultural convictions

Thomas Ziehe

Ever since the publication of his dissertation Puberty and Narcissism *(in German) in 1975, Thomas Ziehe, now Professor at the Hanover University, has been well known in Germany and Scandinavia for his insights and interpretations of youth psychology, youth culture and youth education. In 1982 he published, together with Herbert Stubenrauch, probably his most important book,* Pleading for Unusual Learning *(in German), which broke with prevailing understandings and introduced a new view on youth and education in modern society. Since then, Ziehe has produced a continuous flow of papers and articles closely following the changes and developments in the thinking, feeling, learning, understandings and behaviour of teenagers and suggesting corresponding changes in teaching and schooling. As a sociologist and social psychologist, Ziehe belongs to what has been termed the third generation of the so-called Frankfurt School, and his solid theoretical basis is accompanied by an almost seismographic empathy in the ever-changing conditions and movements of the youth generation. In the following chapter, which compiles three recent papers in German, Ziehe explains his understanding of the basic forces which today are directing learning, development and culture in youth.*

Underlying convictions as symbolic context of learning styles in youth

School research and youth research usually work without any integration. This is a bit curious because the everyday professional experiences of most teachers are profoundly influenced by the fact that the behaviour of their students has changed in many ways. The appearances and consequences of the cultural break in school traditions have only gradually been realized, and what is focused on is then usually how the fascination of youth cultures influences the *habitus* of the students.

In my work I choose another approach. My main interest is to reconstruct theoretically the systems of knowledge and rules as the basic symbolic structures that underlie the socialization of individuals. From the point of view of cultural theory, these basic structures precede any individuation. Most psychological approaches must for methodical reasons omit the level of symbolic–cultural constitution of social reality and relate directly to the internal mental world of the individuals they examine: their motives, attitudes and learning styles. Cultural theory, on the other hand, is occupied with the symbolic conditions of the origin and basic structures of which the single individual has already prepared and which *have always culturally pre-coded* the most intimate relationship of the individual with him- or herself.

When I try to interpret the appearances and problems of learning and school, I use an analytic procedure with three steps which, according to my approach, proceed as follows:

- The investigated school processes should be contextualized with reference to how they are experienced in light of the meaning horizons of the students. This will be a *subject-oriented contextualization.*
- However, the meaning structures of the students, their forms of experience, their social and emotional worlds and their self-thematization cannot just be taken at the words, but must – as any other hermeneutic activity – be interpreted by the social scientist (although most conventional survey inquiry desists from this). A second level of interpretation must therefore be a *meaning structure-oriented contextualization,* in which latent meaning content, which the involved actors do not command intentionally, is also taken into consideration.
- The third level of contextualization includes a further investigation of the latent ascriptions of meaning in order to detect if it is possible to reconstruct meaning patterns and knowledge structures which, in a constitutional way, precede the meaning expressions of the individuals. This will be a *meaning system-oriented contextualization,* which should also include the 'great' semantic changes in supra-subjective meaning patterns, cultural understandings and general social orientations.

I hope that these short references do not sound too boastful. They are intended to indicate the perspectives of my orientation. Whether and to what extent I live up to them is, after all, a question that I am unable to answer myself.

Anyway, *contextualization in a cultural-analytical sense* is what I am dealing with. I try to connect 'learning style' and 'youth culture' as two items of investigation with special attention to available general cultural knowledge structures and rule systems. I take interest in the cultural-analytical question to the extent that changed symbolic meaning structures can be detected *on an underlying level of investigation.* These meaning structures pre-condition what we at any time consider to be 'normal' or unquestionable matters, of course. Therefore these meaning structures are general and abstract and, from a cultural-analytical point of view, they come before the empirical appearances of various youth cultures. The phenomenology of youth cultures can then be regarded as *derived consequences* of changes in the underlying symbolic structures.

Youth cultures are formed by changes in *general underlying convictions* which include a deeply based kind of 'knowledge' fostering our motives, expectations and actions in ways which we are not conscious of in everyday life.

This understanding of knowledge systems includes certain pre-assumptions:

- The cultural-analytical concept of knowledge excludes the question of (at least definitive) truth or validity of cultural knowledge. All the symbolic rules and systems are understood as knowledge that precedes and regulates the ways of observing and experiencing human reality. This conception of knowledge also includes what is regarded as real or considered by the construction of cognitive reality independently of the content of objective reality.
- Furthermore, knowledge is then not understood as being of an individual or subjectively internal origin, but as an elaboration of culturally available and intersubjectively shared schemes of interpretation, functioning as a kind of draft for the individually constructed stock of knowledge.
- The cultural knowledge systems form a *'grammatical' pre-structure,* not only of the cognitive epistemology, but also of the valuations, assessments and expressions of world and self-references. Emotions, wishes and motives are also based on cultural patterns concerning what, in a historically situated culture, can be accepted as expected and normal emotions, wishes and motives.
- From the cultural knowledge systems people build their underlying convictions. They consist of routines, everyday certainties and notions of normality, which are already implied by our experiences of reality. The underlying convictions form a major part of our knowledge. They are accessible to reflection when we convert our life world participant perspectives into observer perspectives, but in 'day-to-day life' the underlying convictions form a nonconscious *implicit context of understanding.* On these nonconscious conditions, our handling of symbols and meanings is then the basis of our conscious, explicit and everyday-life-applicable knowledge.

However, such underlying symbolic structures should not be understood as a rigid and restricting girdle secondarily forced upon a (potentially authentic) individual. The structures are much more ambiguous, in the best meaning of this term. They *restrict* the range of possible symbol elaboration and meaning ascription, but they also have a *disposing* function – in a situation of action they make something topical. They offer the actors world-opening semantics and place, in any context, appropriate interpretations at their disposal.

Thus, the *change of such underlying convictions* is a change of what is typical, a change of what is not striking. If they sometimes may be actualized anyway, the reactions of the actors will be made up of expressions like 'Why, this is really quite simple!' or 'And what then is the problem?' When something is culturally obvious, one does not wonder about it (at least, not as long as one is in a participating position).

The modernization of underlying convictions

In the social sciences, the fundamental concepts of culture, society and personality have a high value of structuring. I shall here present a change to the underlying convictions on these three levels: (1) culture, (2) society and (3) the self. I shall do this in a strongly generalizing way, i.e. abstracting from differences in environments, life circumstances and life ages and focusing on particular *analytical common features* in the heterogeneous.

The changed underlying convictions which I shall here deal with theoretically are not strongly generation-specific. They shall not immediately be fixed as characteristics of the life age of youth, as the underlying convictions change inside society as a whole. What is *generation-specific, but only in a limited way*, is the intensity and the social conventions of the approach to the changed cultural rule systems. For the young generation, they, from a developmental point of view, constitute the 'first' symbolic frames of socialization. For the older generations, they are cultural possibilities and risks, which are already carried by biographical pre-impressions, and thus they are elaborated secondarily. Each age group must, therefore, elaborate the cultural changes and new challenges, which potentially concern all groups, by means that are specific to the generational and social groupings.

Eligibility and noneligibility of knowledge content

The kind of everyday culture, and what is regarded as matters of course, into which the young generation of today grows up is not norm-regulated, as was the case for earlier generations. Rather it is preference-related, i.e. it is oriented towards personal preferences and sensitivity. This is caused by a comprehensive detraditionalization which we have all been through during the last thirty years. For the young that now grow up into this context, it means on the one hand an increase in liberation and more individual scope for interpretation and action, but on the other hand, this detraditionalization for the individual causes a more demanding strain on orientation.

Individuals are today only weakly normatively directed by a general culture. The earlier fall of prestige between high culture and popular culture is today widely dehierarchized, i.e. the importance of high culture has to a great extent become relative. Before, the *high culture* was a kind of symbolic roof of society to which people had to relate (or at least to not damage). By this, I do not indicate that a majority of the population earlier had access to the high culture. But the high culture functioned as a stock of symbols to which it was important to relate positively. In Germany, for instance, a principal speech should include a quotation from Goethe – not because most people had read Goethe, but because he could not be omitted as a symbol. This had considerable consequences for all cultural areas. I think here of the gratitude that earlier has been felt and expressed by people who had no immediate biographical access to cultural knowledge and then later through general adult education opened up to participation in such cultural processes. This moved these people to considerable gratitude – a kind of gratitude which we can hardly find today because the situation has changed radically. Now a much broader understanding of culture has broken through, and it is an individual option whether one will embark on high culture or not.

In a sort of counterbalance to this, *popular culture* at the same time changes its way of banalizing people's forms of knowledge and social conventions, their habits of observation and their mentalities. Popular culture is restless and practicable, integrated in everyday life and omnipresent. What it subjectively provokes is as imperative as noise irrigation in a capital airport. The consequence is a displacement of measures and scales or a gradual permeation of changed cultural normalities.

This places all forms of production and knowledge which differ from current popular culture under a pressure for justification, especially regarding subjective standards of attraction, pleasure, excitement, exaltation, intensity or fun. Popular cultural standards function today as sharp *competitors* with high culture and educational institutions. However, the current distance to high culture is no longer caused by strong social restrictions, but rather by a question of acceptance: high culture is increasingly avoided due to entirely different habits of attention and enjoyment.

The subjective distance of most young people to the products and practices of high culture has therefore become tremendous. Even the historically strongly expanded youth education is hardly able to compensate for this. When Beethoven is mentioned, 11-year-old children think of a dog in a certain movie and only with surprise do they learn that there has also existed a composer by that name. However, the consequences of this big distance are not immediately the end of Western civilization as it has often been claimed, but merely a general *marginalization of high culture*. High culture is pushed back to the level of a subculture among other subcultures. The status of high culture becomes optional: those who want can embark on it, and those who do not can leave it out without any severe loss of reputation. And more and more, young people especially leave it out.

My contrasting of popular culture and high culture should not be understood as a mutually aesthetic theoretical exclusion. I do not share the cultural pessimistic idea of 'arts versus entertainment'. My approach is rather *cultural-sociological*: not a critique of the products of popular culture as such, but a critique of *everyday conventions* turning into 'pop'. This results in *subjective conclusions* about such products and forms of experience which are different from popular culture.

Positively considered, there is in this turning into 'pop' an increased measure of motivational liberty. The mode of optionality, i.e. the possibility and at the same time the necessity of choosing and deciding for one's self, has become part of everyday life, and individuals grow right from childhood into this mode. Optionality includes the possibility of choosing as well as of *not choosing*. It has become easier in everyday culture to say 'no' to any expectations from outside which are experienced as unpleasant or risky. The internal individual space of deviance from what institutions present as knowledge content has clearly expanded. And the *avoidance* of knowledge forms which are subjectively experienced as unpleasant has become a widespread everyday attitude.

Liberation and re-establishment of role patterns

In the social dimension, the symbolic meaning structures are changing the relations between society and the individual. The social integration of the individual in society changes by the process of a social detraditionalization.

In the past era of the modern industrialized society, the normative idea of the 'individuum' expanded. But this individual had to stick to internalized norms of duty, self-discipline and emotional control. This means that the earlier social normativity enjoined the individual to conform, externally as well as internally, with the common role patterns of the class and position to which he or she belonged. In this way the strict lines of the merger of social role and personal individuality had to be followed. The exposition of individuality must be accommodated within the rules of discipline.

In contrast to this, the current modern symbolic order has much less the nature of fixed behaviour programmes. The modern rule systems are not literally to be executed, but only make a frame which can be filled up by the individual in accordance with the context and situation. This means that a higher degree of personal performance is socially left to – and at the same time enjoined on – the modern individual. Simple rule conformity is no longer enough to ensure social recognition.

In this way, a more extensive change of underlying convictions arises. Today there is room for different possibilities *inside* the scope of social roles. At the same time there are demands of individual performance *behind* the system of social roles. The modern social order has normatively become more abstract, implicit and demanding. Jürgen Habermas has characterized this change as the request of a *non-conventional ego identity*. The conventional forms of identity are breaking down – and this means that the duty-oriented dimension of identity is brought into a tension with the ego-ideal-oriented dimension. The guidance of the individual is no longer primarily directed towards the conventional dichotomy between what is forbidden and what is allowed, but towards the subjective dichotomy between what is acceptable and what is not.

Self-observation and recognition of individuals

This change in the direction of a non-conventional form of identity is the core of the much-discussed individualization. From the point of view of social theory, individualization does not mean absolute isolation but rather a change of the *mental self-reference*. The modern social expectations of sanity suggest that the individual, if necessary, is able to give reasons for and discuss his or her social practice. The modern mental self-reference means letting all expectations of and requests from the outside world pass through a 'subjective filter'. It is this type of self-observation which entails the individualizing changes.

In this way, the mental has gotten a public space. Self-references and discussions of relations become part of everyday interaction, and these are not so much based on conformity with the outside social order as on the current awareness of one's own incentives and existential mood.

Consequently the public sphere appears as a extension of the private. The mass media – especially through talk shows, daily soaps and the like – push the semantics of mental self-observation. From a positive point of view, the right to a self-directed private life is in this way consolidated; from a critical point of view, the forms of internal self-conflicts are sharpened. Mass media personify expressions of the outer world and thereby also continue moments of doubt into the area of everyday life.

Thus, the sharpened observation of one's own self does not immediately offer the individual any possibilities of retreat. Rather, the individual comes into a spiral of self-doubt – a diffuse kind of 'identity pain' that makes one more dependent on the recognition of others. A longing for continual recognition of self-confidence also influences the self-reference as well as the social relations to others. Everything must be considered with a view to what it 'does to me'. Identity is then primarily constituted by one's own self-images. The modern underlying conviction includes an implicit rule of action: do it so that it is in accordance with your self-images and so that you *precisely for this reason* are recognized by others.

But at the same time, of course, external compulsion, demands and exclusions are still functioning in individual life connections and limiting the individual possibilities of life management. Thus a perceptible imbalance arises between the demands of self-esteem and self-recognition on the one hand and the sharpened consciousness of lost and withheld life possibilities on the other hand. This may lead to feelings of shame and decreased self-esteem.

The uneasy identity increases action patterns that tend to lead to avoidance. The world is not so much observed through glasses which make visible the increased options. Much more, it is increased objects of avoidance and uneasiness that catch the eye. The symbolic systems of knowledge which are at the disposal of individual preferences will then be applied in ways which make the culturally increased options and spaces for deviance be experienced precisely as possibilities of not choosing and spaces of avoidance. This will typically result in motivational reticence which may sometimes be cautious and sometimes already resistant.

Shortly summarized, the changed underlying convictions lead to the following implicit leitmotifs:

- an increased space for resorting to preferred contents and increased rejection of unpleasant contents;
- a freer management of roles with an increased dependence on an ego-ideal-oriented role administration;
- a sharpened self-observation with an increased dependence on recognition from subjectively important others.

These leitmotifs are, as already stated, only generation-specific in a limited sense. Rather, they are generally distributed independently of age. But I think there are some taperings of these leitmotifs which are totally youth specific and which cause ever-increasing problems for schools in their endeavours to cultivate learning styles.

Consequences for everyday life in youth

Orientation towards personal affairs

I have already stated that symbolic systems up till now have included normative rules about the kinds of knowledge that were relevant in relation to different social roles. In the case of the symbolic functions of the 'old school', i.e. before the break-up of former traditions, this hardly needs further explanation. The former symbolic system pre-defined the knowledge relations. And this was mirrored in the underlying convictions, cognitively and socially as well as motivationally. These pre-definitions followed on available inherent cultural conditions which both relieved and strained the educational institutions, the teachers and the students. Of course, the well-known critique of the 'old school' could here be drawn in. But the symbolic backing of the school, which existed and did not have to be created and maintained all the time, provided a supply of content horizons, social forms and subjective motives anyway.

The 'old school' as an institution relied on the functions of the existing symbolic systems. These symbolic rules made it easy for students on the cognitive level to refer to a cultural *canon*, which was propagated by the historical tradition of education and, as its core programme, had the meeting and opposition with the cultural artifacts. 'Culture' in this connection implies an acquaintance with the various horizons of life philosophy, especially as they were valued by the differentiated branches of high culture.

However, such a symbolic pre-definition worked not only in the cognitive content dimension but also in the social normative dimension. To access the cultural artifacts also implied to meet the institutionalized *aura* of the school, including the hierarchy of generations and the demand of serious 'adult' knowledge. Of course, the experience of this condensed and socially exacting atmosphere included elements of empathy as well as anxiety. But it also produced intensive identifications, even when there is a demarcation from school itself.

Finally, the former symbolic system also pre-stamped ego-ideal images which imposed a positive attitude towards education. The earlier *ascetic* patterns of self-images included encumbrances of self-discipline as well as the potential experiences of pride, which projectively accompanied the efforts of the personal culturing processes: empathetically, it was part of the content of the ego-ideal to culturally become an adult.

Until now, we have been through a huge neutralization of and defascination with the symbolic system elements of *canon*, *aura* and *asceticism*. The former pre-figuration does not work any more. The knowledge references are hardly culturally pre-defined but – at least from the point of view of students and youth – they are individually liberated. The idea of education is no more a strain, but at the same time the former railing of orientation, evaluation and motivation has also disappeared.

The everyday world that surrounds young people today has merged with popular culture to an extent which makes it almost impossible to recognize. Pedestrian precincts, H&M stores, cell phones, text-messaging, hip-hop music, body piercing, daily soaps, MTV and MP3 players are all omnipresent as they are integrated in everyday life, and insistently present as they are absolutely customary. The socializing environment consists of a *merger of everyday life and popular culture*. This allows the young people to keep a distance and when they want it, in any situation, to enter into a space which operates parallel to the space of parents and institutions.

Popular culture as an all-embracing environment allows that one can join an almost full-time entertainment programme and constantly investigate and selectively choose from a worldwide supply of picture, music and information flows. In this situation, individuals tend to assume a position of *cultural self-supporters*. They take note of the mix of symbols, signs, interpretation patterns and ways of behaving offered by the popular culture, but merge it into their own everyday life and 'scenarios' according to their subjective preferences. They do not assume the ready-made products of the popular culture, but they apply them. From these symbolic elements, individuals piece together their own mental world.

These mental worlds should not be understood as places – they are not the local social environment. They are not (only) to be understood as reifications, but they function especially through changes in knowledge and convention styles: the personal mental worlds include the self-determination of particular practices, preferences, priorities and life approaches.

Today such personal mental worlds are forming the structures of the psychological equipment of individuals. They are no longer, as for earlier generations of youth, a recess area which with great trouble must be defended against the demands of the outside world. On the contrary, they can now be understood as the mental centre of the personal lifestyle. Thus the personal worlds are not only important as such. They also, so to speak, radiate into all life areas and give them a special colouring. Therefore, they are not simply a generally accepted parallel world, but they have become real *'leit-cultures'*. The measures of the personal worlds become scales of what is reasonable, meaningful and acceptable. And these measures from the personal worlds are practically unfiltered and then transferred to the various life areas, including the schools. By their implicit scales, they exercise a strong normative pressure, which exposes schools and teachers to intensified conflicts from the students about what can be accepted.

A certain positive effect of the *relativation of high culture* may be seen in the fact that the once so-scary content of the educational canon has decreased extremely, and as a consequence, feelings of educational shame hardly occur today. In an episode of a popular TV quiz programme the following could be observed: a young man in his twenties could repeatedly not answer questions outside the topics of popular culture and sport. In these cases, he said to the moderator, 'This was before my time'. Meaning that everything 'before his time' did not belong to his world – and that's that.

Informalization of the social pattern of behaviour

A second consequence of modernization involves the social conventions in youth. This problem is due to the fundamental informalization of current everyday life. Strict behavioural and disciplining contexts which rigidly and emphatically formed people's internal life belong more or less to the past. A brief look at a school photo, e.g. from the 1950s, would immediately make it clear just how significant facial expressions, body language, dressing conventions and role symbols were in the details of everyday life. The social life worlds were extensively regulated. Disciplinary and role-related behavioural norms ensured the detailed regulation of human interaction and the internal psychological self-observation. The former rule systems also included a clear discrimination between social territories of validity. This especially meant being able to separate between the private and the public spheres, and not to confuse external symbolic systems with internal imagination. Such distinctions between what is 'internal' and 'external' functioned right down to the micro social details of behavioural styles and self-images.

Today this seems like a long time ago. Now the phenomena of abolition of territories of validity and the repeal of self-withdrawal have become extraordinary to the extent that the classical modern diagnosis of 'nervousness' simply appears as an understatement. It is no longer about a temporary loosening or postponement of the rule systems during puberty, but about changes of the *total social habitus*. The everyday life world is characterized by delimitations, confusions and excesses, which have become the state of affairs. Of course, like before, there are institutional and private territories in which things are different, but rather they have the nature of islands in an ocean of obvious informalization.

Thus, when children reach the age of puberty, they do not experience their developmentally conditioned desire for excesses in contrast to the social world of adults, but at most as intensified variations of what is already happening. One only needs to accompany thirty 14-year-olds on a school excursion and, for instance, join the common supper at the youth hostel – impulsive, expansive, unconcentrated behaviour and excessive dropping out of any kind of regulation have become the norm. Everyday behaviour has, just to point out two characteristics, become informalized and unstructured. And it expands in two ways: it expands outwards, i.e. it is 'transferred' almost unfiltered from the private into the institutions, and it expands inwards, i.e. the informalization and lack of structure are also dominating the internal personal conditions.

In the classroom, for instance, the individual 'edginess' in relation to an incalculable interacting mixture of official teaching on the surface and quite different peripheral happenings, which constantly take place, can only be partially settled even by very experienced teachers and only with extreme difficulty and exertion. As to institution-related behaviour, young people have considerable problems with respect to rules, time structures and agreements. This can also be seen as part of the lack of structure, i.e. as a kind of behaviour which usually in no way is personally directed towards the teacher, but just is 'something that happens' for the students in question.

Likewise, the changed modes of individual attention are touched by informalization and lack of structure. Particularly, attention takes on quicker and less concentrated forms. This acceleration of attention implies a habituation to fragmentation, segmentation, interruptions, dissolving and huddling together of moments, and at the same time an inclination to sudden reversals into boredom and loathing. Subjectively, the mode of sliding and jumping is preferred, whereas modes of attention of a slower nature or a linear structure are refused.

Subjectivation of motivation

A third phenomenon of the cultural modernization is about the relation to the self, the personal internal world and its motives. It seems to involve a changed quality of self-observation. The individual cannot avoid a more accurate and isolated observation of him- or herself, as someone also different from and unlike 'society'. The classic questions 'Who am I?' and 'What do I want?' in some ways have become more psychological and part of everyday life. Niklas Luhmann once said about this that the internal lighting has been switched on. Parts of what was earlier professional knowledge of psychology and social science have been included in everyday knowledge. Such knowledge is sometimes even applied for self-description by the participants in afternoon talk shows and simulated therapy programmes. Thus, subjectivation of motivation means that the self-orientation is strongly directed towards very personal standards of valuation. The daily TV soaps are a never-ending demonstration of this urge for subjectivation. There, inside intimate friendship groups, everybody talks about everything, particularly about relational conflicts and self-observations. There is an absolute demand for psychological transparency. Through infinite talking together, everyone must, in the perspective of a pipe dream of self-insight, if possible come to know 'everything' about him- or herself and (relevant) others. This then stands in the way of routine self-delusions – otherwise the soap would lack any kind of dramaturgic tension. Only in ever-repeated loops of talk can an actor finally be convinced that he for a long time has been in love. He has not wanted to recognize it, the others have already known for a long time, and he realizes it himself. Until the next internal mystery turns up ...

The pressure for introspection is not without consequences for self-valuation. There is a considerable need for criteria of an authentic, ego-directed self-valuation. At the same time the mainstream popular culture supply of images of grandiosity and perfection is both invading and importunate. Often, for the individual, unfiltered notions of grandiosity stand without any mediation by negative valuations of personal skills. The notions of grandiosity limit the psychological possibilities of making intermediate aims of efforts and needs attainable and of coping with the lack of grandiosity of such aims. The consequences are internal conflicts of shame, a strong sensitivity to experiences of offence and disregard and permanent occupation with the precarious question of how one is then regarded 'in the eyes of others'.

To protect themselves from such risks of the self-valuation, many individuals develop mechanisms of avoidance, which in a defensive way helps them escape from the conflict. For teachers, these young people typically appear as doped, deprived or drowsing. The consequences of such avoidance strategies for the teachers mean a strong increase in professional demands, because these young students are very difficult to rouse whenever the teachers try to captivate them.

The core problem can then no more be described in the way that the individual wills something, but cannot realize it. Much more these individuals do not know themselves what they could altogether think of realizing. This means that the core problem is now a nondetermination which can hardly be understood or a weakness lying right down in the basic conditions of self-direction.

I hope that it is possible in this perspective of interpretation to understand that these young people are not very inclined to 'swallow' liberal pedagogical offers of thematic participation or self-motivation in highly individual learning arrangements. For these individuals, the problem is, first of all, that they have to learn what it is to 'demonstrate a will'. It is about the acquisition of motivational competence itself. The problem is not so much about the usage of volition, but about the procurement of volition.

The need for meaning supporting structuring

I have now specified the three earlier-mentioned leitmotifs of changed under-lying convictions in relation to contemporary youth, not relating to a cultural pessimistic diagnosis of decay, but to, I particularly see, the possibilities of a productive learning culture being under a pressure from strong risks:

- the larger space for recourse to preferred content and increased possibilities of not choosing 'unpleasant' content can predispose for a kind of 'self-provincialization' which limits the horizons of the personal world;
- the more liberal development of role management can result in a problem promoting a cumulative-nervous way of behaving;
- sharpened self-observation with increased dependence on the achievement of recognition from others can, in relation to the 'will', mount into so complex premises that it becomes nearly habit to define one's self by the sum of what one will not.

I repeat: this does not mean the end of Western civilization, but rather does mean a regrettable drain of symbolic possibilities, which have been nearby because of the liberalization of everyday life.

An atmosphere of 'post-detraditionalization'

However, it is possible to maintain a desirable gain of liberation in comparison with the earlier authoritarian everyday culture. But with a growing distance from the strong detraditionalization of the 1970s, the habitus consequences of this destructing become an important topic, also in the public discourse. In the meantime, it has become clear that a continued push for the delimiting and destructing processes can hardly be a contemporary solution.

Also, interestingly, the young people rarely any longer express their crises about themselves in terms of wishes for liberation. Rather, they explain themselves in relation to the consequences of liberation and destructuring. Thus their identity work seems not to be centred around problems with too many strict rules and bans or too much repression. Essential wishes are much more about how to remove orientation diffusions and instability.

By 'post-detraditionalization', I refer to a context of experience in which counterbalances of the contexts of destructuring are wanted. In this context, rules and structures of the life world are no longer felt as illegitimate constrictions in any way. Quite opposite, it is my impression that 'counter-desires' for liberation and destructuring have arisen, such as

- counter-desires for stable relations, integration and support and community;
- counter-desires for some kind of shielding in relation to continually being observed by society and authorities, a 'quasi-romantic' secrecy and opaqueness (probably the colossal attraction of Harry Potter or movies like *Lord of the Rings* have to do with this); and
- counter-desires for normative clarity, i.e. distinct rules of orientation, security and barriers, and also for an atmosphere of nonrelativism and fixed boundaries.

Current interest in close structures

A comparison between the current youth generation and the preceding generation could somewhat abstractly be expressed as follows: earlier, an individual, after a (relatively) free childhood, at the commencement of adolescence stepped into a life age in which structures gradually became closer. Or expressed more simply: during youth, almost everything became more serious and strict with increasing age. Today, commencement of adolescence in no way means that the surrounding structures become closer. On the contrary, at the commencement of adolescence, the areas in which one can choose for oneself, make decisions and to a high degree follow one's own partiality increase considerably, i.e. structures become looser. Actually, it can be stated that in the age of adolescence today, we have to do a *double destructuring*. The reorganisation of subjectivity – the big internal psychological 'building site', so to speak – must be managed at the same time as the societal environment also becomes increasingly incalculable and unstable. The biographical timetables are no more unambiguous.

In this connection I must to some degree argue anti-cyclically, i.e. towards a *compensation* of experiences of diffusion, respective of problems due to informalization and destructuring. I find it eminently important that young people can learn by experiences of structures.

In the much noteworthy movie *Rhythm Is It!*, it is shown how so-called problematic young people participate in an aesthetic-social project. Under the instruction of a professional choreographer, they prepare a collective dance version of Stravinsky's *Le Sacre du Printemps*, which is finally to be performed together with the Berlin Symphony Orchestra. As the movie shows, this process is both painful and pleasurable. Again and again some of the young actors at the rehearsals over several weeks reject giving up their own habits. At the beginning of each rehearsal, all the participants are requested to assume a certain start position – they must stand motionless in front of the empty wall and concentrate for a while. As could be expected some of the young thwart this small ritual by talking and fooling around. This leads to repeated clashes and symbolic fights with the choreographer. The self-conceit of the young, according to the obvious interpretation of the choreographer, is so small that they can hardly endure any serious demand. However, he is persistent and sensible, and at the end he is able to persuade them. After serious crises, the rehearsals finally lead to a magnificent performance.

I refer to this example here to illustrate the importance of the *setting* of learning processes. In therapeutic and social-pedagogical contexts, the setting designates the totality of rules and agreements that define and regulate the standard work conditions of a field of action. The rules of the setting fix the orders and bans and also imply the communal definitions of what is normal, agreements of objectives and meaning contexts. Thus, a setting not only has technically regulating functions, but also a supporting, meaning-generating and expressive impact. A setting can contain supporting rituals of recognition of formal and personal differences between the persons who are involved. A setting can ensure and explain specific regulations in different places (e.g. the difference between what is public and what is private). And it can contain ego-supporting borderlines and in this way promote self-reassurance, rule observance and relief of ambivalences.

In the movie *Rhythm Is It!*, precisely the regular frames are both conflict-generating and productively extensive, because they provide a provisional abolition of everyday habits – even when it is about such a modest rule as standing and concentrating in front of the wall before the start of the rehearsals. A perfect artificiality in the design of the situation 'seduces' the young people to engage in the alien situation. Not an approximation to what is already familiar, not a levelling of the difference in relation to everyday routines, but on the contrary, the experience of a small and fixed deviation from the usual is offered. Of course, teachers are not choreographers and obviously educational situations are usually not a preparation for a dance performance. But still, educational situations also contain a factor of staging. And to introduce special 'rules of the play' in various situations of educational work in order to establish new self-understanding may be both stabilizing and stimulating.

A simultaneousness of weakness in decision-making and increased self-observation can lead to the unlucky consequence of connecting to an existing self-fixation. The parole of 'not-wanting' will then, so to speak, be omnipresent. A loosening of such paralyzing self-fixations presupposes a distance to the immediate emotions and taking a personal interest in the topic. In this way we can develop ideals of volition or images of how one's volition could be shaped. The way to do so, as already stated, lies in the ability to create an internal distance or an imagination, which encourages one to 'try out internal possibilities'. This is about increasing an internal communication ability which could further be connected to possible abilities of symbol creation – i.e. to learn to find means of articulation in words or images of the valuing determination of our wishes.

Thus, by a loosening of the habitual self-fixations, it is possible to change the ideals of volition – the ideal images about which relations one wants to develop to one's own volition. I suppose that in this connection, an element of narcissism is inevitable. I call this the 'emotional future II'. By this I mean that to be able to realize a long-term wish – e.g. to learn to play a guitar – there must be a force to set up imaginary intermediate aims. This force is in an internal connection with the imaginative ability to make an image of how good it will feel when I 'have learnt' to play the guitar (future II). The anticipation of this condition of pride and self-satisfaction is nothing but the ability to create an intensive expectancy which is resistant to intermediate frustrations. Between the needs of pride, the stable expectancy and the extension of ego-possibilities, in my opinion, there is a narrow connection. But the extension of ego-possibilities is nothing but an extension of one's own horizon of motivation: one becomes more imaginative concerning how and what one is able to will.

Close structures cannot disregard the load of openness, but make it easier to carry. Anyway, an establishment and a valuing attention of settings would be a kind of counter-attention which could be able to completely relieve the diffusing consequences of the destructuring, informalization and subjectivation.

Chapter 14

The practice of learning

Jean Lave

The American anthropologist Jean Lave is Professor at the University of California, Berkeley. She has studied education and schooling in pre-industrial societies and, through comparisons with the corresponding American conditions, she has become a strong advocate of "practice learning." Most significantly this approach has been formulated in the famous book Situated Learning: Legitimate Peripheral Participation *which she published together with Etienne Wenger in 1991. The following chapter is an extract of Lave's introduction to the anthology* Understanding Practice: Perspectives on Activity and Context, *edited together with Seth Chaiklin and published in 1993 as a kind of programmatic update, reformulation and overview of the learning approach of the Russian cultural-historical and activity theoretical school as developed in the 1930s by Lev Vygotsky and others.*

The problem with "context"

Understanding Practice grew out of the work of a two-part conference in which the participants came together to consider what we initially called "the context problem." All of us were involved in research on socially situated activity. We were concerned about conventional limitations on various approaches to the study of activity. In particular, we wished to explore questions about the "socially constituted world" – the context of socially situated activity – that our work often seemed merely to take for granted.

I had tried in previous research to understand how math activity in grocery stores involved being "in" the "store," walking up and down "aisles," looking at "shelves" full of cans, bottles, packages, and jars of food and other commodities. My analyses were about shoppers' activities, sometimes together, and about the relations between these activities and the distractingly material, historically constituted, subjectively selective character of space–time relations and their meaning. Both Seth Chaiklin and I knew that other people conceived of the problem in quite different terms. We decided to hold a collective inquiry into these old, but still perplexing questions.

But why would a diverse group of students of the human condition participate over months, and even years, to try to understand each other's perspective? Seth

Chaiklin and I initially proposed the following rationale: Theories of situated everyday practice insist that persons acting and the social world of activity cannot be separated. This creates a dilemma: Research on everyday practice typically focuses on the activities of persons acting, although there is agreement that such phenomena cannot be analyzed in isolation from the socially material world of that activity. But less attention has been given to the difficult task of conceptualizing *relations* between persons acting and the social world. Nor has there been sufficient attention to rethinking the "social world of activity" in relational terms. Together, these constitute the problem of context.

The participants in the conference agreed to this set of priorities, with the obvious proviso that relational concepts of the social world should not be explored in isolation from conceptions of persons acting and interacting and their activities. That proviso gradually took on a more central meaning and, as a result, our conception of the common task crystallized into a double focus – on context and, to our surprise, learning. A focus on one provided occasions on which to consider the other. If context is viewed as a social world constituted in relation with persons acting, both context and activity seem inescapably flexible and changing. And thus characterized, changing participation and understanding in practice – the problem of learning – cannot help but become central as well.

It is difficult, when looking closely at everyday activity, to avoid the conclusion that learning is ubiquitous in ongoing activity, though often unrecognized as such. Situated activity always involves changes in knowledge and action, and "changes in knowledge and action" are central to what we mean by "learning." It is not the case that the world consists of newcomers who drop unaccompanied into unpeopled problem spaces. People in activity are skillful at, and are more often than not engaged in, helping each other to participate in changing ways in a changing world. So in describing and analyzing people's involvement in practical action in the world, even those authors whose work generally would be least identified with educational foci (e.g. Suchman and Trigg, 1993; Keller and Keller, 1993) are in effect analyzing peoples' engagement in *learning*. We have come to the conclusion, as McDermott (1993) suggests, that there is no such thing as "learning" *sui generis*, but only changing participation in the culturally designed settings of everyday life. Or, to put it the other way around, participation in everyday life may be thought of as a process of changing understanding in practice, that is, as learning.

Learning became one focus of our work, even where unintended, partly because of our concern with everyday activity as social and historical process and with the improvisational, future-creating character of mundane practice; partly, also, because those of us whose research has touched on educational questions have come to insist on denaturalizing the social processes that unfold within educational institutions by turning them into analytic objects. So whether the researchers have approached the problem of context through its temporal dimension, as activity (or practice), or whether they have looked at institutions of learning as contexts, learning has become a central issue.

The discussion of context suggests a problem, however: Conventional theories of learning and schooling appeal to the decontextualized character of some knowledge and forms of knowledge transmission, whereas in a theory of situated activity, "decontextualized learning activity" is a contradiction in terms. These two very different ways of conceiving of learning are hardly compatible. Nonetheless, a belief that the world is divided into contextualized and decontextualized phenomena is not merely an academic speculation that can be discarded when found theoretically inadequate or incomplete.

Craftwork learning and social production

Traditionally, learning researchers have studied learning as if it were a process contained in the mind of the learner and have ignored the lived-in world. This disjuncture, which ratifies a dichotomy of mind and body, sidetracks or derails the question of how to construct a theory that *encompasses* mind and lived-in world. It is not enough to say that some designated cognitive theory of learning could be *amended* by adding a theory of "situation," for this raises crucial questions about the compatibility of particular theories (cf. Soviet psychologists' discussion of the "match" between psychologies and sociologies in the 1920s: Davydov and Radzhikovskii, 1985, p. 49). Nor is it sufficient to pursue a principled account of situated activity armed only with a theory of cognition and good intentions. Without a theoretical conception of the social world one cannot analyze activity *in situ*. A more promising alternative lies in treating relations among person, activity, and situation, as they are *given* in social practice, itself viewed as a single encompassing theoretical entity. It is possible to detect such a trend in most if not all of the research traditions represented in *Understanding Practice* – the chapters are working toward a more inclusive, intensive development of the socially situated character of activity in theoretically consistent terms.

Theories of situated activity do not separate action, thought, feeling, and value and their collective, cultural-historical forms of located, interested, conflictual, meaningful activity. Traditional cognitive theory is "distanced from experience" and divides the learning mind from the world. This "release" from the narrow confines of body and immediate experience is rejected on varied grounds in the chapters collected in *Understanding Practice* in favor of more complex relations between person and world. The idea of learning as cognitive acquisition – whether of facts, knowledge, problem-solving strategies, or metacognitive skills – seems to dissolve when learning is conceived of as the construction of present versions of past experience for several persons acting together (e.g. Hutchins, 1993). And when scientific practice is viewed as just another everyday practice (e.g. Lave, 1988), it is clear that theories of "situated activity" provide different perspectives on "learning" and its "contexts."

Participants in the conference agreed, on the whole, on four premises concerning knowledge and learning in practice:

1 Knowledge always undergoes construction and transformation in use.
2 Learning is an integral aspect of activity in and with the world at all times. That learning occurs is not problematic.
3 What is learned is always complexly problematic.
4 Acquisition of knowledge is not a simple matter of taking in knowledge; rather, things assumed to be natural categories, such as "bodies of knowledge," "learners," and "cultural transmission," require reconceptualization as cultural, social products.

It should be said that the conceptions of craftwork in most of the chapters bear little resemblance to the small-scale problem-solving tasks typical of cognitive learning research: Forging a cooking utensil or taking part in the work of a national university examination committee are substantial, meaningful forms of activity. In all cases the work described takes on meaning from its broader interconnections with(in) other activity systems.

Relations with theory past: Some paradoxes and silences of cognitive theory

Silences and paradoxes are generated in any theoretical problematic: questions that cannot be asked and issues for which no principled resolution is possible. At least four such issues trouble traditional cognitive theory. They concern the conventional divisions between learning and what is not (supposed to be) learning. Resolutions to these difficulties have been anticipated in the four premises concerning knowledge and learning in practice mentioned earlier. The problems include, first, an assumed division between learning and other kinds of activity. Second, both the invention and reinvention of knowledge are difficult problems for cognitive theory if learning is viewed as a matter of acquiring existing knowledge. Third, cognitive theory assumes universal processes of learning and the homogeneous character of knowledge and of learners (save in quantity or capacity). This makes it difficult to account for the richly varied participants and projects in any situation of learning. Finally, there is a problem of reconceptualizing the meaning of erroneous, mistaken understanding in a heterogeneous world.

First, how is "learning" to be distinguished from human activity as such? Within cognitive theories it has been assumed that learning and development are distinctive processes, not to be confused with the more general category of human activity. This involves two theoretical claims that are in question here: One is that actors' relations with knowledge-in-activity are static and do not change except when subject to special periods of "learning" or "development." The other is that institutional arrangements for inculcating knowledge *are* the necessary, special circumstances for learning, separate from everyday practices. The difference may be at heart a very deep epistemological one, between a view of knowledge as a collection of real entities, located in heads, and of learning as a process of internalizing them, versus a view of knowing and learning as engagement in changing processes of human activity. In the latter case, "knowledge" becomes a complex and problematic concept, whereas in the former it is "learning" that is problematic.

A second, related issue concerns the narrow focus of learning theories on the transmission of existing knowledge, while remaining silent about the invention of new knowledge in practice. Engeström (1987) argues that this is a central lacuna in contemporary learning theory. Certainly, any simple assumption that *transmission* or *transfer* or *internalization* are apt descriptors for the circulation of knowledge in society faces the difficulty that they imply *uniformity* of knowledge. They do not acknowledge the fundamental imprint of interested parties, multiple activities, and different goals and circumstances on what constitutes "knowing" on a given occasion or across a multitude of interrelated events. These terms imply that humans engage first and foremost in the reproduction of given knowledge rather than in the production of knowledgeability as a flexible process of engagement with the world. Engeström's conceptualization of how people learn to do things that have not been done before elaborates the idea that zones of proximal development are collective, rather than individual, phenomena and that "the new" is a collective invention in the face of felt dilemmas and contradictions that impede ongoing activity and impel movement and change.

Further, part of what it means to engage in learning activity is extending what one knows beyond the immediate situation, rather than involuting one's understanding "metacognitively" by thinking about one's own cognitive processes. Critical psychologists of the Berlin school (e.g. Dreier, 1991; Holzkamp, 1983) insist on the importance of a distinction between experiencing or knowing the immediate circumstances ("interpretive thinking," "restricted action") and processes of thinking beyond and about the immediate situation in more general terms ("comprehensive thinking," "extended, generalized action"). Together, in a dialectical process by which each helps to generate the other, they produce new understanding (see Wenger, 1991).

Doing and knowing are inventive in another sense: They are open-ended processes of improvisation with the social, material, and experiential resources at hand. Keller and Keller's research illustrates this: The blacksmith's practices as he creates a skimming spoon draw on rich resources of experience, his own and that of other people, present and past. But his understanding of the skimmer also emerges in the forging process. He does not know what it will be until it is finished. At one point he spreads one section of the spoon handle for the second time but goes too far and, in evaluating the work, finds it necessary to reduce the width of the handle again. "It is as though he has to cross a boundary in order to discover the appropriate limits of the design" (Keller and Keller, 1993).

The work of researchers in artificial intelligence appears to have the same character: Suchman and Trigg (1993) describe it as "a skilled improvisation, organized in orderly ways that are designed to maintain a lively openness to the possibilities that the materials at hand present." And "analyses of situated action ... point to the contingencies of practical action on which logic in use, including the production and use of scenarios and formalisms, inevitably and in every instance relies."

Fuhrer (1993) emphasizes the varying emotional effects of the improvisational character of activity. These effects are perhaps most intensely felt by newcomers, but he equates newcomers' predicaments with those of learners in general. He insists that in addition to cognitive and environmental dimensions, there is an emotional dimension to all learning. He argues that:

> to some degree, all individual actions within everyday settings, especially those of newcomers, are somewhat discrepant from what is expected; the settings change continuously. Most emotions within social situations, such as embarrassment, audience anxiety, shyness, or shame, follow such discrepancies, just because these discrepancies produce visceral arousal. And it is the combination of that arousal with an ongoing evaluative cognition that produces the subjective experience of an emotion.

Given these considerations, Fuhrer raises the question of how people manage and coordinate "the various actions that arise from cognitive, social, and environmental demands or goals." Old-timers as well as newcomers try to carry out the usual activities in given settings, but they are also trying to address many other goals, among which are impression management and "developing interpersonal relations to other setting inhabitants ... Thus the newcomers simultaneously pursue several goals and therefore they may simultaneously perform different actions."

The third issue, the assumed homogeneity of actors, goals, motives, and activity itself, is challenged in many chapters, replaced with quite different assumptions that emphasize their heterogeneity. I believe this view is new to discussions of learning. It derives from an intense focus on the multiplicity of actors engaged in activity together and on the interdependencies, conflicts, and relations of power so produced. These views are elaborated in *Understanding Practice* by several authors: Keller and Keller (1993) argue that "the goal of production is not monolithic but multifaceted ... based on considerations aesthetic, stylistic, functional, procedural, financial, and academic as well as conceptions of self and other, and material conditions of work." Dreier (1993) proposes that "different participants' interpretations are based on different contextual social positions with inherent differences in possibilities, interests, and perspectives on conflicts arising from different locations." Suchman and Trigg (1993) describe artificial intelligence research as a socially organized process of craftsmanship consisting of "the crafting together of a complex machinery made of heterogeneous materials, mobilized in the service of developing a theory of mind." And McDermott (1993) proposes that "by institutional arrangements, we must consider everything from the most local level of the classroom to the more inclusive level of inequities throughout the political economy (preferably from both ends of the continuum at the same time)." These statements refer to a wide variety of relations, but each challenges research on knowing and learning that depends implicitly on a homogeneity of community, culture, participants, their motives, and the meaning of events.

The heterogeneous, multifocal character of situated activity implies that conflict is a ubiquitous aspect of human existence. This follows if we assume that people in the same situation, people who are helping to constitute "a situation" together, know different things and speak with different interests and experience from different social locations. Suddenly assumptions concerning the uniformity of opinion, knowledge, and belief become, on the one hand, matters of common historical tradition and complexly shared relations with larger societal forces (whatever these might mean – now an important question) and, on the other hand, matters of imposed conformity and symbolic violence. Analysis focused on conflictual practices of changing understanding in activity is not so likely to concentrate on the truth or error of some knowledge claim. It is more likely to explore disagreements over what is relevant; whether, and how much, something is worth knowing and doing; what to make of ambiguous circumstances; what is convenient for whom; what to do next when one does not know what to expect; and who cares most about what. There are always conflicts of power, so mislearning cannot be understood independently of someone imposing her or his view. There is, of course, and at the same time, much uniformity and agreement in the world. The perspectives represented here differ about whether this is always, or only much of the time, a matter of one party imposing assent, subtly or otherwise, on others.

The fourth and final issue concerns "failure to learn." In mainstream theorizing about learning, this is commonly assumed to result from the inability or refusal on the part of an individual to engage in something called "learning." The alternative view explored earlier is that not-learning and "failure" identities are active normal social locations and processes. The latter generates further questions, however: If failure is a socially arranged identity, what is left to be said about the making of "errors"? Given that several of the authors provide novel construals of failure to learn, question the meaning of "consensus," and call attention to the deficiencies of claims that knowing unfolds without conflict and without engaging the interests of involved participants, does the term *error* still have meaning? The answer depends on whose socially positioned point of view is adopted, and on historically and socially situated conceptions of erroneous action and belief. Several of the chapters in *Understanding Practice* develop powerful ways of conceptualizing socially, historically situated nonlearning or mislearning. They discuss nonlearning activities that occur when embarrassment is too great or that result from anxiety, from the social delegitimation of learning or the learner, and from the retarding effects of denying learners access to connections between immediate appearances and broader, deeper social forces, or to concrete interrelations within and across situations (e.g. Fuhrer, 1993; Levine, 1993). Mehan explores the discoordination of voices in interactions between school psychologist, teacher, and parent, who speak in different "languages" – psychological, sociological, and historical – and between physicians and patients. Engeström (1987) locates unproductive encounters between patients and physicians in the mismatch among historically engendered discourses – thus, in practice, among the biomedical and psychosocial registers or voices the physician and patient use for communicating about medical issues.

Hutchins's analysis (1993) raises questions about the location of error-making in historical systems of activity and in relations among participants. He describes what it is possible for novice navigators to learn in practice in terms of task partitioning, instruments, lines of communication, and limitations and openness of access for observing others, their interactions, and tools. He argues that these define the portion of the task environment that is available as a learning context to each task performer – this constitutes the performer's "horizon of observability." The density of error correction (which helps to make learning possible) depends on the contours of this horizon.

In sum, the assumptions proposed here amount to a preliminary account of what is meant by *situated learning*. Knowledgeability is routinely in a state of change rather than stasis, in the medium of socially, culturally, and historically ongoing systems of activity, involving people who are related in multiple and heterogeneous ways, whose social locations, interests, reasons, and subjective possibilities are different, and who improvise struggles in situated ways with each other over the value of particular definitions of the situation, in both immediate and comprehensive terms, and for whom the production of failure is as much a part of routine collective activity as the production of average, ordinary knowledgeability.

References

Davydov, V. V. and Radzhikovskii, L. A. (1985). Vygotsky's theory and the activity-oriented approach in psychology. In J. V. Wertsch (Ed.), *Culture, communication, and cognition: Vygotskian perspectives* (pp. 35–65). Cambridge, UK: Cambridge University Press.

Dreier, O. (1991). Client interests and possibilities in psychotherapy. In C.W. Tolman and W. Maiers (Eds.), *Critical psychology: Contributions to an historical science of the subject* (pp. 196–211). Cambridge, UK: Cambridge University Press.

Dreier, O. (1993). Re-searching psychotherapeutic practice. In S. Chaiklin and J. Lave (Eds.), *Understanding practice: Perspectives on activity and context*. Cambridge, UK: Cambridge University Press.

Engeström, Y. (1987). *Learning by expanding: An activity-theoretical approach to developmental research*. Helsinki: Orienta-Konsultit.

Fuhrer, U. (1993). Behaviour setting analysis of situated learning: The case of newcomers. In S. Chaiklin and J. Lave (Eds.), *Understanding practice: Perspectives on activity and context*. Cambridge, UK: Cambridge University Press.

Holzkamp, K. (1983). *Grundlegung der Psychologie* [Foundations of psychology]. Frankfurt a.M.: Campus.

Hutchins, E. (1993). Learning to navigate. In S. Chaiklin and J. Lave (Eds.), *Understanding practice: Perspectives on activity and context*. Cambridge, UK: Cambridge University Press.

Keller, C. and Keller, J.D. (1993). Thinking and acting with iron. In S. Chaiklin and J. Lave (Eds.), *Understanding practice: Perspectives on activity and context*. Cambridge, UK: Cambridge University Press.

Lave, J. (1988). *Cognition in practice: Mind, mathematics and culture in everyday life*. Cambridge, UK: Cambridge University Press.

Lave, J. and Wenger, E. (1991). *Situated learning: Legitimate peripheral participation*. Cambridge, UK: Cambridge University Press.

Levine, H.G. (1993). Context and scaffolding in developmental studies of mother–child problem-solving dyads. In S. Chaiklin and J. Lave (Eds.), *Understanding practice: Perspectives on activity and context*. Cambridge, UK: Cambridge University Press.

McDermott, R.P. (1993). The acquisition of a child by a learning disability. In S. Chaiklin and J. Lave (Eds.), *Understanding practice: Perspectives on activity and context*. Cambridge, UK: Cambridge University Press.

Suchman, L.A. and Trigg, R.H. (1993). Artificial intelligence as craftwork. In S. Chaiklin and J. Lave (Eds.), *Understanding practice: Perspectives on activity and context*. Cambridge, UK: Cambridge University Press.

Wenger, E. (1991). *Toward a theory of cultural transparency: Elements of a social discourse of the visible and the invisible*. Unpublished doctoral dissertation, University of California, Irvine.

Chapter 15

A social theory of learning

Etienne Wenger

American Etienne Wenger was born in the French-speaking part of Switzerland and, as a young man, he lived in Hong Kong for three years. Later he studied computer science in Switzerland and the US, finishing by writing a dissertation on artificial intelligence. For ten years he was then a researcher at the Institute for Research on Learning in Palo Alto, California, and it was by the end of this period that he, together with Jean Lave, published the famous book Situated Learning: Legitimate Peripheral Participation *in 1991. This book also launched the concept of "communities of practice" as the environment of important learning, a term Wenger cemented in 1998 and elaborated further in his book* Communities of Practice: Learning, meaning, and identity. *The following chapter is made up of the more programmatic part of the introduction to that book and a note in which Wenger gives an account of his understanding of other important approaches to learning.*

Introduction

Our institutions, to the extent that they address issues of learning explicitly, are largely based on the assumption that learning is an individual process, that it has a beginning and an end, that it is best separated from the rest of our activities, and that it is the result of teaching. Hence we arrange classrooms where students – free from the distractions of their participation in the outside world – can pay attention to a teacher or focus on exercises. We design computer-based training programs that walk students through individualized sessions covering reams of information and drill practice. To assess learning, we use tests with which students struggle in one-on-one combat, where knowledge must be demonstrated out of context, and where collaborating is considered cheating. As a result, much of our institutionalized teaching and training is perceived by would-be learners as irrelevant, and most of us come out of this treatment feeling that learning is boring and arduous, and that we are not really cut out for it.

So, what if we adopted a different perspective, one that placed learning in the context of our lived experience of participation in the world? What if we assumed that learning is as much a part of our human nature as eating or sleeping, that it is both life-sustaining and inevitable, and that – given a chance – we are quite good at it? And what if, in addition, we assumed that learning is, in its essence, a fundamentally social phenomenon, reflecting our own deeply social nature as human beings capable of knowing? What kind of understanding would such a perspective yield on how learning takes place and on what is required to support it? In this chapter, I will try to develop such a perspective.

A conceptual perspective: theory and practice

There are many different kinds of learning theory. Each emphasizes different aspects of learning, and each is therefore useful for different purposes. To some extent these differences in emphasis reflect a deliberate focus on a slice of the multidimensional problem of learning, and to some extent they reflect more fundamental differences in assumptions about the nature of knowledge, knowing, and knowers, and consequently about what matters in learning. (For those who are interested, a number of such theories with a brief description of their focus are listed in a note at the end of this chapter.)

The kind of social theory of learning I propose is not a replacement for other theories of learning that address different aspects of the problem. But it does have its own set of assumptions and its own focus. Within this context, it does constitute a coherent level of analysis; it does yield a conceptual framework from which to derive a consistent set of general principles and recommendations for understanding and enabling learning.

My assumptions as to what matters about learning and as to the nature of knowledge, knowing, and knowers can be succinctly summarized as follows. I start with four premises:

*   We are social beings. Far from being trivially true, this fact is a central aspect of learning.
*   Knowledge is a matter of competence with respect to valued enterprises – such as singing in tune, discovering scientific facts, fixing machines, writing poetry, being convivial, growing up as a boy or a girl, and so forth.
*   Knowing is a matter of participating in the pursuit of such enterprises, that is, of active engagement in the world.
*   Meaning – our ability to experience the world and our engagement with it as meaningful – is ultimately what learning is to produce.

As a reflection of these assumptions, the primary focus of this theory is on learning as social participation. Participation here refers not just to local events of engagement in certain activities with certain people, but to a more encompassing process of being active participants in the *practices* of social communities and constructing *identities* in relation to these communities. Participating in a playground clique or in a work team, for instance, is both

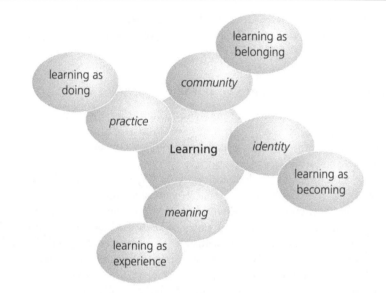

Figure 15.1 Components of a social theory of learning: an initial inventory.

a kind of action and a form of belonging. Such participation shapes not only what we do, but also who we are and how we interpret what we do.

A social theory of learning must therefore integrate the components necessary to characterize social participation as a process of learning and of knowing. These components, shown in Figure 15.1, include the following:

- *meaning:* a way of talking about our (changing) ability – individually and collectively – to experience our life and the world as meaningful;
- *practice:* a way of talking about the shared historical and social resources, frameworks, and perspectives that can sustain mutual engagement in action;
- *community:* a way of talking about the social configurations in which our enterprises are defined as worth pursuing and our participation is recognizable as competence;
- *identity:* a way of talking about how learning changes who we are and creates personal histories of becoming in the context of our communities.

Clearly, these elements are deeply interconnected and mutually defining. In fact, looking at Figure 15.1, you could switch any of the four peripheral components with learning, place it in the center as the primary focus, and the figure would still make sense.

Therefore, when I use the concept of "community of practice" in the title of the book, I really use it as a point of entry into a broader conceptual framework of which it is a constitutive element. The analytical power of the concept lies precisely in that it integrates the components of Figure 15.1 while referring to a familiar experience.

Communities of practice are everywhere

We all belong to communities of practice. At home, at work, at school, in our hobbies – we belong to several communities of practice at any given time. And the communities of practice to which we belong change over the course of our lives. In fact, communities of practice are everywhere.

Families struggle to establish an habitable way of life. They develop their own practices, routines, rituals, artifacts, symbols, conventions, stories, and histories. Family members hate each other and they love each other; they agree and they disagree. They do what it takes to keep going. Even when families fall apart, members create ways of dealing with each other. Surviving together is an important enterprise, whether surviving consists of the search for food and shelter or of the quest for a viable identity.

Workers organize their lives with their immediate colleagues and customers to get their jobs done. In doing so, they develop or preserve a sense of themselves they can live with, have some fun, and fulfill the requirements of their employers and clients. No matter what their official job description may be, they create a practice to do what needs to be done. Although workers may be contractually employed by a large institution, in day-to-day practice they work with – and, in a sense, for – a much smaller set of people and communities.

Students go to school and, as they come together to deal in their own fashion with the agenda of the imposing institution and the unsettling mysteries of youth, communities of practice sprout everywhere – in the classroom as well as on the playground, officially or in the cracks. And in spite of curriculum, discipline, and exhortation, the learning that is most personally transformative turns out to be the learning that involves membership in these communities of practice.

In garages, bands rehearse the same songs for yet another wedding gig. In attics, ham radio enthusiasts become part of worldwide clusters of communicators. In the back rooms of churches, recovering alcoholics go to their weekly meetings to find the courage to remain sober. In laboratories, scientists correspond with colleagues, near and far, in order to advance their inquiries. Across a worldwide web of computers, people congregate in virtual spaces and develop shared ways of pursuing their common interests. In offices, computer users count on each other to cope with the intricacies of obscure systems. In neighborhoods, youths gang together to configure their life on the street and their sense of themselves.

Communities of practice are an integral part of our daily lives. They are so informal and so pervasive that they rarely come into explicit focus, but for the same reasons they are also quite familiar. Although the term may be new, the experience is not. Most communities of practice do not have a name and do not issue membership cards. Yet, if we care to consider our own life from that perspective for a moment, we can all construct a fairly good picture of the communities of practice we belong to now, those we belonged to in the past, and those we would like to belong to in the future. We also have a fairly good idea of who belongs to our communities of practice and why, even though membership is rarely made explicit on a roster or a checklist of qualifying criteria. Furthermore, we can probably distinguish a few communities of practice in which we are core members from a larger number of communities in which we have a more peripheral kind of membership.

In all these ways, the concept of community of practice is not unfamiliar. By exploring it more systematically, I mean only to sharpen it, to make it more useful as a thinking tool. Toward this end, its familiarity will serve me well. Articulating a familiar phenomenon is a chance to push our intuitions: to deepen and expand them, to examine and rethink them. The perspective that results is not foreign, yet it can shed new light on our world. In this sense, the concept of community of practice is neither new nor old. It has both the eye-opening character of novelty and the forgotten familiarity of obviousness – but perhaps that is the mark of our most useful insights.

Rethinking learning

Placing the focus on participation has broad implications for what it takes to understand and support learning:

* For *individuals*, it means that learning is an issue of engaging in and contributing to the practices of their communities.
* For *communities*, it means that learning is an issue of refining their practice and ensuring new generations of members.
* For *organizations*, it means that learning is an issue of sustaining the interconnected communities of practice through which an organization knows what it knows and thus becomes effective and valuable as an organization.

Learning in this sense is not a separate activity. It is not something we do when we do nothing else or stop doing when we do something else. There are times in our lives when learning is intensified: when situations shake our sense of familiarity, when we are challenged beyond our ability to respond, when we wish to engage in new practices and seek to join new communities. There are also times when society explicitly places us in situations where the issue of learning becomes problematic and requires our focus: we attend classes, memorize, take exams, and receive a diploma. And there are times when learning gels: an infant utters a first word, we have a sudden insight when someone's remark provides a missing link, we are finally recognized as a full member of a community. But situations that bring learning into focus are not necessarily those in which we learn most, or most deeply. The events of learning we can point to are perhaps more like volcanic eruptions whose fiery bursts reveal for one dramatic moment the ongoing labor of the earth. Learning is something we can assume – whether we see it or not, whether we like the way it goes or not, whether what we are learning is to repeat the past or to shake it off. Even failing to learn what is expected in a given situation usually involves learning something else instead.

For many of us, the concept of learning immediately conjures up images of classrooms, training sessions, teachers, textbooks, homework, and exercises. Yet in our experience, learning is an integral part of our everyday lives. It is part of our participation in our communities and organizations. The problem is not that we do not know this, but rather that we do not have very systematic ways of talking about this familiar experience. Even though the topic of *Communities of Practice* covers mostly things that everybody knows in some ways, having a systematic vocabulary to talk about it does make a difference. An adequate vocabulary is important because the concepts we use to make sense of the world direct both our perception and our actions. We pay attention to what we expect to see, we hear what we can place in our understanding, and we act according to our worldviews.

Although learning can be assumed to take place, modern societies have come to see it as a topic of concern – in all sorts of ways and for a host of different reasons. We develop national curriculums, ambitious corporate training programs, complex schooling systems. We wish to cause learning, to take charge of it, direct it, accelerate it, demand it, or even simply stop getting in the way of it. In any case, we want to do something about it. Therefore, our perspectives on learning matter: what we think about learning influences where we recognize learning, as well as what we do when we decide that we must do something about it – as individuals, as communities, and as organizations.

If we proceed without reflecting on our fundamental assumptions about the nature of learning, we run an increasing risk that our conceptions will have misleading ramifications. In a world that is changing and becoming more complexly interconnected at an accelerating pace, concerns about learning are certainly justified. But perhaps more than learning itself, it is our *conception* of learning that needs urgent attention when we choose to meddle with it on the scale on which we do today. Indeed, the more we concern ourselves with any kind of design, the more profound are the effects of our discourses on the topic we want to address. The farther you aim, the more an initial error matters. As we become more ambitious in attempts to organize our lives and our environment, the implications of our perspectives, theories, and beliefs extend further. As we take more responsibility for our future on larger and larger scales, it becomes more imperative that we reflect on the perspectives that inform our enterprises. A key implication of our attempts to organize learning is that we must become reflective with regard to our own discourses of learning and to their effects on the ways we design for learning. By proposing a framework that considers learning in social terms, I hope to contribute to this urgent need for reflection and rethinking.

The practicality of theory

A perspective is not a recipe; it does not tell you just what to do. Rather, it acts as a guide about what to pay attention to, what difficulties to expect, and how to approach problems.

- If we believe, for instance, that knowledge consists of pieces of information explicitly stored in the brain, then it makes sense to package this information in well-designed units, to assemble prospective recipients of this information in a classroom where they are perfectly still and isolated from any distraction, and to deliver this information to them as succinctly and articulately as possible. From that perspective, what has come to stand for the epitome of a learning event makes sense: a teacher lecturing a class, whether in a school, in a corporate training center, or in the back room of a library. But if we believe that information stored in explicit ways is only a small part of knowing, and that knowing involves primarily active participation in social communities, then the traditional format does not look so productive. What does look promising are inventive ways of engaging students in meaningful practices, of providing access to resources that enhance their participation, of opening their horizons so they can put themselves on learning trajectories they can identify with, and of involving them in actions, discussions, and reflections that make a difference to the communities that they value.

- Similarly, if we believe that productive people in organizations are the diligent implementers of organizational processes and that the key to organizational performance is therefore the definition of increasingly more efficient and detailed processes by which people's actions are prescribed, then it makes sense to engineer and re-engineer these processes in abstract ways and then roll them out for implementation. But if we believe that people in organizations contribute to organizational goals by participating inventively in practices that can never be fully captured by institutionalized processes, then we will minimize prescription, suspecting that too much of it discourages the very inventiveness that makes practices effective. We will have to make sure that our organizations are contexts within which the communities that develop these practices may prosper. We will have to value the work of community building and make sure that participants have access to the resources necessary to learn what they need to learn in order to take actions and make decisions that fully engage their own knowledgeability.

If all this seems like common sense, then we must ask ourselves why our institutions so often seem not merely to fail to bring about these outcomes but to work against them with a relentless zeal. Of course, some of the blame can justifiably be attributed to conflicts of interest, power struggles, and even human wickedness. But that is too simple an answer and unnecessarily pessimistic. We must also remember that our institutions are designs and that our designs are hostage to our understanding, perspectives, and theories. In this sense, our theories are very practical because they frame not just the ways we act, but also – and perhaps most importantly when design involves social systems – the ways we justify our actions to ourselves and to each other. In an institutional context, it is difficult to act without justifying your actions in the discourse of the institution.

A social theory of learning is therefore not exclusively an academic enterprise. While its perspective can indeed inform our academic investigations, it is also relevant to our daily actions, our policies, and the technical, organizational, and educational systems we design. A new conceptual framework for thinking about learning is thus of value not only to theorists but to all of us – teachers, students, parents, youths, spouses, health practitioners, patients, managers, workers, policy makers, citizens – who in one way or another must take steps to foster learning (our own and that of others) in our relationships, our communities, and our organizations. In this spirit, *Communities of Practice* is written with both the theoretician and the practitioner in mind.

Note

I am not claiming that a social perspective of the sort proposed here says everything there is to say about learning. It takes for granted the biological, neurophysiological, cultural, linguistic, and historical developments that have made our human experience possible. Nor do I make any sweeping claim that the assumptions that underlie my approach are incompatible with those of other theories. There is no room here to go into very much detail, but for contrast it is useful to mention the themes and pedagogical focus of some other theories in order to sketch the landscape in which this perspective is situated.

Learning is a natural concern for students of *neurological* functions.

- Neurophysiological theories focus on the biological mechanisms of learning. They are informative about physiological limits and rhythms and about issues of stimulation and optimization of memory processes (Edelman 1993; Sylwester 1995).

Learning has traditionally been the province of *psychological* theories.

- *Behaviorist* theories focus on behavior modification via stimulus-response pairs and selective reinforcement. Their pedagogical focus is on control and adaptive response. Because they completely ignore issues of meaning, their usefulness lies in cases where addressing issues of social meaning is made impossible or is not relevant, such as automatisms, severe social dysfunctionality, or animal training (Skinner 1974).

- *Cognitive* theories focus on internal cognitive structures and view learning as transformations in these cognitive structures. Their pedagogical focus is on the processing and transmission of information through communication, explanation, recombination, contrast, inference, and problem solving. They are useful for designing sequences of conceptual material that build upon existing information structures. (Anderson 1983; Wenger 1987; Hutchins 1995).

- *Constructivist* theories focus on the processes by which learners build their own mental structures when interacting with an environment. Their pedagogical focus is task-oriented. They favor hands-on, self-directed activities oriented towards design and discovery. They are useful for structuring learning environments, such as simulated worlds, so as to afford the construction of certain conceptual structures through engagement in self-directed tasks (Piaget 1954; Papert 1980).

- *Social learning* theories take social interactions into account, but still from a primarily psychological perspective. They place the emphasis on interpersonal relations involving imitation and modeling, and thus focus on the study of cognitive processes by which observation can become a source of learning. They are useful for understanding the detailed information-processing mechanisms by which social interactions affect behavior (Bandura 1977).

Some theories are moving away from an exclusively psychological approach, but with a different focus from mine.

- *Activity* theories focus on the structure of activities as historically constituted entities. Their pedagogical focus is on bridging the gap between the historical state of an activity and the developmental stage of a person with respect to that activity – for instance, the gap between the current state of a language and a child's ability to speak that language. The purpose is to define a "zone of proximal development" in which learners who receive help can perform an activity they would not be able to perform by themselves (Vygotsky 1934; Wertsch 1985; Engeström 1987).

- *Socialization* theories focus on the acquisition of membership by newcomers within a functionalist framework where acquiring membership is defined as internalizing the norms of a social group (Parsons 1962). As I argue, there is a subtle difference between imitation or the internalization of norms by individuals and the construction of identities within communities of practice.

- *Organizational* theories concern themselves both with the ways individuals learn in organizational contexts and with the ways in which organizations can be said to learn as organizations. Their pedagogical focus is on organizational systems, structures, and politics and on institutional forms of memory (Argyris and Schön 1978; Senge 1990; Brown 1991; Brown and Duguid 1991; Hock 1995; Leonard-Barton 1995; Nonaka and Takeuchi 1995; Snyder 1996).

References

Anderson, J.R. (1983). *The Architecture of Cognition.* Cambridge, MA: Harvard University Press.
Argyris, C. and Schön, D.A. (1978). *Organizational Learning: A Theory of Action Perspective.* Reading, MA: Addison-Wesley.
Bandura, A. (1977). *Social Learning Theory.* Englewood Cliffs, NJ: Prentice-Hall.
Brown, J.S. (1991). Research that reinvents the corporation. *Harvard Business Review,* Jan.–Feb., pp. 102–11.
Brown, J.S. and Duguid, P. (1991). Organizational learning and communities-of-practice: Toward a unified view of working, learning, and innovation. *Organization Science,* 2(1): pp. 40–57.
Edelman, G. (1993). *Bright Air, Brilliant Fire: On the Matter of the Mind.* New York: Basic Books.
Engeström, Y. (1987): *Learning by Expanding: An Activity-Theoretical Approach to Developmental Research.* Helsinki: Orienta-Konsultit.
Hock, D.W. (1995). The chaordic century: The rise of enabling organizations. Governors State University Consortium and The South Metropolitan College/University Consortium, University Park, IL.
Hutchins, E. (1995). *Cognition in the Wild.* Cambridge, MA: MIT Press.
Leonard-Barton, D. (1995). *Wellsprings of Knowledge: Building and Sustaining the Sources of Innovation.* Boston: Harvard Business School Press.
Nonaka, I. and Takeuchi, H. (1995). *The Knowledge-Creating Company: How Japanese Companies Create the Dynamics of Innovation.* New York: Oxford University Press.
Papert, S. (1980). *Mindstorms.* New York: Basic Books.
Parsons, T. (1962). *The Structure of Social Action.* New York: Free Press.
Piaget, J. (1954). *The Construction of Reality in the Child.* New York: Basic Books.
Senge, P.M. (1990). *The Fifth Discipline: The Art and Practice of the Learning Organization.* New York: Doubleday.
Skinner, B.F. (1974). *About Behaviorism.* New York: Knopf.
Snyder, W. (1996). Organization, learning and performance: An exploration of the linkages between organization learning, knowledge, and performance. Doctoral dissertation, University of Southern California, Los Angeles.
Sylwester, R. (1995). *A Celebration of Neurons: An Educator's Guide to the Human Brain.* Alexandria, VA: Association for Supervision and Curriculum Development.
Vygotsky, L.S. (1934). *Thought and Language.* Cambridge, MA: MIT Press.
Wenger, E. (1987). *Artificial Intelligence and Tutoring Systems: Computational and Cognitive Approaches to the Communication of Knowledge.* San Francisco: Morgan Kaufmann.
Wenger, E. (1998). *Communities of Practice: Learning, Meaning, and Identity.* Cambridge, MA: Harvard University Press.
Wertsch, J. (1985). *Vygotsky and the Social Formation of Mind.* Cambridge, MA: Harvard University Press.

Chapter 16

Transitional learning and reflexive facilitation

The case of learning for work

Danny Wildemeersch and Veerle Stroobants

Danny Wildemeersch, Professor at the Catholic University of Leuven (Belgium), is a well-known scholar in European youth and adult education research. He has a special interest in educational and learning activities in grassroots movements, initiatives and organisations dealing with social exclusion, participation, sustainable development, etc. For ten years, from 1993 to 2003, he worked closely together with two younger researchers, Veerle Stroobants and Marc Jans, among others, in a cross-national EU research project, investigating the situation and possibilities of socially vulnerable youth in six European countries. The research resulted in various contributions, including the book Unemployed Youth and Social Exclusion in Europe: Learning for Inclusion? *(Weil, Wildemeersch and Jansen, 2005). The following chapter is written by Wildemeersch and Stroobants and presents a framework on transitional learning, building on Stroobants' dissertation (2001) and on findings from the European research. Some of these insights were presented earlier in a 2001 article 'Making sense of learning for work: Towards a framework of transitional learning' by Stroobants, Jans and Wildemeersch in the* International Journal of Lifelong Education.

Introduction

In this contribution we look back at some ten years of research in which we have tried to interpret the processes of transitional learning taking place in the context of various education, training and guidance practices, mostly in support of people who have difficulty in finding or in keeping a job. One of the outcomes of this research is a framework that helps to interpret the changing conditions of individual learning processes and educational practices against the background of transformations in present-day society. Various observers describe the changes in society today in terms of individualisation. Individuals are said to be at the same time free, obliged and responsible to make adequate choices and decisions regarding their own private and professional lives. Such processes of individualisation increase the need for individual and social reflexivity. Consequently, individualisation processes go together with interrelated developments in the learning of people on the one hand and with challenges to educational models and practices on the other hand. People are faced with the task of developing self-reflexive biographies to anticipate and cope with changing circumstances (Beck, 1992; Giddens, 1991). Meanwhile, educational practitioners need to reflexively reconsider their role as facilitators of this learning for personal and social change.

We do not want to interpret these developments exclusively in terms of individualisation processes. In line with various theories that try to avoid one-sided structural determinism or naive voluntarism (Giddens, 1984; Bourdieu, 1990; Hodkinson and Sparkes, 1997), we argue that reflexive biographies not only may allow people to adapt to rapidly evolving conditions, but that they possibly create opportunities to develop alternative, singularised answers to the changing conditions and to influence the social context (Alheit, 1995; Fischer-Rosenthal, 1995; Biesta, 2006). In this respect, we believe that educational practices, just like educational research, can and even should play their part. The theory on transitional learning we present here (see also Stroobants *et al.*, 2001) is a descriptive and explanatory framework aimed at making sense of the learning processes of individuals in relation to work and their participation in initiatives of adult and continuing education. We are convinced that this theory of transitional learning will be helpful to support the decision-making process of the reflexive professional whose role is said to be dramatically shifting today from a position of 'legislator' to a position of 'interpreter' (Bauman, 1987). For this reason, a genuine understanding of the way in which learning is related to one's biography is of utmost importance.

Between reflexive and restrictive activation

In 1998 we started the first international research project on the education, training and guidance of unemployed young people (Wildemeersch, 2001). Over the course of this project and later on, when we wrote a book about our observations, we noted significant shifts in social policy discourses (Weil *et al.*, 2005; Wildemeersch and Weil, 2008). The naming and framing of programmes for unemployed young people as 'activation practices' became more and more apparent. During the previous decade, an emphasis on active citizens, active job-seekers, active senior citizens, active communities and the active welfare state has become prominent in social policy discourses all across Europe. In this context, individuals are meant to assume active responsibility for their own learning, employment and community welfare. In line with this, a more 'client-centred' approach towards the unemployed has engendered increased 'humanistic' modes of activation where individual counselling, trajectory guidance and continuous monitoring are important principles. Activation practitioners are nowadays very well aware that their clients – such as unemployed young adults, women and the long-term unemployed – need special rather than standardised treatments and approaches. Most practitioners acknowledge, although to different degrees across the projects we studied, that an approach characterised by open communication and understanding, by consideration of the clients' lifeworld and by an attitude of respect is of great importance. Our research revealed that they favour what we called 'reflexive' forms of activation. Yet, we will notice further on that in these practices, reflexive activation is sometimes the espoused theory, whereas restrictive activation is the theory-in-use (Argyris and Schön, 1978).

Furthermore, reflexive activation implies the need to balance respect for the singularity of young adults on the one hand with the needs and demands of the labour market on the other hand. Moreover, the ideal balance seems to be different for each particular individual. This tension makes the activation practice a rather delicate and sometimes frustrating experience, requiring careful reflexivity on behalf of the facilitator. This implies that professionals and young adults co-interpret and negotiate possibilities and limitations of particular activation strategies, given the complex nature of labour markets and social policies, but also given the context of ambivalent relationships between young adults and professionals. Respect for the singularity of the young adults inevitably moves the facilitators towards a more biographical approach. They have to construct concrete actions based on insecure interpretations. Problem solving in practice is a reflexive activity of an 'interpretive professional' (Wildemeersch, 2000).

> Interpreting and negotiating in this perspective constitute an open-ended process. Professionals use the information coming out of boundary tensions between their own and their participant's lifeworlds and those of the system, by staying critical and creative about the choices that cannot be seen except through new forms of dialogue, inquiry, and action research in practice'
>
> (Weil *et al.*, 2005, p. 159)

Transitional learning

In another research project in our research centre (Stroobants, 2001), we focused on biographical learning processes in which women make sense of work through the construction of their life courses and their life stories. Presupposing an ambiguous relationship between the promise of emancipation through paid labour, women's actual work experiences and the current opportunity structures on the labour market, we researched the way women learn to handle the different and changing meanings of work in their lives and in overall society. We started the research with some scepticism about the emancipatory potential of paid labour for women as well as of lifelong learning and participation in adult and continuing education. However, we were equally fascinated by the way women have to look for adequate ways to connect their own biography to broader social issues and, in one way or another, also seem to succeed in doing so, often via work and/or education, be it with or in spite of the help of education and training professionals.

Throughout the research process we began to understand that the real 'job' women perform, during their life, is the (re)construction of the self in relation to society (Fenwick, 1998; Rossiter, 1999; Tennant, 1998). In this process of searching for and developing the self, work does represent a possible and desirable way for women to structure and make sense of their life and to widen their action space in society. However, finding a job attuned to their own capacities and personal and social aspirations on the one hand, and to the demands and structures of the labour market on the other hand, is not taken for granted. We consider the search for meaningful connections between self and society when engaging with work, as a process of transitional learning.

Transitional learning and meaningful connections

Transitional learning emerges when individuals are faced with unpredictable changes in the dynamics between their life course and the transforming context, and when they are confronted with the need to (learn to) anticipate, handle and reorganise these changing conditions. This situation triggers a continuous process of constructing meaning, making choices, taking up responsibilities and dealing with the changes in the personal and societal context. In line with Alheit (1995) we refer to this lifelong process of shaping one's own biography as a process of transitional learning. It is about creating meaningful connections between one's narrative understanding of the self as an actor in past, present and future on the one side, and one's understanding of the context in which one operates and lives in terms of broader themes and issues on the other. While transitional learning refers to a permanent learning process, meaningful connections are its varying and concrete stakes and possible outcomes at a specific moment. It is important to mention here that this process of creating meaningful connections is not a process that is located 'in' the person. The telling of a story – who one is, where one stands, where one goes to – is always a 'response' to a question coming from someone else. Therefore, the development of a singular life story relates to the act of 'coming into presence' into an intersubjective space that is constituted by the company of others who 'interrupt' the self-evidence of one's biography. 'To ask the question of human subjectivity in this way, as a question about where the subject as a unique singular being – as someone – comes into presence, allows us to get away from the determination of the human subject as a substance or essence' (Biesta, 2006, p. 43).

Adaptation, growth, distinction and resistance: Four basic strategies

Processes of transitional learning are located in the centre of a symbolic space created by two dimensions (see Figure 16.1). The first – horizontal – dimension, relates to action and reflection dealing with tensions between societal demands and personal demands. These demands are needs, values, norms and aspirations that may converge or diverge. Priority may be given to societal criteria or to personal criteria or, what is more real, to a combination of both criteria. The second dimension – the vertical one – is about the actor's perception of the extent to which the fields in which s/he operates (e.g. the field of work, training, leisure, etc.) can be altered in view of individual or social/societal expectations, plans and projects. In other words, it concerns the subjectively experienced and perceived possibilities and limitations to influence or change arrangements and structures (e.g. a distribution of opportunities) within a particular domain of life and within society at large.

Within this two-dimensional space, four basic strategies or logics of making meaningful connections can be distinguished: adaptation, growth, distinction and resistance.

Adaptation is a strategy which gives priority to societal demands and which takes as a point of departure the alleged unchangeable character of the opportunity structures on the labour market. With respect to this position, the process of connecting the self and the context is mainly directed by the (changing) needs and conditions of the labour market. Adaptation is about trying to acquire the necessary competencies to meet these needs and to come to terms with the social expectations.

Growth is the person-oriented counterpart of adaptation within a societal

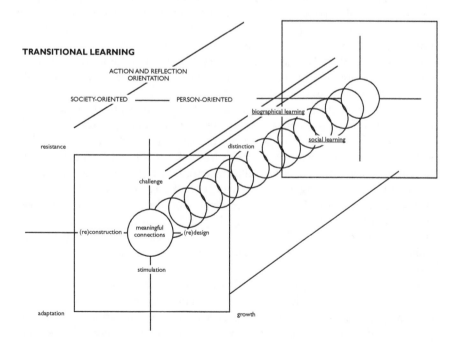

Figure 16.1 Transitional learning.

context that is predominantly perceived as hard to influence. It refers to the holistic development of the individual as an authentic, free and responsible subject, both in the sense of developing all aspects and potentialities of the whole person and in the sense of caring for the well-being and recovery of the self in order to personally cope with the society-in-transformation.

In both strategies, actors direct and interpret their lives in the best possible way within the given social context. Yet, when the changeability of societal opportunity structures is taken as a starting point, activities of critical reflection and action come into focus, in combination with attempts to shape particular social fields and life contexts, e.g. labour market practices, in a wilful way.

In the strategy of distinction, the development of an alternative, individual lifestyle, in view of finding a personalised way out of societal demands that are experienced as oppressive, is at stake (e.g. the demands of the labour market which are at odds with images of freedom, creativity and authenticity).

Resistance, on the other hand, directs critical reflection and action explicitly towards influencing and maybe transforming the demands of society. It refers to social commitment. In order to demonstrate the relevance of these four strategies, we now present some of the interpretations made by Stroobants (2001) on the basis of biographical interviews with a selective group of women.

Anita's search for a job can be interpreted with reference to the strategies discussed above. She is a young married woman without children, looking for 'the right job' after some frustrating work experiences. She wants to continue a training trajectory preparing her for a 'male' job. Yet, she is not allowed to finish it because the counsellors are convinced that there is no way to get work for her in that sector. Instead, she is guided towards a nursing job. Having no alternative option and because in that sector employment is guaranteed, she goes for it (adaptation). Soon she realises that this job is not what she expected. She cannot attune it to her own aspirations, competencies and dreams. The job is getting her down and undermines her self-esteem. Therapy helps her to gain back her self-respect and to cope with the situation (growth). By attending evening courses in pottery and furniture making, she tries to develop the forgotten creative aspects of her self (growth). In a certain way, she develops a proper lifestyle by doing all sorts of courses and evening classes (distinction). Actually, she wants to be a furniture maker and dreams of starting her own little business, but at the moment, taking into account the limitations of the context in which she has to operate, this is not a realistic option. She decides to become a cab driver, for she wants to prove that she is able to do a man's job (resistance).

The four strategies or logics mentioned above are more-or-less ideal-typical and theoretical constructions and are to be understood as combinations of two extreme poles of the two structuring dimensions. As the tensions with other poles cannot really be ignored in the construction of meaningful connections, these strategies do not often occur in their pure form. When they seem to do so, like in Anita's story, they make sense in view of coping with a concrete situation (e.g. she can only continue with her nursing job because she finds compensation in courses and therapy), but – from a biographical point of view – they are not really connected. At the same time, through acts of resistance, Anita creates space to relate her personal development to her own lifestyle that she wants to develop further. It thus seems more true to assume that most of the time, a combination or a mix of strategies – at the crossroads of the two dimensions – is applied so as to achieve meaningful connections. It is important to see that the fields of tension either have opportunities to produce dynamic and productive outcomes which can be converted to one's own use, or that they stimulate activities of control within the subject. The combined strategies of stimulation, challenge, (re)design and (re)construction described below explicitly take into account the tension on one of the two dimensions. Thereby, the poles of the dimensions are connected in such a way that and–and combinations do occur rather than or–or combinations.

Stimulation, challenge, (re)design and (re)construction: Four combined strategies

Stimulation is the first combined strategy operating within the given opportunity structures, by attuning societal and personal demands. It tries to meet the changing needs produced by a society in transformation on the one hand (adaptation) and to take individual orientations into consideration (growth) on the other. In view of the importance nowadays attached to inte-gration in the labour market, this combined strategy is frequently applied. However, because the demands of the labour market are considered to be hard to transform, some risks may occur. For example, mechanisms of exclusion remain tangible in the context of practices that cultivate the myth of individual liberty and responsibility, as is the case with the employability discourse that tends to reproduce the 'blaming-the-victim model' (Jansen and Wildemeersch, 1996).

As a second combined strategy, challenge equally relates to the tension between societal and personal demands, yet takes the changeability of the social context as a point of departure. It means that resistance can find an individualized expression in particular lifestyle practices and in reverse order, that distinction is allowed to play a role in activities of resistance. The remaining one-sidedness here is that the possibility to transform the social order may be overestimated, or that existing restrictive mechanisms are not taken into account well enough. This may lead to disappointment, despair and even self-exclusion.

The third combined strategy of (re)design is situated on the borderline of two opposing perceptions concerning the transformability of opportunity structures and is preoccupied exclusively with the meeting of personal demands. It refers to a personal developmental process, not only within (personal growth) or beyond (distinction through lifestyle) existing opportunity structures, but by calculating realistically the opportunities, possibilities and limitations of the self and of the action environment and by actively interacting with these. The (re)design strategy does not address societal demands.

(Re)construction as the fourth combined strategy counterbalances the strategy of designing. It is directed to societal demands rather than to personal demands. It is about the (re)establishment of practices based on a critical (resistance) and yet pragmatic and realistic (adaptation) perception of opportunity structures and their moral and political dimensions. (Re)construction runs the risk of turning a blind eye to the individual perspective of the issues at stake.

Monique is a single mother who eventually, after several moves in and out of the labour market, has found a job that fits her chosen lifestyle. As a vegetarian who lives in accordance with anthroposophic principles, she is a co-owner of a natural health shop. She experiences her work as a continuation of her way of living and being. One could say that she has created ((re)designed) her own life, finding personal development in a particular lifestyle. By extending it to an income-generating activity and attaching her own profile and meaning to work as a self-employed woman, her example represents an alternative way for women to relate to the labour market ((re)construction).

Remarks and nuances

When explaining the combined strategies, we pointed to some risks resulting from the one-sided focus on only one of the two dimensions against which we situate transitional learning. The process of creating meaningful connections tries to take into account the tensions on both dimensions. Taking social agency within dynamic social structures as a point of departure, it is about attuning social and personal demands and realistically integrating acceptance of and change in the surrounding context. To this goal, several of the presented strategies will be followed in a creative and changing order and direction.

Yet, transitional learning is not an intentional linear process towards meaningful connections that can be directed in a systematic and rational way. Nor is it always successful or even possible. Coincidence, luck, differences in opportunity structures, unexpected possibilities and structural limitations, amongst other things, play an important role in the generation of meaningful connections that shape the process of transitional learning. What matters is that one is (or learns to be) able to react in an adequate way to this situation of serendipity or 'happenstance' (Hodkinson and Sparkes, 1997).

From Denise's story we learn that finding a meaningful connection is not always easy or evident. She tries out different strategies to enter the labour market, none of which have been successful thus far. She is a single woman without children. Although she has a university degree, she doesn't feel able to meet the corresponding social demands. She has worked in several different jobs and sectors but has not yet found the suitable and useful job she is looking for. She has been out of a regular job for a few years now and attends various labour market-oriented training (adaptation) and counselling (growth) activities. Denise is almost desperately looking for a job, trying to develop her own competencies in harmony with the demands on the labour market (stimulation/activation). But at the same time, she is very critical of the current flexible and stressful labour market. She cannot fit in her proper values and principles and she does not actually want to be part of it (resistance). She wants to work on her own terms, while also countering the labour market, but she has not yet found a way to do so.

However, this relative unpredictability on the individual level does not mean that it is not important to create positive opportunity structures and enable meaningful connections on a societal level. Though our theoretical approach is not meant to offer a normative framework, we do stress that the processes of deliberation and choice with regard to work do not take place in a neutral social context. They are explicitly related to different opinions that exist about the way in which the field of work and labour operates, to the public debate concerning issues of social responsibility and to the obligation to (re)organise this field in view of a (re)distribution of opportunity structures. New balances or relations between individual autonomy and responsibility on the one hand and collective arrangements and opportunities on the other can bring about and facilitate meaningful connections on the personal and social levels alike.

An educational perspective on transitional learning

Meaningful connections through adult and continuing education

In the lives and life stories of the interviewees of our biographical research, not only work, but also participation in adult and continuing education initiatives, is experienced as a structuring and meaningful activity. In many, often-surprising and changing ways, adult and continuing education initiatives, amongst other media, are often considered helpful for the process of transitional learning that they experienced. The participants in this research on women and work attended several educational and counselling activities, thereby inevitably giving personal meaning to their learning from a biographical and situated perspective. They more or less believe in education as a means of responding to the demands of the labour market and of society in transformation. If education fails to do so, it still retains relevancy for the sake of personal growth and self-development, or as a means of helping to design a proper lifestyle or to construct alternative ways of being employed. The way in which the interviewees at various occasions integrate education and learning experiences into their particular life plan and life story sometimes questions or counters outcomes which have been constructed from an educational framework.

Magda's story illustrates well the way in which the female interviewees give meaning to educational experiences, thereby relating their learning to different strategies of transitional learning. She grows up as the youngest of nine children in a family of merchants. It is her childhood dream to one day have a shop of her own. When she gets married and has children of her own, she stops working as an office assistant. She takes the role of mother and housewife to heart and helps her husband with the bookkeeping of his business. After a few years, Magda looks for ways to break free from the 'patterns' that limit her actions. Eventually, she decides to attend evening classes orienting her towards the bakery business. At that moment, it is not certain what the outcome of that commitment will be. Retrospectively, it is clear from Magda's life story that she succeeded in making her dream come true. Attending the baker's training, however, must be understood as a multilayered strategy possibly serving several aims, sometimes opposing the predetermined educational objectives. For Magda, it is a way to exercise her hobby (personal growth fitting her role as a mother and housewife), to get qualified in bookkeeping (useful for her 'job' as cooperating spouse – stimulation) and to keep open the possibility of starting her own business (and realise her dream – construct/design/challenge).

Meaningful connections and activation strategies: The case of 'Flexi Job'

The theory of transitional learning can also be of interest from a facilitation point of view, as the entire framework is not limited to the perspective of the learner. It is also applicable to the activities of professionals of education, training, guidance and counselling who try to support individual learning processes. The framework also refers to the ways in which these professionals make sense of their own position and practices as facilitators and to the (mix of) strategies they use. Their actions vis-à-vis the learning individuals can be understood in terms of either facilitating and stimulating or inhibiting each of the strategies we distinguished. The framework of transitional learning can thus be approached from different perspectives. This makes it possible to interpret some of the tensions, conflicts and contradictions in the interactions between professionals and participants. In order to illustrate the relevance of the theory of transitional learning in this respect, we briefly present the case of 'Flexi Job' (Weil *et al.*, 2005, p. 38). The data we present here were collected on the occasion of a case study organised in the context of the 'Balancing Competencies' project about which we report extensively in our book *Unemployed Youth and Social Exclusion in Europe* (Weil *et al.*, 2005). The interpretation of these data also helped us to develop the framework of transitional learning. Simultaneously, this emerging framework gave us a better understanding of some of the tensions and contradictions at stake in this case. The case we present below is indeed an interpretation based on a partial observation. Therefore, this interpretation should not be considered as the ultimate truth about this case. On the contrary, it is an invitation – also for the practitioners involved – to consider this practice with the help of the framework of transitional learning and to experience that this framework may reveal elements which they have not yet taken into consideration.

Flexi Job is a fictitious name for a 'social' employment agency in Belgium. It is purposefully located in an underprivileged area in the bigger cities of Flanders and Antwerp, in contrast with other agencies that are located in the centre of the city. The agency has the ambition to create a connection between the lifeworld of disadvantaged young people and the present-day situation of the labour market. The model which has been developed and which seems promising in the eyes of policy-makers and the Flemish Employment Agency (VDAB) is based on a long and intensive outreach contact of the youth worker involved in the project with the target group of long-term unemployed young adults. These experiences gave rise to the hypotheses that the envisaged group is not really ready for, or willing to accept, steady jobs and that it is better to look for unconventional ways to create work experience for them. Therefore, Flexi Job wants to support the young unemployed adults in their attempt to alternate periods of leisure and employment. The concept of Flexi Job is based on the principle that short-term jobs (1–30 days) should be offered to this particular group. These jobs are supposed to encourage young adults who want an income but are not motivated to subject themselves to regular labour market discipline. The 'maximum 30 days' slogan is thought to match their relation to labour and therefore is used to attract them. It promises a combination of 'work' and 'freedom', of 'stability' and some sort of 'nomadic lifestyle'. Flexi Job wants to support these young adults in experimenting with 'new ways of life' that reflect their culture of 'resistance'. This culture is considered to reflect their opposition to mainstream society, including the norm of lifelong work, and their ambition to 'distinguish' themselves through alternative lifestyles.

However, the interviews we had with these young people revealed other aspirations. We did not find much evidence of this form of resistance espoused by the group. On the contrary, we encountered many traditional dreams of 'lifelong work'. In the eyes of these young people, temporary employment is either an emergency solution or an intermediate step towards a long-term contract. Let us just consider the group of 'alternative dreamers' to develop our argument. The form of resistance that Flexi Job refers to may eventually not be resistance at all, but rather a new trajectory to adaptation. Three arguments support this viewpoint:

- The resistance can be meaningful for young people who productively succeed in juggling this flexibility as an introductory step in their career development. It is then a resistance strategy or maybe some kind of lifestyle distinction strategy that relates at the same time to a growth strategy.

Take the examples of the highly qualified young graduate who succeeds in building a career, while making use of several short assignments in close connection with his/her personality and individual agenda. The alternation of periods of work and non-work is, for instance, exemplified in the trend of travelling around the world for a couple of months.

This perspective makes sense, especially for the highly qualified young adults. Yet, the opportunity structures of low-qualified people are so restricted that this form of resistance or distinction may eventually turn into conditions of mere adaptation and even self-exclusion for those who are in disadvantaged positions in society and on the labour market.

- The labour market is not indifferent to this kind of resistance. The resistance matches the flexibility discourse perfectly well. In that way, the resistance is not resistance in the first place, but rather an invitation to adapt to the flexibility demands of the labour market. Some young adults experience this shift in the labour market as disturbing. Adaptation is considered a necessity: the best of all unsatisfactory solutions or a survival strategy rather than a new way of life. Temporary employment goes together with a crisis in their lives and helps them to overcome acute financial problems. There seems to be a gap between the new 'values' of the labour market, notably flexibility, and the expectation of low-skilled people in general to find a long-term job.
- Flexi Job seems to create the illusion that there is some kind of experimental moratorium where the young adults can alternate between work and non-work while simultaneously developing their own plans so as to arrive at a point where they find sustainable employment in harmony with their own plans and agenda. Yet, the real experimental room is restricted by the defective opportunity structures of an unschooled, flexible workforce. The young people in the interviews discussed their dreams, such as becoming a telephone operator, a policeman or a security agent. There is no place to experiment with these plans and dreams within Flexi Job, unless they earn enough money to be able to afford training at a later stage.

In conclusion we would argue that Flexi Job predominantly meets the short-term needs of the young unemployed adults. The young people it addresses indeed want a job, and they want it fast, because they need instant money. Temporary employment perfectly meets this need. However, the difference in aspirations between Flexi Job and some of its participants has to do with the long-term perspective. In some respects, Flexi Job supports a new way of life, in which temporary employment takes a central place, and thus contributes to new understandings of quality of life. Yet, the perspective of the young adults that we interviewed is different. Temporary employment for them has the character of emergency help. What they actually clearly strive for (and prefer as soon as possible) are long-term contracts in sustainable jobs, enabling them to develop traditional lifestyles rather than the unconventional lifestyles that the mentor has in mind. For this reason we would argue that this case is an example of 'restrictive activation', which we characterised as a strategy that problematises the excluded rather than exclusion, that gives limited responsibilities to the participants to co-direct their trajectory and that does little to create meaningful connections while learning for jobs (Weil *et al.*, 2005, p. 200). With the help of our framework on transitional learning, we were able to reconsider some of the assumptions which directed the actions of Flexi Job. We hope to have convincingly demonstrated that the framework indeed helps to further explore and discuss the relevance of particular activation strategies.

Conclusions

We have argued in this chapter that transitional learning is a process that takes place not only 'in' the person, but also, to an important extent, through the interaction initiated by external people who ask for a response. That is why in this chapter we have also brought practices of adult and continuing education into the picture. Adult and continuing education today increasingly operate as providers of vocational and market-oriented training activities aimed at activating individuals to fit economic demands. Yet, adult and continuing education initiatives can also play a role in other learning practices. They can stimulate the search for work and the creation of meaningful work in relation to self and society. They can help people to develop an overview of personal and structural possibilities for and limitations to the realisation of alternative ways of living and working. They can help to create new opportunities. They can invite people to develop their life stories and thereby create opportunities for them to come into presence as 'singularised persons'. In such cases it may be relevant to 'interrupt' the taken-for-granted stories of participants. In doing so, they can also create new significant connections between the initiatives' own aims and missions and the surrounding society by attaching a social significance to the choices and decisions of individuals, by strengthening signals to society and in this way influencing social structures and creating possibilities to design new realities and construct new practices. Such activity today is to a large extent a 'reflexive facilitation practice'. The cases we have presented based on different research experiences in the last decade make clear how such practices can be inspired by emerging theories, both on transitional learning and on reflexive activation. Such theories can be an important basis for reflection, dialogue and decision-making among practitioners and policy-makers and within the organisations that provide education, training and guidance. We hope our considerations in this chapter will help to deepen such processes.

References

Alheit, P. (1995). Biographical learning: Theoretical outlines, challenges and contradictions of a new approach in adult education. In P. Alheit, A. Bron-Wojciechowska, E. Brugger and P. Dominicé (eds.), *The Biographical Approach in European Adult Education* (pp. 57–74). Vienna: Verband Wiener Volksbildung.

Argyris, C. and Schön, D. (1978). *Organizational Learning: A Theory of Action Perspective.* Reading, MA: Addison-Wesley.

Bauman, Z. (1987). *Legislators and Interpreters: On Modernity, Post-Modernity and Intellectuals.* Ithaca, NY: Cornell University Press.

Beck, U. (1992 [1986]). *Risk Society: Towards a New Modernity.* Cambridge, UK: Polity Press.

Biesta, G. (2006). *Beyond Learning: Democratic Education for a Human Future.* Boulder, CO: Paradigm.

Bourdieu, P. (1990 [1987]). *In Other Words: Essays Towards a Reflexive Sociology.* London: Routledge.

Fenwick, T. (1998). Women composing selves, seeking authenticity: A study of women's development in the workplace. *International Journal of Lifelong Education*, 17(3), 199–217.

Fischer-Rosenthal, W. (1995). The problem with identity: Biography as solution to some (post)-modernist dilemmas. *Comenius*, 15, 250–265.

Giddens, A. (1984). *The Constitution of Society: Outline of the Theory of Structuration.* Cambridge, UK: Polity Press.

Giddens, A. (1991). *Modernity and Self-Identity: Self and Society in Late Modern Age.* Stanford, CA: Stanford University Press.

Hodkinson, P. and Sparkes, A.C. (1997). Careership: A sociological theory of career decision making. *British Journal of Sociology of Education*, 18(1), 29–44.

Jansen, T. and Wildemeersch, D. (1996). Adult education and critical identity development: From a deficiency towards a competency approach. *International Journal of Lifelong Education*, 15(5), 325–340.

Rossiter, M. (1999). A narrative approach to development: Implications for adult education. *Adult Education Quarterly*, 50(1), 56–71.

Stroobants, V. (2001). Baanbrekend leren – een levenswerk: Een biografisch onderzoek naar het leren, leven en werken van vrouwen [Learning for work: A biographical research into learning, living and working of women]. Leuven, Belgium: K.U. Leuven, Faculty of Psychology and Educational Sciences (doctoral dissertation).

Stroobants, V., Jans, M. and Wildemeersch, D. (2001). Making sense of learning for work: Towards a framework of transitional learning. *International Journal of Lifelong Education*, 20(1/2), 114–126.

Tennant, M. (1998). Adult education as a technology of the self. *International Journal of Lifelong Education*, 4(13), 364–376.

Weil, S., Wildemeersch, D. and Jansen, T. (2005). *Unemployed Youth and Social Exclusion in Europe: Learning for Inclusion?* Aldershot, UK: Ashgate.

Wildemeersch, D. (2000). Lifelong learning and the significance of the interpretive professional. In K. Illeris (ed.), *Adult Education in the Perspective of the Learners* (pp. 158–176). Copenhagen: Roskilde University Press.

Wildemeersch, D. (ed.) (2001). *Balancing Competencies: Enhancing the Participation of Young Adults in Economic and Social Processes.* (Report for the European Commission – Targeted Socio-Economic Research, FP4). Leuven, Belgium: Katholieke Universiteit Leuven, Centre for the Research on Lifelong Learning and Participation.

Wildemeersch, D. and Weil, S. (2008). Social sustainability and activation strategies with unemployed young adults. In P. Willis, S. McKenzie and R. Harris (eds.), *Rethinking Work and Learning: Adult and Vocational Education for Social Sustainability.* Berlin: Springer.

Index

Also by Knud Illeris

How We Learn
Learning and Non-Learning in School and Beyond
Knud Illeris

How We Learn deals with the fundamental issues of the processes of learning. It considers a broad range of important questions, such as: modern research into learning and brain functions; self-perception, motivation and competence development; teaching, intelligence and learning style; learning in relation to gender and life age.

The book provides a comprehensive introduction to both traditional learning theory and the newest international research into learning processes, while at the same time being an innovative contribution to a new and more holistic understanding of learning, including discussion on school-based learning, net-based learning, workplace learning and educational politics. It is a refreshing and thought-provoking piece of scholarly work as it adds new research material, new understandings and new points of view.

2007

Hardback

978-0-415-43846-9

Paperback

978-0-415-43847-6

International Perspectives on Competence Development
Developing Skills and Capabilities
Knud Illeris

The issue of Competence Development is at the core of contemporary educational politics all over the world. It is celebrated by governments and international bodies such as the OECD, EU and UNESCO, in close relationship to such other popular issues as Lifelong Learning and Human Resource Development. In contrast, the international academic literature on the issue of Competence Development is rather limited and scarce, perhaps because the concept of Competence scarce.

This book brings a broad range of qualified contributions from selected scholars in Competence Development all over the world. It presents a comprehensive and international selection of different understandings and viewpoints, offering a differentiated insight into the many perspectives and opinions that are at stake.

2009
Hardback: 978-0-415-49210-2
Paperback: 978-0-415-49211-9

Also by Peter Jarvis

Lifelong Learning and the Learning Society Trilogy
Peter Jarvis

With the release of the final volume of his trilogy, Peter Jarvis completes his comprehensive, multi-disciplinary study of lifelong learning and the learning society. Between them, these three volumes analyse every aspect of learning, from the fundamental psychology of the human drive to learn, to the global sociological apparatus in which learning takes place.

In Volume 1, **Towards a Comprehensive Theory of Human Learning**, Jarvis demonstrates how learning underpins humanity. By assessing theories of learning across all ages, he constructs a new model for analysing how people learn.

Volume 2, **Globalization, Lifelong Learning and the Learning Society**, considers the effects on the learning society of sociological structures, politics and economics, alongside the moral and ethical basis of such a society.

In the brand new Volume 3, **Democracy, Lifelong Learning and the Learning Society**, the arguments of the first two volumes are brought together and furthered, asking what kind of society is possible as a result of learning? The book concludes that since human beings continue to learn, so the learning society must be a process within the incomplete project of humanity.

All three books in the trilogy will be essential reading for students in education, HRD and teaching and learning generally, in addition to academics and informed practitioners.

Vol 1 (2005) Hb: 978-0-415-35540-7   Pb: 978-0-415-35541-4
Vol 2 (2007) Hb: 978-0-415-35542-1   Pb: 978-0-415-35543-8
Vol 3 (2008) Hb: 978-0-415-35545-5   Pb: 978-0-415-35545-2
Complete Trilogy 978-0-415-47788-8

The Routledge International Handbook of Lifelong Learning
Peter Jarvis

As lifelong learning grows in popularity, few comprehensive pictures of the phenomenon have emerged. **The Routledge International Handbook of Lifelong Learning** provides a disciplined and complete overview of lifelong learning internationally.

The theoretical structure puts the learner at the centre and the book emanates from there, pointing to the social context beyond the learner. Up-to-the-minute syntheses from many of the leading international experts in the field give vital snapshots of this rapidly evolving subject.

This authoritative volume, essential reading for academics in the field of Lifelong Learning, examines the complexities of the subject within a systematic global framework and places it in its socio-historic context.

2008 Hb: 978-0-415-41904-8

Also by Yrjö Engeström

Activity Theory in Practice:
Promoting Learning Across Boundaries and Agencies

Harry Daniels, Anne Edwards, Yrjö Engeström, Tony Gallagher, Sten Ludvigsen

This ground-breaking book brings together cutting-edge researchers studying the transformation of practice through the enhancement and transformation of expertise. Expertise is in transition, moving toward collaboration in inter-organizational fields and toward continuous shaping of transformations. To understand and master this transition, powerful new conceptual tools are needed and are provided here.

Working as part of an integrated international team the authors have identified a number of specific findings whose implications are of proven interest to the policy field. Examples are:

- approaches to the analysis of vertical learning between operational and strategic levels within complex organizations
- the refinement of notions of identity and subject position within Cultural Historical Activity Theory (CHAT)
- the introduction of the concept of labour power into CHAT and
- the development of a method of analyzing discourse which theoretically coheres with CHAT and the design of projects.

Essential reading for the growing international CHAT research community, **Activity Theory in Practice** will also prove highly useful to all researchers and research students who are interested in conceptual and empirical issues in activity-based research.

2009
Hb: 978-0-415-47724-6
Pb: 978-0-415-47725-3

Also by Howard Gardner

Development and Education of the Mind
The Selected Works of Howard Gardner

The Development and Education of the Mind

The selected works of
HOWARD GARDNER

HOWARD GARDNER

In this book American psychologist and educator Howard Gardner has assembled his most important writings about education. Spanning over thirty years, these papers reveal the thinking, the concepts, and the empirical research that have made Gardner one of the most respected and cited educational authorities of our time.

Trained originally as a psychologist at Harvard University, Gardner begins with personal sketches and tributes to his major teachers and mentors. He then presents the work for which he is best known—the theory of multiple intelligences; included are a summary of the original theory as well as accounts of how it has been updated over the years.

Included additionally are seminal papers on the nature of understanding; education in the arts; powerful ways in which to assess learning; broad statements about the educational enterprise; and two accounts of how education is likely to evolve in the globalized world of the 21st century.

Following the tradition of John Dewey, Jean Piaget, and Jerome Bruner, Gardner views education as the optimal development of the mind. This volume illustrates how a broad and generous psychological perspective, drawing as well on other disciplines, can bring powerful insights to the processes of education.

This book is part of the World Library of Educationalists series, which celebrates the contributions made to education by leading figures. Each scholar has selected his or her own key writings from across numerous books and journal articles, and often spread across two or more decades to be presented in a single volume. Through these books, readers can chase up the themes and strands that have been lodged in a lifetime's work, and so follow the development of these scholars' contributions to the field, as well as the development of the fields themselves. Other scholars included in the series: Richard Aldrich, Stephen J. Ball, Elliot W. Eisner, John Elliott, Howard Gardner, John Gilbert, Ivor F. Goodson, David Hargreaves, David Labaree and E.C Wragg.

2005
Hb: 978-0-415-36729-5
Pb: 978-0-415-36728-8

Also by Mark Tennant

Psychology and Adult Learning
3rd edition

The 3rd edition of this popular book examines the role of psychology in informing adult education practice, and has been fully updated to reflect the impact of changes to the structure of society, globalization, technology, and the impact of postmodernism.

It explores the traditions of key psychological theories, and discusses issues and problems in applying them to an understanding of adult learning and development. It also examines the formation of identities, and places increased emphasis on what it means to be a lifelong learning. Dealing with adult learning in a variety of contexts, topics considered include:

'an excellent text to concentrate the minds of all those coming into adult education, community or social work for the first time'
EDUCATION

Psychology and Adult Learning

Mark Tennant | THIRD EDITION

- humanistic psychology
- self directed learners
- psychoanalytic approaches
- the formation of identities
- development of intelligence
- learning styles
- behaviourism
- group dynamics and group facilitator
- critical awareness

Hb: 978-0-415-37334-0
Pb: 978-0-415-37335-7

Also by Robin Usher

Globalisation and Pedagogy
Space, Place and Identity
2nd Ed.

Richard Edwards and Robin Usher

The reconfiguration of pedagogical practices around the globe has taken on a momentum that an earlier generation might well have considered startling and disorientating. Many still working in the education and training arenas do experience a high degree of disorientation and dislocation. With different pedagogic practices come different ways of examining them and fresh understandings of their implications and assumptions. It is the examination of these changes and developments that is the subject of this book.

The authors examine a number of questions posed by the rapid march of globalisation, including:

•What is the role of the teacher, and how do we teach in the context of globalisation?

•What curriculum is appropriate when people and ideas become more mobile?

•How do the technologies of the Internet and mobile phone impact upon what is learnt and by whom?

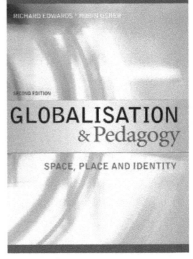

2007

Hardback
978-0-415-42895-8

Paperback ISBN
978-0-415-42896-5

The second edition of this important book has been fully updated and extended to take account of developments in technology, pedagogy and practice, in particular the growth of workplace, distance and e-learning. Drawing upon a wide range of literature, it explores the changing configurations of pedagogy in response to and as part of globalising processes and raises questions about identity and difference, homogeneity and heterogeneity, in the practices of education and training.